The Modern Prison Paradox

In *The Modern Prison Paradox*, Amy E. Lerman examines the shift from rehabilitation to punitivism that has taken place in the politics of American corrections and explores its consequences for both crime control and community life. Professor Lerman's research shows that spending time in more violent and castigatory prisons strengthens inmates' criminal networks and fosters social norms that increase the likelihood of criminal activity following parole. Additionally, Professor Lerman assesses whether harsher prisons similarly shape the attitudes of correctional staff. Her analysis reveals that working in more punitive prisons causes officers to develop an "us against them" mentality while on the job, affecting their orientations toward inmates and support for rehabilitation. Moreover, the wariness and stress officers develop at work carry over into their personal lives, straining relationships with partners, children, and friends. These results make clear that time spent within the confines of a correctional institution is not a deep freeze, during which individuals remain unchanged. Rather, prisons are small communities unto themselves, and the context of life inside them determines the kinds of people they produce.

Amy E. Lerman is Assistant Professor of Politics and Public Affairs at Princeton University. She previously served as Vice President of Policy Studies for the consulting firm Attention America, worked as a freelance political speechwriter, and was a faculty member of the college program at San Quentin State Prison.

Administrative segregation prisoners take part in a group therapy session at San Quentin State Prison, June 8, 2012.

Photo by Lucy Nicholson for Reuters. Reprinted with permission.

The Modern Prison Paradox

Politics, Punishment, and Social Community

AMY E. LERMAN

Assistant Professor of Politics and Public Affairs
Princeton University

CAMBRIDGE
UNIVERSITY PRESS

CAMBRIDGE
UNIVERSITY PRESS

32 Avenue of the Americas, New York, NY 10013-2473, USA

Cambridge University Press is part of the University of Cambridge.

It furthers the University's mission by disseminating knowledge in the pursuit of education, learning, and research at the highest international levels of excellence.

www.cambridge.org
Information on this title: www.cambridge.org/9781107613850

First published 2013

Printed in the United States of America

A catalog record for this publication is available from the British Library.

Library of Congress Cataloging in Publication data
Lerman, Amy E., 1978–
The modern prison paradox : politics, punishment, and social community / Amy E. Lerman, Assistant Professor of Politics and Public Affairs, Princeton University.
    pages   cm
Includes bibliographical references and index.
ISBN 978-1-107-04145-5 (hardback) – ISBN 978-1-107-61385-0 (pbk.)
1. Prisons – United States.   2. Prisoners – United States – Social conditions.   3. Corrections – United States.   4. Criminal justice, Administration of – United States.   I. Title.
HV9471.L439   2014
365'.973 – dc23   2013006875

ISBN 978-1-107-04145-5 Hardback
ISBN 978-1-107-61385-0 Paperback

He thought that in the history of the world it might even be that there was more punishment than crime but he took small comfort from it.

Cormack McCarthy, *The Road* (2006)

Contents

Acknowledgments

It is a truism that books are not written by the author alone. This has certainly been my experience.

First, a million thanks to the following organizations for their financial support of this project: the Survey Research Center, Institute of Governmental Studies, Goldman School of Public Policy, and Graduate Division at the University of California, Berkeley; the Center for Evidence-Based Corrections at the University of California, Irvine; the Fox Leadership Center at the University of Pennsylvania; the Bobst Center for Peace and Justice at Princeton University; and the National Science Foundation. Thanks also to the wonderful people at Cambridge University Press, particularly Robert Dreesen, who saw promise in this project, and Jayashree Prabhu, who expertly helped usher this book toward publication.

In addition, I could not have completed this project without a series of truly excellent research assistants. Thanks to Matt Incantalupo, Katherine McCabe, Jennifer Onofrio, Meredith Sadin, Lisa Steacy, Matt Tokeshi, and Natalie Torres. Thanks also to the fabulous Michele Epstein and Helene Wood for their tremendous administrative (and emotional) support.

Thanks to the many people at the California Department of Corrections and Rehabilitation for their patience, advice, and assistance in helping me put together the data for this project. Special thanks to Jay Atkinson, Daniel Johnson, and Carrie Davies, who all went above and beyond. Thanks also to Joan Petersilia, a formidable expert on the California prison system and a truly lovely person, for her very early comments on this project.

Appreciation is also due to the many people who have supported and guided this work throughout, especially the respective faculties of the UC Berkeley Political Science Department and the Department of Politics and the Woodrow Wilson School of Public and International Affairs at Princeton University. Special gratitude to Chris Achen, Doug Arnold, Paul Frymer, Marty Gilens, Doug Massey, Tali Mendelberg, Devah Pager, Paul Pierson, Markus Prior, Steve Raphael, Matt Salganik, Jasjeet Sekhon, Jonathan Simon, Laura Stoker, Rocio Titiunik, and Ali Valenzuela for their thoughts and comments on various drafts of this book. Much gratitude is also due to Mary Katzenstein, Lisa Miller, and Bruce Western for their incredible generosity with their time and willingness to provide me with valuable input on the manuscript.

I am extremely grateful to the California Correctional Peace Officers Association for agreeing to assist with the 2006 California Correctional Officer Survey and for allowing me the opportunity to dialogue with members at various state board meetings and conventions. Thanks especially to Mike Jimenez, Chuck Alexander, and Joe Baumann. You are remarkable human beings who continue to surprise and educate me. And, of course, thank you to the thousands of men and women who work each day in California's prisons, for participating in the survey and sharing your thoughts and experiences.

To the students of the Prison University Project's college program at San Quentin State Prison: I am forever indebted to you for your willingness to let me teach you and learn with you, and for telling me your stories. I hope I have done them justice.

To Jack Citrin, who gave me a chance to see firsthand how good research is done, and who remains the first person (other than my mother) who thought I could become a "real" political scientist.

To Henry Brady, who believed that this project was important enough to write, and who believed that I could write it: I could not have completed this book, my degree, or my first few years of professional life without your moral support and continued professional guidance.

To my friends and colleagues from Berkeley, Princeton, NYU, WHS, and scattered to the wind (you know who you are): More than you could possibly be aware – particularly since I too often fail to pick up the phone to tell you – I appreciate all the times you listened to me talk about this project, even when I didn't know where it was going or how to get there. Your advice and support have gotten me through the darker times. Thanks especially to the good folks of the CAPER, CAPER Reloaded, and Builders and Beer (aka the Vice Club) for keeping me in and out of trouble at (mostly) the appropriate times.

To Jody Lewen, the Patron Saint of Lost Souls and Complicated Lives, who taught me by example that literally anyone can be won over – from the most hardened inmate to the most cynical officer – if you just listen carefully enough to find out where their real fears are rooted: You constantly challenge me to be a better teacher, scholar, and human being.

To my parents, Lori and Steve; my siblings, Deb, Scott, and Dave; my grandparents, Gladys, Jerry, Rima, and Bern; and the many extended family members and family members-in-law who have loved and supported me through the sundry twists and turns: There are no words for how lucky I am to have you all as my booster club, teachers, and friends.

And to my Britt Boys, the Dukes of Trenton: You are my Haven, my two-man cheerleading team, and the loves of my life. This book is for you.

The Modern Prison Paradox

The test of every religious, political, or educational system, is the man which it forms.
If a system injures the intelligence it is bad. If it injures the character it is vicious.
If it injures the conscience it is criminal.

Henri Frederic Amiel, *Journal (June 17, 1852)*

In the early morning hours of Sunday, August 14, 1971, police cars in the small city of Palo Alto, California, were dispatched to the homes of 12 young men. Uniformed officers knocked on their doors and notified the men that they were being charged with armed robbery and burglary. They were read their rights, searched, handcuffed, and put in the back of a squad car. Each was taken to the police station, where he was summarily processed: photographed, fingerprinted, and led to a holding cell. These dozen men were then transferred to prison, where they were to be incarcerated together for 14 days under the watchful eye of the warden and a rotating cast of 12 young prison guards.

Thus began a landmark experiment that offered scholars a remarkable window on the socializing effects of prison. The experimental protocol was fairly straightforward. Twenty-four research subjects, all healthy and normal college-aged men, had been randomly assigned to play the part of either a prisoner or a prison guard. For two weeks, these men would live full time (in the case of the inmates) or work long shifts (in the case of the guards) in a simulated prison that had been carefully constructed in the basement of a building at Stanford University.

The goal of the study, which would come to be known as the Stanford Prison Experiment, was to examine "the extraordinary power of institutional environments to influence those who passed through them."[1] In particular, the researchers were interested in the way that individuals adapt to the rules and roles of their situational context. The relatively long time frame of the study and the nearly total immersion of the research subjects in the prison environment were necessary, according to the researchers, to "allow sufficient time for situational norms to develop and patterns of social interaction to emerge, change and become crystallized."[2] Essentially, the researchers set out to show that even "normal" people could be shaped by the contours of their environment and their relative position within it.

The results of the Stanford Prison Experiment are by now well known to any student who has taken an introductory psychology class: the experimental subjects quickly began to adapt to prison life. By only the second day, participants had begun to display intense emotional behaviors according to their assigned role. Prison guards developed an "us against them" mentality, becoming belligerent toward their charges. Inmates also succumbed to their new role. Some pushed back against their captors, refusing to comply with institutional rules. Others became depressed and in many cases withdrawn. The extent and speed of this adaptation surprised even the researchers.

The situation escalated in the days that followed. Officers resorted to increasingly punitive tactics to force compliance with their edicts. The researchers witnessed prison guards intentionally humiliating inmates, calling them derogatory names, and punishing them for insubordination or other behaviors deemed unacceptable. In addition, the researchers noted that "none of the less actively cruel mock-guards ever intervened or complained about the abuses they witnessed."[3] Those who occupied the inmate role likewise became deeply immersed. Several inmates staged a rebellion, barricading themselves in a room. By the middle of the first week, others showed signs of severe psychological distress. The lead researcher, Philip Zimbardo, describes the scene that unfolded:

The most dramatic of the coping behaviour utilised by half of the prisoners in adapting to this stressful situation was the development of acute emotional disturbance – severe enough to warrant their early release. At least a third of the guards were judged to have become far more aggressive and dehumanising toward the prisoners than would ordinarily be predicted in a simulation study.[4]

Faced with an environment that encouraged nearly total adaption to their respective roles of the powerful and the powerless, these seemingly normal men began to act out in ways that would have been completely out of place in their regular lives; indeed, the demands of the institutional environment seemed to override their individual dispositions. Zimbardo writes, "We had created a dominating behavioral context whose power insidiously frayed the seemingly impervious values of compassion, fair play, and belief in a just world. The situation won; humanity lost."[5] Confronted by a rapidly deteriorating situation and concerned for the health and safety of the research subjects, Zimbardo and his colleagues terminated the experiment after only six days.[6]

Crime and Punishment in America

Over the past half-century, America has enacted a real-life version of the Stanford prison on an unprecedented scale. In just four decades, the size of the state prison population has grown by more than 700 percent (see Figure 1.1).[7] By 2008, the number of incarcerated individuals in the United States hit an all-time high, with 1 in 100 adults in either prison or jail[8] and fully 1 in every 31 American adults under some form of correctional jurisdiction (including incarceration, probation, and parole).[9] In the size of its incarcerated populations, America now has no equal; it houses about a quarter of the world's prisoners, despite having less than 5 percent of the world's population. China, which has a population four times larger than that of the United States, is a distant second in the size of its imprisoned population, and most European nations have only about one-seventh the per capita incarcerated population of the United States.[10]

These snapshots are startling. However, there are two important ways in which even these numbers underestimate the true scale of mass imprisonment. First, the incarcerated are highly concentrated by race, class, age, and geography. In America today, the prison has become an increasingly prevalent institution in citizens' lives, but it is particularly so for youth, racial minorities, and the poor. For example, while "1 in 100" describes the proportion of incarcerated among the nation's total

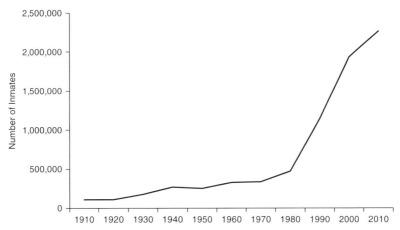

FIGURE I.I. Estimated number of jail and prison inmates in the United States, 1910–2010.

Source: For 1910–1990: Justice Policy Institute, *The Punishing Decade: Prison and Jail Estimates at the Millennium*; for 2000 and 2010, Bureau of Justice Statistics, *Correctional Populations in the United States, 2010*.

adult population, the figure is 1 in every 9 for young black men and a whopping 1 in every 3 for young black men without a high school education.[11] Among young male Latinos who did not complete high school, 1 in every 14 is behind bars.

For these groups of citizens, rates of contact with criminal justice now rival the likelihood of experiencing more traditional landmarks of the life course, including getting married and owning a home. Today, a black man without a high school education is more likely to be found in a prison or jail than at work.[12] Prison institutions have likewise replaced other, more conventional points of citizen contact with the state, emerging as "a major institutional competitor" to military service and secondary public education, particularly for racial minorities.[13] As Senator Jim Webb recently observed, "[T]he principal nexus between young African-American men and our society is increasingly the criminal justice system."[14] For these individuals, imprisonment has become a "predictable part of experience."[15]

Likewise, the experience of incarceration is highly concentrated in certain geographic areas. For instance, taxpayers in Pennsylvania spend more than $40 million a year to incarcerate residents sharing just a single low-income zip code in the state.[16] In Michigan, one-third of prisoners are sent back to a single county. About 80 percent live in Detroit, 41 percent in only eight zip codes.[17] A greater number of prisoners return to just seven neighborhoods in Houston than come home to several whole counties in Texas. And of the more than 50 community board districts in New York City, nearly three-quarters of prisoners in the entire state hail from just seven.[18] Simply put, some areas have become "deep reservoirs of criminal justice involvement," where punishment and prisons help to construct the "architecture of community life."[19] This has led some to criticize the very concept of "mass incarceration," arguing that it is not the "masses" who are imprisoned so much as highly concentrated groups within certain locales. As Todd Clear notes, "[I]ncarceration is not an equal opportunity activity."[20]

The second way in which acknowledging only a general upward trend of American incarceration obscures its true impact is that "1 in 100" includes only those who are in prison or jail *on any given day*. The Bureau of Justice Statistics estimates that by 2001 the proportion of adults who had *ever* spent time in prison had reached nearly 3 percent, and it was well over 16 percent for black men.[21] These proportions would be significantly higher if jail time were included. To the extent that the effects of prison persist beyond the prison gates, the accumulation of ex-prisoners in the population is certainly as important as the number of individuals imprisoned at any one time.[22]

Not surprisingly, researchers have noted these patterns and trends with some alarm. However, scholars interested in the consequences of incarceration, particularly its effects on recidivism, have so far attended primarily to the effects of imprisonment relative to other forms of punishment (e.g., probation).[23] This focus reflects a legitimate concern about recent growth in the total correctional population, and extant studies provide crucial commentary on the implications of America's increasing reliance (and many would argue over-reliance) on incarceration. However, while the rapidly rising number of people serving time behind bars is important, so, too, are recent changes in the way that U.S. prisons are constituted. That is to say, *we must be concerned not only with who is being incarcerated in America, but also with how they are being incarcerated*. In this book, I analyze changes in the culture of American prisons over the last half century and assess the consequences of variation in correctional administration for the types of people and communities that prisons produce.

The Politics and Practice of Punishment

The modern period has been marked by two significant trends in the culture of American corrections. First, the American criminal justice system over the past half-century has largely abandoned the goal of reforming inmates. Rehabilitation-oriented programming retrenched, leaving prisons to serve little more than a "waste management function."[24] Famously summing up this new approach to crime control, James Q. Wilson commented: "Wicked people exist. Nothing avails except to set them apart from innocent people."[25] In the contemporary era of warehousing and incapacitation, what goes on inside the nation's prisons has become largely beside the point, with the exception of regular reassurances to the public that prisoners are being treated with the tough justice they deserve.

The second change that accompanied the modern politics of crime control was the arrival of a new language of criminal justice, what Malcolm Feeley and Jonathan Simon term the "new penology," which focused on "the efficient control of internal system processes in place of the traditional objectives of rehabilitation and crime control." The cornerstone of this penological approach was a heightened attention to risk management.[26] In essence, as policymakers and prison practitioners began to doubt that prisons could really reduce recidivism, rehabilitation became subordinated to the more concrete task of efficient operational control; if criminal populations could not be transformed, they could at least be effectively managed.

These shifting tides were compelled by substantial changes in the politics of crime control. In the first half of the 20th century, crime was largely absent from the national political agenda. Prisons were barely discussed in Congress, and imprisonment was used only sparingly by states.[27] For most of this period, the design and operation of correctional institutions were instead left largely to specialists within the state and federal bureaucracy, such as criminal psychologists, social workers, and custodial staff. This began to change in the 1950s and 1960s, however, as elected officials on both sides of the aisle began to realize that appearing "tough on crime" was a winning political strategy that offered few, if any, strategic downsides. Against a background of urban unrest and rising rates of crime, punishment quickly became a high-profile political issue. The emergent view of offenders as violent and immoral predators left little public sympathy for prison-based services that might make incarceration a comfortable experience. Moreover, on the heels of this "new punitiveness"[28] in political rhetoric came an influential report, titled "What Works? Questions and Answers About Prison Reform,"[29] which cast doubt on whether prisons could actually reform criminal offenders. As faith in the rehabilitative potential of prisons began to wane, support for continued funding of prison-based programs rapidly eroded.

The end result of these dynamics is a modern correctional model that employs prisons as little more than tools for temporary containment, a set of institutions designed for "selectively incapacitating the wicked."[30] As David Garland points out, "Treatment modalities still operate within [prison] walls, and lip service is still paid to the ideal of the rehabilitative prison. But the walls themselves are now seen as the institution's most important and valuable element.... [T]he walls have been fortified, literally and figuratively."[31]

The results I uncover, however, make clear that time spent within the confines of a correctional institution is not a "deep freeze"[32] during which individuals simply serve out their time unchanged. Rather, prisons are small communities unto themselves, and the context of life inside these state institutions has important consequences for the kinds of people they produce. In the chapters that follow I argue that, for both incarcerated individuals and their keepers, navigating a more punitive prison entails the adoption of new social relationships and collective norms. However, rather than the generalized trust and cooperation that are often posited to follow from strong social connections,[33] America's harsher prisons produce citizens who are less interested in – and arguably less capable of – healthy (re-)integration into a broad and inclusive social community. In this way, the culture of the correctional institution has important repercussions for the ways in which a growing group of citizens think, behave, and interact.

The Social Effects of the Punitive Prison

In uncovering the effects of more punitive prisons, I start by examining the effect of incarceration on the social orientations of the imprisoned. Inmates often form close relationships with peers while behind bars, but this is particularly true in higher-security prisons, where social ties result from the desire for companionship, but also the need for protection. For example, I find that inmates incarcerated in these harsher prison settings become significantly more likely to report that they have friends who "help me when I have troubles" and with whom they can talk "about everything" than do inmates who serve time in less punitive settings.

This expansion of personal friendship networks, despite providing meaningful camaraderie and confidants, does little to ameliorate feelings of loneliness, however. Inmates in more punitive prisons are no less likely to say that they "feel lonely" or that "no one really knows [them] very well." Instead, the expansion of social networks that occurs in this type of prison results in the adoption of criminogenic attitudes; those assigned to harsher prison settings are significantly more likely to agree that "some people must be treated roughly or beaten up just to send them a clear message" and to assert that they "won't hesitate to hit or threaten people if they have done something to hurt [their] family or friends." In sum, I argue that the social networks built between inmates in a more punitive prison seem at best to promote a particularized trust that does not substantially mitigate feelings of isolation. At worst, harsher prison environments inculcate inmates with an increased propensity for interpersonal violence and aggression, and ultimately increase the likelihood of re-offending following parole. In fact, I find that assignment to a harsher prison setting significantly increases recidivism. Using fairly conservative assumptions, I estimate that a more punitive prison culture might account for more than 64,500 crimes in the coming decade in California alone, which would be expected to include more than 13,000 violent crimes, such as murder, rape, and violent assault.

As in the Stanford Prison Experiment, I also find that the culture of prison institutions affects those individuals who hold formal power within the prison environment: the officers tasked with the maintenance of order and security. Like the number of people incarcerated, the ranks of people employed by the U.S. criminal justice system have increased substantially, growing by 86 percent between 1982 and 2003 to more than 2.36 million people (see Figure 1.2). As of March 2003, almost 13 percent of all public employees (and a larger percentage of public employees in 15 states and the District of Columbia) worked in the criminal justice sector.[34] Much of this growth has been driven by the number of correctional employees. Between 1982 and

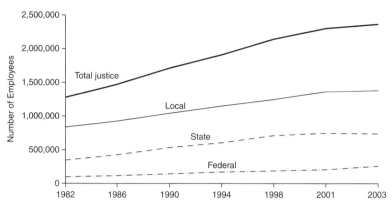

FIGURE 1.2. Justice employees by level of government, 1982–2003.
Source: Bureau of Justice Statistics.

2003, corrections employment more than doubled, rising from about 300,000 to more than 748,000. Corrections now accounts for more than 63 percent of state criminal justice employees, with police protection and judicial/legal employees accounting for the other 14 and 22 percent, respectively.[35] Today, the criminal justice system employs more people than General Motors, Ford, and Wal-Mart combined.[36]

Just as more punitive settings shape inmates' social ties, I find that harsher prisons affect the social relationships and attitudes of those who work behind their walls. In fact, the particular social patterns of inmates are mirrored in those of correctional staff. For correctional officers, prison work often requires long hours spent in a hostile and chaotic work environment, marked by the need for constant surveillance and feelings of threat. The result of this institutional context is the development of meaningful bonds between officers, but also the adoption of an "us against them" mentality. In particular, officers who find themselves working in harsher prisons develop harsher ideas about inmates than do their counterparts in less punitive prisons: they are more likely to express the belief that "most people who end up in prison are there because of personal failure" rather than "because they did not have advantages like strong families, good education and job opportunities." They are also less likely to support the provision of rehabilitation programs and more likely to say that "rehabilitation programs don't work because most inmates don't want to change." Even more striking are officers' own assessments of how imprisonment shapes inmates; officers assigned to more punitive prisons become more likely to say that the institution where they work causes inmates to become more violent and that inmates actually leave prison less prepared to be law-abiding citizens than when they entered.

The prison environment also shapes the interactions that officers have with each other, with their superiors, and with friends and family. Officers working in harsher prisons are more likely to report that they would turn to the union to help resolve work-related problems. Conversely, they become less likely to turn to their direct supervisors for assistance. This is particularly true of officers who feel unsafe in the workplace. Prison work and experiences of violence likewise impose substantial costs on officers' lives outside prison. Unlike inmates, officers must move between home and prison on a daily basis. For many, this transition can be a difficult one. In his searing account of time spent as an officer at Sing Sing Correctional Facility, Ted Conover describes the personal toll that the job took on him:

"Leave it at the gate," you hear time and again in corrections. Leave all the stress and bullshit at work; don't bring it home to your family. This was good in theory. In reality, though, I was like my friend who had worked the pumps at a service station: Even after she got home and took a shower, you can still smell the gasoline on her hands. Prison got into your skin, or under it. If you stayed long enough, some of it probably seeped into your soul.[37]

I find that officers working in harsher prison environments are especially likely to experience work–family conflict; these officers are more likely to say that they have "become harsher or less trusting towards family members since I took this job" and that "what happens at work negatively affects my relationship with my spouse/partner or children."

In the last empirical chapter of the book, I turn my attention to the types of communities to which prisoners return. I start by analyzing survey data from 515 individuals living in diverse areas of Los Angeles County, a geographic area that alone receives almost a third of all people returning from prison in California. Within this one county, there is significant variation in the concentration of parolees. For instance, less than 1 parolee returns to the wealthy Beverly Hills zip code 90210 in a typical year; in comparison, several consecutive zip codes in south central LA receive roughly 15 parolees for every 100 residents. This variation in communities' ex-prisoner concentration is highly predictive of the social orientations of the individuals who reside there. I find that individuals living in areas of high ex-prisoner concentration are equally likely to say that they have friends and people in whom they can confide as those in areas of lower concentration, and there is even some evidence that they engage in more frequent informal social interactions. However, their social networks are smaller; individuals living in higher-concentration localities report a lesser number of close friends and confidants. At the same time, people who reside in areas that receive a higher concentration of ex-prisoners also report significantly less generalized social trust. They are less likely to believe that "most people can be trusted" and substantially more likely to instead endorse the idea that "you can't be too careful in dealing with people."

In order to see whether this pattern holds beyond this one county and state, I then expand my analysis to a larger and more geographically diverse dataset. Using survey data from nearly 12,000 individuals residing in 2,083 unique zip codes and spread across 13 states, I show that the patterns in Los Angeles County are not unique to this locale. Rather, the same patterns of atomized community that are evident among correctional officers and inmates serving time in more punitive prisons are characteristic of the many poor, urban neighborhoods across the nation to which ex-prisoners predominantly return.

Prisons are sometimes described as "total institutions,"[38] in that for a period of time they segregate individuals from the rest of society. This would seem to suggest that they are most productively studied as isolated communities rather than as extensions of the low-income cities and towns from which most incarcerated people come. However, nearly 95 percent of the imprisoned will eventually be released.[39] In California, for instance, which operates the largest of the nation's state prison systems, the average time in prison is 26 months.[40] This means that more than 40 percent of people who are currently incarcerated in that state will be released from prison *this year*. In total, some 650,000 of America's incarcerated move back and forth – and some then back and forth again – between prison and their neighborhoods each year.[41] When they leave the confines of the prison, these individuals are likely to bring with them the attitudes and behaviors they have learned. As the journalist Sasha Abramsky warns, noting that conflicts begun or sustained in prison are increasingly spilling out onto the street: "There is an awful lot of potential rage coming out of prison to haunt our future."[42]

The Modern Prison Paradox

Institutions of punishment are often considered to be a necessary, if unfortunate, prerequisite of a thriving civil society and the establishment of a legitimate state.[43] Indeed, protecting the lives and property of citizens through the creation and enforcement of criminal law is inarguably a fundamental role of government. In the liberal democratic tradition, law and order is at the heart of the social contract and provides the foundation on which organized society is built. On this, John Locke wrote: "Government being for the preservation of every man's right and property, by preserving him from the violence or injury of others, is for the good of the governed."[44]

Yet in this regard, the modern American prison presents us with a troubling paradox. In the chapters that follow, I argue that the crime control politics of the past half-century have given rise to institutions that (re-)create the conditions that arguably gave rise to criminality in the first place, and they do so in a particularly intense and toxic form. Within the harsh environment of the nation's most punitive prisons, strategic social connections are formed, as individuals band together for mutual protection and exchange. However, the social ties forged in prison ultimately foster social norms that are anathema to broad-based, cooperative community engagement.

The result is that, by sending people to increasingly punitive and dangerous prisons, we do not resocialize them into the norms and roles of American culture. Rather, we socialize them into the norms and roles of *prison* culture. And "as one inmate serving a life term at East Jersey State Prison puts it, 'You create Spartan conditions, you're gonna get gladiators.'"[45] To the extent that the nation's modern "law and order" institutions shape the social order in ways that weaken, rather than sustain, our communities and civil society, prisons may undermine the very collectivities they were designed to serve and perpetuate the problems of crime and disorder they are tasked with preventing.

Departures

In making the argument that prisons in the modern era shape Americans' social orientations in salient ways, I depart from existing literature on political institutions, prison effects, and social connectedness in four important respects:

1. Centralizing the State

In most accounts, social networks and norms are construed to be a positive resource, a social good that inheres within formal and informal relationships. For instance, in his seminal work *Bowling Alone*, Robert Putnam implicates the "collapse" of social community in the emergence of a host of social ills.[46] Strong social ties provide individuals with emotional benefits, including the chance for fraternization, group identity, and the feeling of solidarity that comes with being part of a shared effort.[47] More extensive and deeper social ties can also promote a generalized sense of trust and feelings of communal belonging.[48] In turn, people who possess high levels of generalized trust are more involved than others in community life and are more likely to engage in economic exchange and cooperative behavior outside their immediate social group.[49] As Eric Uslaner writes, "Trust is the chicken soup of social life."[50]

The idea that social relationships can serve a pro-social purpose is formalized in Pierre Bourdieu's classic conception of "social capital," wherein he invokes a "species of capital" that "allows its possessors to wield a power, an influence, and thus to exist, in the field under consideration, instead of being considered a negligible quantity."[51] Social capital can be leveraged by individuals toward varied ends – for example, to help find employment,[52] to mobilize political action,[53] or to trade and share property in informal markets.[54] Likewise, in the aggregate, social networks and the norms they engender foster a range of collective goods, from education and children's welfare, and safe and productive neighborhoods, to economic prosperity, and health and happiness.[55] Interpersonal trust can help promote and sustain a productive economy, a peaceful and cooperative society, and a democratic government.[56]

In contrast, we know sizably less about the potential "dark side"[57] of social ties, the "down side"[58] of social networks, or the possible "unsocial"[59] forms of interpersonal association. Social networks may be more or less present, but they may also take different forms.[60] Just as economic capital can be applied toward both charity and war, social connections can be deployed toward either more or less cooperative ends. As Francis Fukuyama remarks, "This does not disqualify it as a form of capital; physical capital can take the form of assault rifles or tasteless entertainment, while human capital can be used to devise new ways of torturing people."[61] While "darker"[62] incarnations of social connection have received substantially less attention than their more pro-social counterparts, they are no less a part of what gives social relations their broader meaning.

Even more significantly, there has been little systematic theorizing on the role of the state in shaping less pro-social kinds of interpersonal connectedness. This is true even in the many studies that have been attentive to the interrelations between crime, community, and social organization. These studies regularly cite poverty, residential instability, urbanization, and other macro trends as primary contributors to a decline in social activity. However, with few exceptions,[63] the state as purposive actor is peculiarly absent from these accounts. What is still therefore missing is a *political* accounting of negative social capital – how it arises and what its relationship is to state power and public policy.

While recognizing the importance of existing work, my intention in this book is to locate the state front and center within the study of social community and collective well-being. The argument I make seeks to avoid attributing the diffusion of countercultural norms to "indigenous, self-sustaining social organizational capacity."[64] Instead, I start from the proposition that the state, through its policies and institutions, helps to shape the particular types of social attitudes and behaviors that form and persist within communities. This argument rests on two central claims. First, I argue here that government can play a formative role in shaping social organization in even its least pro-social incarnations. Second, I argue that it does this not only when it is derelict in its responsibility to mitigate poverty or when it otherwise passively fails to ameliorate systematic disadvantage,[65] but also directly and proactively through its punitive policy choices and the culture of its carceral institutions.

Understanding the collateral effects of the modern prison institution is therefore critical, first and foremost because mass incarceration represents what is arguably the most significant public policy shift of the modern era. As Elliot Currie has observed, "Short of major wars, mass incarceration has been the most thoroughly implemented government social program of our time."[66] With mass incarceration, the United States "embarked on one of the largest public policy experiments in our history";[67] it is the "great public works project of our time."[68]

Moreover, with the exception of lethal force, confinement is the most extreme power that the state regularly exercises against its citizens.[69] Prisons therefore maintain a unique position among democratic institutions, and their culture provides "a key index of the state of a democracy."[70] As Nicola Lacey remarks: "The state of criminal justice – the scope and content of criminal law, the performance of criminal justice officials, public attitudes to crime, *and the extent and intensity of the penal system* – is often used as a broad index of how 'civilized,' 'progressive,' or indeed 'truly democratic' a country is."[71]More broadly, criminal justice institutions are an especially important site for empirical investigation because they are a feature of nearly every organized state[72] and central to liberal notions of the social contract.[73] As political scientist John DiIulio notes, "Prison workers perform what is arguably one of the most essential functions of the sovereign state."[74] The effects of prison institutions on individuals and communities should thus be of interest to any serious scholar of politics and the nation state.

2. *Emphasizing Institutional Variation*

Scholars have long been concerned with the economic, social, and psychological effects of incarceration. Indeed, interest in prison effects dates as far back as Gustave de Beaumont and Alexis de Tocqueville's *Du système pénitentiaire aux États-Unis et de son application en France*, written following their tour of the southern United States in 1831.[75] Since this first foray into American prison research, myriad studies have scrutinized the attitudes and behaviors individuals develop when they are exposed to the correctional environment. Researchers concerned with mental health and post-traumatic stress have examined the psychological pressures of incarceration,[76] the difficulties of prison adjustment have dominated prison memoirs,[77] and the contours of the inmate subculture have been addressed in scholarly studies of the sociology of prisons.[78] Recently, the topic has even surfaced in the popular press, with *Time* magazine posing the question "Are Prisons Driving Prisoners Mad?"[79]

Craig Haney, a prominent author on the "pains of imprisonment," notes that by the end of the 20th century, there was relative agreement among scholars that prisons caused little serious psychological harm for most inmates. Summarizing the existing empirical literature, Frank Porporino suggested that "imprisonment is not generally or uniformly devastating."[80] Yet Haney rightly notes that this was hardly an endorsement; "statements to the effect that not everyone who passed through prison is irreparably harmed, devastated, or made insane by the experience represent fairly faint praise."[81] Moreover, these studies too often obscured important ways in which the conditions of confinement could vary across prisons, variation that could substantially affect the potential of imprisonment to help or harm.

My aim in this book is to map this variation in the form and culture of the prison institution and to document its consequences for individuals and community life. This focus provides a new empirical leverage on the consequences of the prison boom. Scholars of the carceral state have sometimes portrayed the American prison system as a monolith and written of the "punitive turn" as a whole-scale shift in the culture of corrections. Yet, even in the 1950s, when Gresham Sykes and his contemporaries were penning their landmark prison studies, it is unlikely to have truly been the case that there existed "a remarkable tendency to override the variations of time, place and purpose [such that prisons were] apt to present a common social structure."[82] Rather, as I detail in Chapter 2, at least since the 1970s there has been substantial variation in the management of American prisons across states and regions. In addition, the rise of highly sophisticated inmate classification schemes has introduced greater and more systematic variation into the prison prototype.

In the following chapters, I measure prison variation – how harsh or punitive a prison environment is – by relying on the security-level designation(s) of a given facility: whether it is a low-, medium-, high-, or maximum-security setting. Using a facility's security-level designation is theoretically advantageous in several respects. First, as I describe in Chapter 4, prison security levels in many ways approximate historical variation, in that higher-security prisons place a greater emphasis on order and control over rehabilitation: they offer less freedom of movement, greater oversight, and a more limited range of programs. They are also marked by higher rates of violence than lower-security settings. In contrast, lower-security prisons in many ways retain a more rehabilitative focus and less violent inmate culture. In this way, lower-security prisons provide an (albeit imperfect) proxy for a pre-1970s model of prison administration, and higher-security prisons more fully embody the new punitiveness.

More important, however, is that security level is one of the most identifiable signifiers of institutional variation in the modern American prison system; as Gerald Gaes and Scott Camp observe, "Prison security level, more than any other prison level variable, identifies variation in [both institutional and social] dimensions of prison regime."[83] Prison management and design may differ across institutions of the same security level,[84] but generally speaking, higher-security prisons are marked by more restrictive rules and protocols. Similarly, through increasingly mechanized classification procedures,[85] the security level of a prison serves as a primary predictor of inmate composition, including the prevalence of gangs, levels of violence, and the "criminal propensity" of individual inmates.

By focusing on prison variation, I emphasize that prisons in the United States can and do take many forms; prisons are not homogeneous, and "the prison" as an undifferentiated concept is not all that useful. This variation has important implications, as correctional institutions can play a critical role in shaping social communities; as I show, variation in the way that imprisonment is practiced can produce widely disparate results.

Understanding the effects of prison design also has important implications for public policy. Given the relatively low likelihood that the nation will ever abolish prisons, custodial versus non-custodial sanctions is not the only or even the most pressing policy-relevant dichotomy. Instead, we must consider the consequences of different forms of incarceration – the various and varied ways that prison institutions are (or could be) designed and run.

3. Going Beyond "Just" Inmates

Extant research on correctional officers is far less expansive than scholarship on inmates. However, interest in the "street-level bureaucrats"[86] who work inside America's prisons has grown exponentially over the past few decades. What was once an overly simplistic and even hostile literature depicting prison custody staff as predominantly "less than quick witted" or "sadists," and their jobs as requiring only "20/20 vision, the IQ of an imbecile, [and] a high threshold for boredom," now encompasses a diverse set of descriptive and empirical studies that explore many aspects of correctional officers' attitudes and behavior.[87] Despite this, however, published studies of prison officers are still extremely rare in comparison with examinations of inmates.

Understanding the orientations of prison workers is a critical part of assessing the formal culture of the modern prison. Correctional officers, on the front lines of the prison system, are responsible for the day-to-day execution of almost every aspect of prison life. They therefore play a primary role in shaping the institutional culture that inmates confront. Indeed, if the relatively casual contact that clients have with welfare administrators or their brief encounters with police officers can have an impact on their attitudes, as previous research has suggested,[88] then the more intense and sustained contact that inmates have with correctional workers likely also has considerable effects. With this in mind, studies of correctional workers have begun to high-light how officers adopt and embody their professional norms and how they communicate these norms through their professional practice.[89]

We can consider correctional officers not only as representatives of the state, though, but also as citizens who themselves may be affected by correctional policies and prison management. As I detail in the fol-lowing chapters, correctional officers often face extremely high lev-els of violence in the workplace – according to the Bureau of Labor Statistics, this occupational group has one of the highest rates of non-fatal work-related injuries[90] – and I find that many of these workers feel they are not given the training and resources they require to keep themselves safe on the job. As bureaucrats, these individuals shape the administration of criminal justice, but as people and as citizens, they are also affected by it. Like inmates, correctional officers have daily experiences within the confines of a prison that are mediated by the design and implementation of institutional policies and practices. In fact, many career correctional officers will spend more time in prison over the course of their lives than a large fraction of inmates. Thus, in addition to examining the socialization of prisoners, I explore the flip side of the correctional coin: the ways in which prison work shapes the social lives, norms, and values of officers.

In expanding the subject of inquiry, I hope to emphasize that choices about how to manage and organize prisons do not affect only inmates. Rather, they have consequences for a much broader array of people who are both directly and indirectly affected by the culture of this increasingly predominant state institution. Consider the following:

even if correctional employees and inmates are each linked to only three other individuals outside prison or jail – a child, a mother, and a friend, for example – the affected population *at any given time* reaches a total of about 12 million Americans. That is roughly equivalent to the combined populations of Hawaii, Rhode Island, Montana, Delaware, South Dakota, North Dakota, Alaska, Vermont, Maine, New Hampshire, Idaho, and Wyoming.[91] The population either directly or vicariously affected by incarceration increases dramatically once we also include the previously incarcerated, retired officers, and the host of others who have encountered correctional institutions as prison counselors, teachers, medical staff, or program volunteers.

4. *Testing Causality*

Several recent, rigorous empirical studies have shown that incarceration in a harsher prison environment may actually increase rates of recidivism.[92] However, despite extensive theorizing, we are still missing evidence for *how* different prison environments might shape criminal behavior. What happens during imprisonment that affects subsequent proclivities for crime? The handful of quasi-experimental studies that exist on this topic have left the mechanisms that link in-prison socialization and post-prison behavior largely unexplored, with prison as a proverbial black box in which some indeterminate change occurs. In this study, I argue that the social roles and attachments that are formed or solidified in prison play a pivotal role in determining the effects of different types of institutions.

Inmates assigned to harsher, higher-security prisons are not placed there by random chance, however, but rather because of who they are and what they have done. In particular, inmates are placed in higher-security settings because they have characteristics that make them more likely to engage in misconduct or to attempt escape. Thus, in higher-security prisons, the average inmate has a higher likelihood of being affiliated with a gang, is serving more time for a more violent offense, and has a longer and more violent criminal record. We might therefore reasonably expect that differences in the social orientations of higher- and lower-security prisoners pre-date their incarceration.

The same is true of correctional officers. For prison staff, demographic and attitudinal characteristics are likely to predict the type of institution to which they feel best suited and, over time, officers will select into the prison environment that conforms to their pre-existing orientations and beliefs. For instance, officers who hold more punitive attitudes may prefer working in more punitive prisons. This makes it difficult to determine the effects of different types of prison, as distinct from the differences individuals bring with them from the beginning.

In a perfect world, we would randomly assign both inmates and correctional officers to different types of prison and evaluate the outcome. This would allow us to isolate the impact of the prison environment. Of course, this is both infeasible and wildly unethical. For this reason, extant scholarship on prison effects remains primarily "anecdotal, qualitative and phenomenological."[93] This is not to say that we have learned little from these examinations and also from the many excellent quantitative, descriptive inquiries into prison effects that have emerged in recent years. However, only a handful of existing studies allow for the successful establishment of cause-and-effect relationships. For example, of the 300 relevant studies reviewed by Patrice Villettaz and her colleagues that estimated the effects of incarceration relative to non-custodial sanctions, the authors were able to find only four randomized experimental studies, one natural experiment, and an additional 23 non-randomized quasi-experimental studies that employed a sufficiently large number of control variables.[94] Even fewer experimental or quasi-experimental studies examine the effects of incarceration in different *types* of prison, and nearly all such studies examine imprisonment's effects on recidivism only.[95] This has left open the question of whether social orientations following imprisonment are *caused* by the prison or whether they are instead a reflection of the pre-existing resources and constraints that inmates and officers bring with them from the start. The analyses that follow are therefore distinct in that they help to adjudicate between these potential explanations.

By relying on two unique sources of data and two quasi-experiments, the analyses presented in the coming chapters help establish that prison institutions actually *change* the social attitudes and behavior of individuals. (I describe the specifics of these research designs in Chapter 4.) My contention is that the particular contours of the prison environment actively shape the ways in which social groups coalesce, the collective norms that groups develop, and the ways that individuals behave when they return to society at large. Just as in the mock prison of the Stanford

Prison Experiment more than 40 years ago, "the negative, anti-social reactions observed were not [only] the product of an environment created by combining a collection of deviant personalities, but rather the result of an intrinsically pathological situation.... The abnormality here resided in the psychological nature of the situation and not [just] those who passed through it."[96]

Separating "cause" from "correlate" is important not just as a methodological exercise, but also for its public policy implications. The dominant model of inmate rehabilitation is often solely "person-centered and dispositional in nature (focusing entirely on individual-level change)."[97] Yet addressing only the stable characteristics of individuals that make them likely to recidivate following release from prison serves to obscure the ways that imprisonment itself can encourage criminality. I find that it is the environment to which individuals are exposed, in addition to the pre-existing features of these individuals, that explain their attitudes and behavior. If this is the case, then focusing exclusively on the dispositions of individuals is not enough. Instead, we must also seek to reform the institutional contexts in which they are placed. This is not to deny that people have agency; individuals are surely responsible for the choices they make. However, the results I present in the following chapters suggest that those choices are also a product of the circumstances in which they are made.

How Institutions Make Citizens

By locating prisons as important state-centered sites of socialization, I do not mean to suggest that they are the primary places where social networks are produced, or even that they are the only arena in which social ties are transformed by the "right hand of the state."[98] As Dietlind Stolle's comprehensive review of social capital makes clear, "the spread of generalized trust, and norms of reciprocity and social participation are complex phenomena and cannot be explained by one factor alone."[99] Rather, my broader point is that social connectedness and the state are interdependent and reciprocal; civil society and the state work together in a "dynamic and cooperative relationship"[100] to build the strong social dynamics that enable effective collective problem solving.[101]

In this regard, the prison social context can help us to specify the dynamics of a more general set of processes. Prisons have a number of features that make them a strategic site for theoretical inquiry into how state policies and institutions "make citizens,"[102] shaping their social attitudes and behavior.[103] First, decisions about the particular prison institution to which an individual will be assigned are largely outside of his or her control. While some attributes of the individual will determine the type of prison to which he or she will be assigned, these characteristics are predictable, consistent, and observable. This helps to alleviate concerns that individuals are "selecting" into and out of their preferred social context. In addition, the boundaries for interpersonal interaction in prison are highly constrained. Prisons are extremely controlled environments, in which individuals are limited in their freedom of movement; once inside the prison walls, individuals cannot freely choose where they will go and with whom they will associate.

Second, prisons place people into social interactions of lengthy duration – the average prison sentence in 2008 was about two years,[104] and many correctional officers work 10- to 12-hour shifts for years or even decades on the job – and the context in which these interactions occur can lend social solidarities a particular intensity and importance. As Devah Pager and Michelle Phelps write, "Prisons can be unpredictable and dangerous environments, [so] access to the right social networks may be integral to a successful survival strategy."[105]

Finally, although the correctional institution represents a particularly stark form of state intervention, prison culture provides a useful microcosm of the social world. Prisons are small communities unto themselves. Like any small city or town, many prisons have schools and churches, factories and stores. Most residents get up every morning, eat breakfast, and go to work. After a long day, they eat dinner. Then they read or exercise; they play games, write letters, or watch television. They make friends; they make enemies; they change and adapt. Many features of modern prisons – in particular, the extent to which they manage violence, provide resources, and promote cooperative interaction between individuals and groups – are not unique to these particular social environments, but are instead reflective of the state's capacity to administer to these concerns in a variety of contexts.

In important respects, then, the results I present in the following chapters provide a general reflection on how the culture and constraints people face in their daily lives help shape their social adaptation. This book is about prisons, but it is also a broader story about why political institutions matter for how citizens come to view their social world, how they interact with others, and how they experience and respond to the particular context in which they are placed.

2

Politics and the Punitive Turn

> *The founders of a new colony, whatever Utopia of human virtue and*
> *happiness they might originally project, have invariably recognized it*
> *among their earliest practical necessities to allot a portion of the virgin*
> *soil as a cemetery, and another portion as the site of a prison.*
> Nathaniel Hawthorne, *The Scarlet Letter* (1850)

Over the past half-century, the United States has vastly expanded its
powers to punish, rapidly increasing institutional capacity, public
expenditures, and personnel devoted to this task. The most obvious
reflection of these changing trends in governance is the nation's rising rate of incarceration. During the latter half of the 20th century,
the prison admission rate skyrocketed. In 1960, there were roughly
330,000 prison and jail inmates in America; there were almost 2.3 million by 2010.[1]

Scholars have long argued that this precipitous growth in the correctional population was not purely a functional response to changes
in the crime rate, however.[2] In fact, rates of violent crime in the period
from 1960 to 2004 increased most precipitously during the 1960s and
1970s, rising about 125 percent. The same is true of property crime,
which increased roughly 100 percent from 1960 to 1969. In contrast, the number of adults under correctional jurisdiction remained
relatively stable until the mid-1970s, and only then did it begin to
rise. This growth subsequently continued during the mid-1990s and

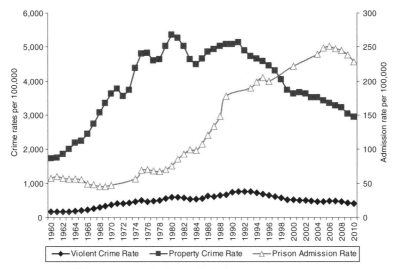

FIGURE 2.1. Crime rates and prison admissions, 1960–2010.
Source: Incarceration rate for 2000–2010 is from the *Sourcebook of Criminal Justice Statistics*, table 6.009.2010; for 1960–1998 is from the *Historical Statistics of the United States*, table Ec298–308; crime rates are from the *Sourcebook of Criminal Justice Statistics*, Table 3.106.2011.

beyond. Even as crime rates began to fall, prison admissions continued to climb (see Figure 2.1).

Crime, then, is only part of the story of how the prison population has grown; crime and criminal justice are not equivalencies.[3] Instead, while incarceration rates in the United States are not wholly disconnected from rates of crime,[4] growth in the number of the nation's imprisoned resulted from of a set of concerted public policy shifts at the federal, state, and local levels.[5] As Kevin Smith concludes, "[T]he explosive increase in prison populations since the mid-1970s is largely a product of the most basic elements of the political environment."[6] The changing use and culture of incarceration reflects the political values, priorities, and incentives of those in power.

My aim in this chapter is to review the contours of these changes and to explore their roots in the politicization of American corrections over the past half-century. I start by describing the partisan politics of crime control and the decline of the rehabilitative ideal. I then examine the ways that modern prison institutions vary both across and within states, arguing that despite a national trend toward greater punitiveness, systematic variation across prison facilities has actually increased over time.

The Politics of Crime Control

The emergence of crime as a key political issue is a relatively recent occurrence. In fact, prior to the 1960s, the federal government made little mention of punishment, preferring instead to leave crime control policies primarily to the states.[7] This began to change in the mid-20th century, however, as crime rates around the country began to rise. Seizing on growing public unease over civil unrest, urban riots, and disorder,[8] Barry Goldwater and other leaders in the Republican Party began to decry "violence in our streets, corruption in our highest offices, aimlessness among our youth, anxiety among our elderly."[9] Scholars now widely view this strategy as an implicit appeal to southern white voters who were growing uncomfortable with the substantial gains of the civil rights movement and urban riots,[10] a tactic that proved effective in mobilizing these voters for partisan political gain.[11]

Building on this implicitly racial rhetoric, Richard Nixon's subsequent campaign for president helped launch a "tough on crime" movement that would define the politics of criminal justice for decades to come.[12] Pointing to the Supreme Court's due process revolution as responsible for weakening efforts at crime control,[13] Nixon promised to put an end to the coddling of prisoners, appoint more conservative justices to the bench, and return authority to police officers. As Gregory Caldeira suggests, "[T]he rate of crime did skyrocket in the midst of the Warren Court's heyday, a time when the accused and convicted seemed to win a victory every week, and so it is not surprising that some should conclude that the Supreme Court was at fault."[14] In a strategic move to paint themselves as the law and order party, Republicans promised to crack down on crime, painted criminals (and, implicitly, urban blacks) as a threat to the social order, and advocated for more and harsher punishment.[15] Some conservatives even called for the impeachment of Justice Warren.[16]

Quickly realizing that they were being outflanked on crime control, Democrats soon began their own calls to ratchet up state and federal punishment.[17] Indeed, in some respects, liberal legislators in this period were caught in a political catch-22. Although some Democrats might in principle have supported a focus on rehabilitation and the root causes of crime, most feared the political cost of appearing too "soft on crime." This anxiety was personified in the unexpected defeat of Michael Dukakis, whose presidential ambitions were brought down at least in part by the specter of William Horton, a black convicted murderer who kidnapped and assaulted a white couple while on a weekend pass from prison during the candidate's tenure as governor. In their description of this period, Philip Klinkner and Rogers Smith write: "The 'Willie' Horton imagery served several purposes for the Republicans – it not only conjured up white fears of black crime, but also reinforced the perception of many white voters that the Democrats were overly tolerant of social deviants (read, blacks)."[18]

The Democratic Party quickly learned its lesson, launching a punitive policy "bidding war" to outdo Republicans on punishment. Of the "ideological confusion" that would serve subsequently to delimit the conversation over crime control, Michael Dukakis's 1988 campaign manager, Susan Estrich, suggests: "The traditional structure of the liberal-conservative crime debate is a debate between punishment and rehabilitation, between their responsibility for breaking the law and our responsibility for creating a rotten society. It is a debate you don't hear very much, except when conservative talk show hosts are debating themselves, for the very reason that the liberal position is politically untenable."[19]

The momentum of this "punitive turn" in criminal justice politics continued to build through the 1980s and beyond. Driven by the war on drugs and so-called quality-of-life policing, incarceration was imposed as punishment on a wider swath of individuals and for increasingly minor crimes. From 1984 to 1998, the chance of receiving a prison sentence after an arrest increased by more than 50 percent.[20] This represented a sizable change in the centrality of prisons to state crime control activities; in both political discourse and policy practice, incarceration went from a last resort to a central tool in the nation's crime control arsenal. In addition, more punitive sentencing reforms, such as "three strikes" policies, sentencing enhancements, and mandatory minimum sentences increased the amount of time individuals served. Meanwhile, indeterminate sentencing laws that had been designed to take into account the psychological growth of inmates gave way to truth-in-sentencing laws that required inmates to serve the full length of their terms.[21] The result was a truly unprecedented growth in the use and scale of imprisonment. In 1970, there were roughly 20 inmates for every 1,000 crimes committed. By 2000, there were 112 inmates for every 1,000 crimes.[22]

Politics and Prison Culture

Growth in the size of the American prison population, as well as its changing composition, has engendered a great deal of discussion among policymakers, practitioners, and scholars of punishment and the penal state. At the same time that incarceration rates were rising, however, another important trend was taking hold: the country's correctional system underwent a significant cultural shift,[23] a concurrent trend that was motivated largely by the same strategic partisan concerns. Scholars now widely agree that this period was marked by the "decline of the rehabilitative ideal," a movement away from a guiding view of criminal justice institutions (and prisons in particular) as reformatory and toward a model that emphasized deterrence, retribution, and (especially) incapacitation.[24]

This was not so much a new occurrence as a return to an earlier model of prison practice. In fact, since its founding in the American colonies, the nation's prison system has largely maintained a consistent focus on deterrence as its primary goal.[25] It was not until the early 19th century that prison reformers began to seriously introduce the idea that prisons could also serve to rehabilitate individuals, a goal that was based on the psychological, sociological, and moral belief that "an offender is someone who has erred but is capable of change."[26] This rehabilitative philosophy, or "medical model" of corrections, which would come to characterize the field for a time, posited that correctional experts could administer "treatment" to inmates to cure them of the "disease" of crime and eventually allow them to return to society.[27] The belief was that reformation could be accomplished through the delivery of "constructive activity," such as rehabilitation-oriented programs in prison, combined with the use of indeterminate sentencing and parole, which allowed authorities to hold inmates for as long as it took to see positive behavioral change. Public support for this ideal was extremely high well into the middle of the 20th century; Marc Mauer writes that "as late as 1968, a Harris poll showed that 48 percent of the public thought that the primary purpose of prison *was* rehabilitation and that 72 percent believed the emphasis *should be* on rehabilitation."[28]

Scholars place the death knell of the rehabilitation ethic sometime in the 1970s. In both responding to, and fanning the flames of, growing public concerns about crime and disorder during this period, politicians on both sides of the aisle worked to outdo one another in showing how punitive they could be.[29] Over the ensuing decades, elected officials became hesitant to seem overly sympathetic to "bad" criminals who were threatening the lives and property of the "good," law-abiding public.[30] Instead, the ratcheting up of punishment became a powerful way for politicians to publicly express the "retributive urge" and appeal to voters who were seen as responsive to calls for vengeance. In the words of David Garland, the "language of condemnation and punishment…re-entered official discourse."[31]

In addition, politicians argued that harsher prisons could serve as a potential deterrent to criminal behavior. The idea was that, if the experience of incarceration could be made truly unappealing, those who served time would be loath to return, and those who had never been to prison might think twice before committing a crime that would send them there. This logic echoes the "principle of less eligibility," expressed by Jeremy Bentham more than a hundred years earlier, that the "ordinary condition of a convict ought not to be made more eligible than that of the poorest class of subjects who work for an honest living."[32] In other words, prison should not be made so appealing that it could incentivize those in the lowest stratum of society to commit crimes and thereby become eligible for the lifestyle incarceration provides. This notion swiftly took hold. By 2001, 59 percent of the public agreed with the statement "Prisons are too comfortable and criminals don't mind being sent to prison."[33]

Moreover, in the absence of serving any successful deterrent function, imprisonment would at least incapacitate offenders for the length of their term. In this regard, a "new penology" emerged in correctional administration after the 1970s that found prison managers increasingly consumed by "obsessive attempts to monitor risky individuals, to isolate dangerous populations, and to impose situational controls on otherwise open and fluid settings." This change is clearly articulated in work by Malcolm Feeley and Jonathan Simon. They describe the replacement of older models of penal administration, which were focused on the individual – his or her "responsibility, fault, moral sensibility, diagnosis, or intervention and treatment" – with a new model of correctional management that is "neither about punishing nor about rehabilitating individuals. It is about identifying and managing unruly groups.... The task is managerial, not transformative."[34]

The rise to prominence of these new models of imprisonment had help from within criminal justice circles, where conceptions of prison practice were also being rapidly transformed. Like the political transformations already described, the 1970s were a turning point for ideologies within the correctional bureaucracy. Most notably, in 1974, Robert Martinson released a controversial report titled "What Works? Questions and Answers About Prison Reform," in which he concluded that "with few and isolated exceptions, the rehabilitative efforts that have been reported so far have had no appreciable effect on recidivism."[35] Long-standing critics of the rehabilitation philosophy seized on this "nothing works" report to bolster their argument that current correctional practice was irrevocably flawed and to urge a transition toward a more punitive approach.

The Martinson report brought together strange bedfellows. Liberals embraced the report, citing it as confirmation of their growing concern, drawn also from recent experiences with mental hospitals, that rehabilitation could not successfully be accomplished in a coercive institution of forced confinement. Furthermore, they argued that indeterminate sentencing – providing inmates with a sentencing range and then periodically convening a panel of experts to judge whether they had been sufficiently rehabilitated to warrant release – gave too much flexibility to so-called professionals, resulting in inconsistent decisions. In particular, liberal critics drew attention to the racial disparities they believed discretion produced. Conservatives likewise welcomed Martinson's conclusions. For those on the right, the report served as confirmation of their contention that coddling criminals was ineffective and that the state should take a tougher approach. As James Q. Wilson and others argued, the role of the prison should be to "isolate and punish," not to rehabilitate and cure.[36]

What emerged was a reconceptualization of the rationale that undergirds punishment.[37] Explanations of criminal offending under the rehabilitation model often portrayed offenders as products or even victims of their circumstances, and crime as at least in part attributable to society's failure to provide adequate educational and employment opportunities. In marked contrast, the new punitiveness positioned criminals as having transgressed the moral code by making poor choices. Crime, like poverty, was "the consequence of individual failure."[38] Emerging from this new idea of criminality was the principle of just deserts: the proposition that individuals should take responsibility for their actions and reap the (harsh) punishment they were rightfully due. And while voices outside the Beltway continued to push for an older conceptualization of criminals as the canary in the coal mine – a visible symptom of the underlying problems of economic inequality, urban decay, and racial injustice – this frame was largely downplayed in popular political rhetoric.

As the medical model of rehabilitation was discredited, it made room for a new vision of offenders "as evildoers of society who are supposed to be punished and deterred through determinate and harsh sentences."[39] At the heart of this new rhetoric were concerns about "the new dangerous class"[40] and the supposed threat posed by a violent new breed of intransigent criminal. This idea is perhaps best typified in *Body Count*, a book by three highly esteemed conservative voices on crime control, including political scientist John DiIulio. The book warned of "a new generation of street criminals"[41] that posed a potential crisis-level threat to American law and order:

Based on all that we have witnessed, researched and heard from people who are close to the action, here is what we believe: America is now home to thickening ranks of juvenile 'superpredators' – radically impulsive, brutally remorseless youngsters, including ever more preteenage boys, who murder, assault, rape, rob, burglarize, deal deadly drugs, join gun-toting gangs and create serious communal disorders.[42]

According to the authors of *Body Count*, this new breed of superpredator was emerging not as a result of economic inequality or a historical legacy of systemic racial discrimination, but rather from a growing "moral poverty." Broken families and weakened civil society had resulted in a generation of people who failed to take personal responsibility for their own choices and had no meaningful moral compass to guide them toward pro-social behavior. From this starting point of both individual and cultural failings, the authors advocated a hardline approach to crime that would make unstinting use of incarceration.

This "personal responsibility" frame for criminality proscribed a particular function for the prison. If criminality was rooted in the failure of social and political institutions to provide adequate social safety nets and afford ample opportunities for education and employment, then rehabilitation programs and restorative justice might be appropriate policy responses. However, if criminal behavior instead stemmed from poor choices and moral failings, then long sentences and harsh prisons were the better means to curb crime.

Data in the years after *Body Count* made clear that the darker predictions of the superpredator claim had failed to materialize; in the ensuing period, rates of juvenile crime fell precipitously. In fact, Professor DiIulio later softened his position, writing articles that advocated a broader approach to crime control and "zero prison growth."[43] Once the punitive movement had taken hold, however, there was little room for older or more nuanced arguments; the punitive horse had already left the proverbial barn. As DiIulio put it in a *New York Times* interview published a few years after the book: "I couldn't write fast enough to curb the reaction."[44] Tellingly, Martinson (of the Martinson Report) also later revisited some of his earlier conclusions, noting that some rehabilitation programs did appear to lower recidivism.[45] Yet as one historical account of correctional policy describes, "whereas Martinson's nothing works article is among the most cited of criminological writings, his revisionist 1979 essay earned scant attention."[46]

The Modern American Prison

What were the consequences of these political and policy developments for the practice of American corrections? Some scholars suggest that there actually has been relative stability in the operation of American prisons over time,[47] citing a sizable disconnect between emerging "tough on crime" rhetoric calling for harsher prisons and the "lived experience of rehabilitation"[48] on the ground.[49] These authors note that changes in public discourse over corrections do not necessarily translate into substantive administrative reforms.[50] Others suggest that there has always been some combination of goals and perspectives guiding prison practice; prisons have long "braided" punishment and rehabilitation, practicing a penology that is both "volatile and contradictory."[51]

However, while it may be true that the "punitive turn" was not a whole-scale and undifferentiated break with the recent past, it is also the case that modern shifts in the meaning and purpose of imprisonment called for practical changes in the form and function of American prisons. Punitive reforms at the state level were further encouraged by federal dollars, provided in large amounts during the second half of the 20th century to any state willing to increase its capacity to convict and confine. For example, the federal government incentivized states to increase prison sentences by providing "truth-in-sentencing" grants, which lowered the cost of imprisonment.

Many states also began to reconceptualize the culture of corrections as it was practiced within prison institutions. In describing the political backlash against what were perceived by many to be the nation's "county club prisons," Robert Worth writes:

Punishment is in vogue, along with hard labor and "no frills" prisons, stripped of weight rooms, TVs, and computers. Republicans in Congress have added a no-frills-prison section to the Contract With America's "Take Back Our Streets Act," and they have passed it as an amendment to the 1994 crime bill. Massachusetts Governor William F. Weld has argued that prisons should be "a tour through the circles of hell," where inmates should learn only "the joys of busting rocks." Alabama has already reinstituted the chain gang, forcing inmates to do hard labor in leg irons for up to ten hours a day. State administrators and sheriffs, sniffing the political wind, have begun to crack down ... making prison life as harsh as possible.[52]

During this period, Congress sought to "prevent luxurious conditions in prisons" by withholding federal funds to state prisons that allowed inmates access to privileges, such as weightlifting equipment, televisions, and unmonitored phone calls.[53] In Alaska, for instance, voters adopted state constitutional language in 1994 that expressly added "community condemnation" to its list of standards for prison administration in that state. This served as an important precursor to the subsequent passage of a "No Frills Prison Act" in 1997, which sought to make sure that prisons were not "overly comfortable."[54] Sociologist Francis Cullen writes that, in launching a "penal harm movement," the United States entered into a "mean season in which it has become politically correct ... to devise creative strategies to make offenders suffer ... we are witnessing a movement whose supreme aim is the infliction of penal harm."[55]

Other states similarly pursued reforms. For example, author Mona Lynch documents the practices of a sheriff in Arizona who became well known for his extreme form of justice. Lynch reports that inmates in one 8,400-person county jail facility were forced to live in a "tent city" in the desert, located next to "an animal shelter, a waste treatment plant and a garbage dump"; were served "post-date 'green bologna' and other surplus foods" and had their daily meals reduced from three to two; and were exposed to summer temperatures that regularly reached 110–120 degrees. In addition, in order to "emasculate his male inmates," the sheriff had their underwear dyed bright pink; and men, women, and juveniles alike were assigned to work on "publicly displayed 'chain gangs'" whose mandated tasks included "public projects, such as burying the indigent in county owned cemeteries."[56]

The effects of this paradigm shift went beyond the physical discomfort and psychic humiliations faced by inmates, however. Once practitioners and policymakers began to question the basic idea that offenders could be successfully transformed into law-abiding citizens, rehabilitation-oriented programs within prisons quickly lost their appeal. The central question, as David Rothman rhetorically poses, became: "If education and training programs are seen as futile, why should the state spend money on them?"[57] Indeed, perhaps most often cited as a key marker of the "new punitiveness" was that state and federal funding for rehabilitation programs substantially diminished.

This devolution was particularly evident in prison-based higher education.[58] Prior to 1994, there were at least 350 of these programs in correctional facilities spread across most of the 50 states and the majority of their funding came from public financing. The "punitive turn" aggressively targeted these expenditures, though; from 1982 through 1994, conservatives in Congress annually proposed legislation that would bar receipt of federal Pell Grants to any incarcerated person. Finally, in 1994, Congress passed the Violent Crime Control and Law Enforcement Act. While only 1 percent of money distributed by the Pell Grant program was at the time going to pay tuition for people in prison, the 1994 legislation had devastating effects on prison college programs. Virtually overnight, programs across the country closed their doors.[59]

The disappearance of higher education programs from American prisons was a remarkable break from the past. However, as criminologist Joan Petersilia notes:

The Pell controversy was but a small part of a huge and largely undocumented trend to drastically scale back all prison vocational and education programs. At least 25 states report having made cuts in vocational technical training, the areas most likely to provide inmates with an alternative career when they leave prison. Most states now have long waiting lists for classes of any kind. Even in states where programs have not been cut, prison crowding has rendered them almost useless. Class size has increased so rapidly that the standard approach for elementary-level courses, according to one prison teacher, is "throw them the GED handbook and say 'let me know when you're finished.' "[60]

Not surprisingly, the decreasing availability of in-prison programs (and most likely their diminishing quality) described by Petersilia also led to declining participation rates. "Just over one-fourth (29 percent) of those released from prison in 1997 participated in vocational training programs (down from 31 percent in 1991), and only 35 percent participated in education programs (down from 43 percent in 1991). Just 13 percent of all inmates leaving prison in 1997 were involved in any pre-release education program."[61] Bert Useem and Anne Piehl find similar trends in data from the Bureau of Justice Statistics. They report that participation in academic programs in state prisons increased slightly from 22 percent in 1974 to 45 percent in 1986, but had declined again by 2007 to 36 percent. In addition, in-prison work assignments shrank from a high of 74 percent participation in 1974 to 60 percent in 1997.[62]

Useem and Piehl observe, too, that although the quality of these programs is difficult to gauge, it almost certainly varies across prisons. As evidence, they cite Ann Chih Lin's study of education programs in five prisons, noting that "real education" could be found in only three of the five facilities. In the other two, Lin reports, "staff's first priority was to protect one another, especially from inmate assaults and manipulation. Any relaxation of this cultural solidarity, which might be fostered by staff–inmate communication, threatened to initiate a spiral toward disorder."[63] Lin suggests that such marked differences in the quality of prison education were reflected in student outcomes; after all, she chides, "there is little reason to expect that sleeping in a classroom would have an effect on test scores or recidivism rates."[64]

Prison Variation and the Culture of Institutions

In the preceding sections, I described substantial changes in the trajectory of prison management, and suggested that the politicization of crime urged a broad shift toward a new style of corrections. However, there is also a more nuanced version of this recent history, which complicates the idea of a straightforward and homogeneous transformation. In fact, it is clear that focusing exclusively on a national return to punitiveness masks wide variation across regions and states, and even within state systems.

Most basically, scholars have documented wide disparities in state incarceration rates, as well as in the length of state prison terms, parole revocation rates, and levels of state spending on punishment.[65] Incarceration rates range from the low levels in states like Maine and Minnesota, approximately 150–200 inmates per 100,000 residents, to the high levels maintained by Louisiana, Texas, and others, which are above 700 per 100,000 (Figure 2.2).[66] In fact, rates of incarceration are more diverse across U.S. states than they are across all of Western Europe.[67]

Less is known about how the *culture* of prison varies across state contexts. However, some accounts suggest that states also deviate in their administrative rules and day-to-day operations, as well as in their more informal inmate organization.[68] For instance, in *Governing Prisons*, John DiIulio focuses his attention on classifying the formal, or administrative, state prison regime, identifying different models of correctional management across states that are predicated on different correctional philosophies. Through extensive site visits and interviews with correctional staff and management, DiIulio compares three different state prison systems: Texas, Michigan, and California. He argues that these three systems represent three distinct "keeper philosophies," typifying a control model, a responsibility model, and a consensual/ mixed model, respectively.[69]

Texas's control model is marked by a highly regulated, restrictive environment, which mandates clearly communicated punishments for

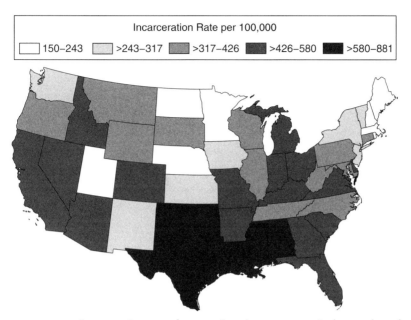

FIGURE 2.2. Incarceration rates by state. Imprisonment rate is the number of prisoners sentenced to more than one year per 100,000 U.S. residents. Based on census estimates for January 1, 2010.
Source: Bureau of Justice Statistics, Prisoners Series, National Prison Statistics, 1997–2010.

poor behavior and rewards for good behavior. All rules are strictly enforced, movement is tightly controlled, and inmates are exhorted to "do their own time" and stay out of trouble. The responsibility model in Michigan, by comparison, focuses on inmates' accountability for their own conduct. "Whereas the control model involved policies and procedures intended to maximize the paramilitary content of prison life, the responsibility model involved measures that minimized the symbols and substance of formal administrative authority over inmates."[70] The responsibility system has an elaborate classification system and grievance process, as well as an inmate self-government body and a wide variety of rehabilitation programs.

The California system is in turn described by DiIulio as a mixed model, which is not focused exclusively either on control or on responsibility. Rather, it stresses a less restrictive inmate environment while simultaneously promoting a strong formal hierarchy. The central tenet of this model "is the notion that prison government rests ultimately on the consent of the governed – that is, the inmates."[71] DiIulio notes that the Golden State's powerful correctional officers' union had sought and won such concessions as the right of correctional officers to carry concealed weapons while off-duty and that on-duty officers wear military-style uniforms. At the same time, though, many officers in the California system reported to DiIulio that they prided themselves on an informal relationship with inmates and the ability to speak to inmates in their own language.

DiIulio stops short of claiming that one model of management is superior to the others, but he does argue that each form of management ultimately leads to a different "quality" of prison life. He measures this using a trichotomy of characteristics: order, amenity, and service. Order is operationalized through concrete measures such as the number of violent incidents – assaults, rapes, riots, murders – and also subjectively by descriptors like "calm, stable, and predictable."[72] Amenity is measured with indicators such as the nutritional value and quality of food, as well as access to things like television, recreation, books, and exercise. Service is measured with traditionally rehabilitative considerations such as work opportunities, educational programming, and vocational training.

Other scholars have likewise developed systematic typologies for measuring variation across individual prisons and prison systems. In a study of criminal justice performance measures, Charles Logan expands on DiIulio's tripartite measurement, identifying eight dimensions on which prisons can be evaluated – Security, Safety, Order, Care, Activity, Justice, Conditions, and Management – and listing a wide variety of indicators describing each dimension (Table 2.1).[73] Each of these dimensions might reasonably be expected to affect the experience of inmates serving time in prison.

To the best of my knowledge, there has been no comprehensive effort to classify state systems on all of these variables. However, several studies have outlined variation across two or more states on key dimensions of the prison regime.[74] For instance, Mona Lynch argues that prisons in Arizona and nearby states remained largely punitive even during the height of the rehabilitative era, operating according to the laws of "Sunbelt" or "frontier justice"[75] even as progressive reforms took hold in the Northeast. In a similar tradition, Robert Perkinson

TABLE 2.1. *Dimensions of Quality of Confinement*

Security	**Justice**
Security Procedures	Staff Fairness
Drug Use	Limited Use of Force
Significant Incidents	Grievances, Number and Type
Community Exposure	The Grievance Process
Freedom of Movement	The Discipline Process
Staffing Adequacy	Legal Resources and Access
Safety	Justice Delays
Safety of Inmates	**Conditions**
Safety of Staff	Space in Living Areas
Dangerousness of Inmates	Social Density and Privacy
Safety of Environment	Internal Freedom of Movement
Staffing Adequacy	Facilities and Maintenance
Order	Sanitation, Noise, Food
Inmate Misconduct	Commissary, Visitation
Staff Use of Force	Community Access
Perceived Control	**Management**
Strictness of Enforcement	Job Satisfaction
Care	Stress and Burn-Out
Stress and Illness	Staff Turnover
Health Care Delivered	Staff and Management Relations
Dental Care	Staff Experience
Counseling	Education, Training
Staffing for Programs and Services	Staffing Efficiency
Activity	
Involvement and Evaluation	
Work and Industry	
Education and Training	
Recreation	
Religious Services	

Source: Charles Logan, "Criminal Justice Performance Measures for Prisons," *Study Group on Criminal Justice Performance Measures* (1993).

has traced the history of race and criminal justice with an emphasis on the Lone Star State's tradition of being "Texas Tough."[76] To explain these regional differences, scholars have pointed to disparities in the development of state penal cultures over time, which left a legacy of geographic inconsistency in how prisons are managed.[77]

A more complete accounting is offered by Michelle Phelps, who compares state prison systems according to their relative focus on rehabilitation, as expressed in the proportion of prison staff who are

dedicated to programming relative to security-related tasks.[78] She finds
that the overall proportion of education and other inmate services
staff has declined somewhat over time, particularly in the most recent
decades. For instance, the ratio of education staff to inmates was nearly
halved between 1990 and 2005. In addition, the proportion of inmates
participating in such programs declined substantially.[79] However, she
finds that, in every decade since the 1970s, there has been greater variation across states than over time. This means that "many states provided
more inmate services staff members [such as teachers, mental health
professionals, and librarians] well into the 2000s than other states did
as far back as 1979, with a range of practices co-existing at every point
in time."[80]

Intra-State Variation in Prison Administration

At least in part, wide variation within modern state correctional systems was made possible by changes in the legal environment. During
the 1960s,[81] courts gave greater scrutiny to prison conditions, expanded
inmate habeas corpus, and intervened on behalf of inmates' rights under
the Eighth Amendment, ruling in *Wolff v. MacDonnell* (1974) that
"[t]here is no iron curtain drawn between the Constitution and the prisons of this country."[82] The courts began to take a different tone in the
1970s, though, reversing course from the expansion of rights that had
occurred under Warren and Burger to the more conservative approach
of Rehnquist and Roberts. "It is not so much that the courts reversed
themselves … as that the courts drew a line in the sand: 'this and no
further.'"[83] The "hands-off" approach of the pre-1960s was replaced by
a "one hand on, one hand off era" characterized by renewed deference
to prisons and their administrators.[84]

   The defining moment for this change was the Supreme Court decision of *Bell v. Wolfish* (1979), which was "heralded apocalyptically"
by prisoner reformers and rights advocates as "a fatal blow to the
[prisoners' rights] movement and by prison officials as a vindica-
tion of their authority and competence."[85] In *Bell*, the Court argued
that prison officials should be allowed a great deal of discretion in
determining how prisons should be run, including whether and how
certain rights should be afforded.[86] This allowed states extraordinary flexibility in deciding what policies to implement within their
correctional systems.

In addition, greater institutional variation was made possible by a more intensive focus on streamlining and mechanizing correctional procedures. As the "new penology" took hold, prisons became more offense-centered than client-centered, and risk replaced welfare as the dominant framework guiding correctional practice.[87] What resulted was a renewed focus on matching the "right" prison environment with the appropriately designated group of offenders, through the process of custody classification. In addition to ensuring that risk was managed appropriately,[88] classification was seen as a way to increase efficiency and consistency, by focusing limited resources where they were most needed.[89]

The history of prison classification dates as far back as the workhouses of 1500s Europe, where certain subgroups of inmates, including juveniles, women, and first-time offenders, were separated from the general prison population. However, the classification of inmates into discrete categories was not routine in American prisons until the mid-1800s, when "increasing humanitarian concerns" led to some inmates – juveniles, the mentally ill, women, the sick and infirm – being systematically isolated from the rest. In addition, prisons at this time sorted inmates by race, with specific facilities designated to hold black offenders.[90] As late as 1940, though, a national survey found that half of all institutions had not established a classification scheme for new inmates.[91]

Emerging technologies in the science of risk management helped usher in a set of modernized classification systems. While the clinical assessment tools that dominated the early practice of risk evaluation came under attack as being too subjective, a number of highly quantitative actuarial tools have been developed for correctional risk assessment, including the VRAG, the SIR scale, Static 99, and the SONAR.[92] These instruments bear little resemblance to the older "holistic but subjective" model that fell out of favor in the 1970s and 1980s.[93]

Thus, increased discretion at the institution level, combined with a new emphasis on empirical classification and risk management, yielded a network of state prison systems that are each composed of a widely varied set of institutions. For instance, relying on the same marker of rehabilitation employed by Phelps – the ratio of inmate services staff to inmates in a given year – we see only a slight increase in mean values across institutions over the period from 1979 to 2005. However, there has been a substantial increase in the standard deviation of this ratio over time (Figure 2.3).

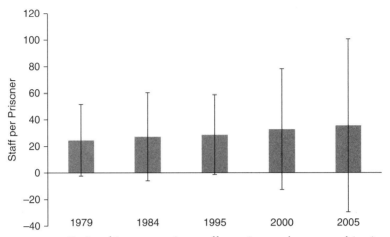

FIGURE 2.3. Ratio of inmate services staff to prisoners by year and institution. Bars show mean ratios across institutions, with SD lines.
Source: Census of State and Federal Correctional Facilities.

Conclusion

Terry Moe writes that political institutions serve two fundamental roles. First, they enable cooperation. By enforcing contracts and ensuring commitment, they assist in overcoming collective action problems. A second important role of political institutions is as "weapons of coercion and redistribution."[94] Political institutions structure the political process, providing the "rules of the game" that help to determine "who gets what, when and how."[95] At the same time, however, I would argue that political institutions can serve a third function: institutions are symbolic representations of collective values, meanings, and norms. In this way, political institutions are not purely instrumental; they also serve an expressive function that is manifested in both their prevalence and form. As Matthew Holden notes, institutions are *embedded in structures of meaning.* Indeed, "[t]he very meaning of 'institution' is that values are settled within it."[96]

In the politics of criminal justice, the modern prison has become in many ways a physical expression of public condemnation and an outlet for the retributive urge. In the classic formulation of this idea, Emile Durkheim argued that punishment helps to reinforce moral solidarity among law-abiding citizens. Through the visible enforcement of society's moral code, punishment serves to delineate the rules of civilized society and create a sense of cohesion among the populace. The culling of lawbreakers from the ranks of the compliant serves as a way of fortifying the unity of "us, the good guys" by providing a visible "them, the bad guys."[97] Yet, in modern debates over crime control, symbol has in many ways overtaken substance; in effect, more punitive prisons became political leverage as much as policy tool.

This occurrence alone might not have altered the ways in which prisons operate. After all, political rhetoric often lacks substantive depth and leaves the more mundane details of policy implementation to academics, bureaucrats, and others within the policy community, a group John Kingdon describes as "hum[ming] along on its own, independent of … political events."[98] As I have already described, however, the role of these potentially more insulated bureaucratic actors was concurrently altered, such that their influence on prisons began to wane. As Jonathan Simon notes, in the modern era, "the social scientist has less of a reason to be inside the prison and perhaps less of a welcome."[99] The result was a fundamental change in the cultural context of the prison institution, as prisons became both more punitive in focus and more managerial in practice. Where the rehabilitation ethic concerned itself with what went on inside the prison, the new politics of crime control championed a focus primarily on high walls (incapacitation) and long sentences (retribution).

This transformation did not come without a cost. In the coming chapter, I will argue that the institutional variation I have just described has important consequences for how inmates and officers experience and adapt to prison life. Both for incarcerated individuals and for their keepers, navigating the more punitive prisons of the modern era entails the adoption of new social relationships. The result, I suggest, is a disjointed form of community, which is best described as a collection of *densely knit* but *tightly bounded* social groups. Within these groups, strong ties are formed. However, competition over scarce resources and exposure to pervasive violence results in inter-group distrust and hostility, and ultimately perpetuates a cycle of violence and criminality.

3

Public Policy and the Creation of Community

Neither a man nor a crowd nor a nation can be trusted to act humanely or to think sanely under the influence of great fear.
Bertrand Russell, *An Outline
of Intellectual Rubbish, Unpopular Essays* (1950)

The English philosopher Thomas Hobbes identified crime control as the primary motivation for the creation of an organized state. In *Leviathan*, Hobbes describes the state of nature as a place where competition for power abounds, and each individual views all others primarily as an obstacle to his own satisfaction.[1] Thus, "war of all against all" is inevitable. In this dismal scenario, wherein life is "solitary, poor, nasty, brutish, and short," people will willingly give up some measure of individual liberty in order to ensure their survival. For Hobbes, it is thus people's desire for protection from robbery and violence that serves as a catalyst for the formation of government and justifies the subjugation of natural rights to a centralized authority that can enforce law and order.

In this conception of state power, government's role as punisher is central, "because it is of the nature of punishment to have for end the disposing of men to obey the law."[2] Through punishment, the state provides for the collective peace and order that, in turn, allows individuals to enjoy their freedoms. Punishment must therefore be severe enough to have a "contrary effect" rather than simply being viewed by the public as the (acceptable) cost of crime.[3]

For John Locke, as for Hobbes, people enter into civilized society for protection from each other and to impose the moral restrictions necessary for peaceful co-existence.[4] And while Locke, the father of liberalism, diverges from Hobbes concerning the state of man in nature and the nature of individual rights, he likewise underscores the fundamental role of government as the enforcer of legal compliance. While in nature anyone may punish transgressors, government creates a common judge to interpret the rules of natural law, safeguard property, and arbitrate disputes. Punishment is therefore equally central to the liberal notion of political authority; the state constitutes a neutral authority able to judge the severity of an offense and dictate a proportionate response.[5]

In practice, as in theory, crime control is central to the liberal democratic state, as is the process through which the government may legitimately infringe on citizens' liberties in order to punish lawbreakers. For instance, the U.S. Declaration of Independence echoes John Locke's sentiments that citizens have "inalienable rights" that government may not impede, that government is created to secure those rights, and that such a government derives its "just power from the Consent of the Governed." At the same time, however, the writers of the Constitution were acutely aware of the need to impose order and to create a system of justice and accountability. It is perhaps not surprising, given this tension, that fully half of the amendments included in the Bill of Rights deal explicitly with the rights of the criminal and accused.[6]

These conceptions of state power make clear that civil society, state power, and punishment are tightly interwoven. It is somewhat surprising, then, that there has been little rigorous research into the role of crime and punishment policies in shaping social and political communities. In fact, extant literature probing the source of social ties focuses most often on the role of non-governmental actors, especially voluntary organizations.[7] Though Robert Putnam has become well known for this strain of research,[8] he was not the first to recognize the importance of associational activity to American society and governance. As early as the 1830s, Alexis de Tocqueville asserted that "only by the reciprocal action of men upon another can feelings and ideas be renewed, the heart enlarged, and human mind developed.... This, only associations can do." To de Tocqueville, participation in civic organizations was an integral part of American democratic life, as through such activity the average citizen "will discover, without its being shown to him, the close tie that unites private to general interest." Thus, in his view, "[n]othing ... deserves more attention than the intellectual and moral associations in America."[9] Samuel Huntington's *Political Development and Political Decay* likewise addresses the role and character of associations and organizations, asserting their significance in providing stability and enabling democracy.[10]

While important, these studies have been criticized for their "curious neglect of politics"[11] and general inattention to the role of the state in shaping patterns of social interaction.[12] Moreover, even those scholars who do incorporate some role for the state in shaping social connectedness and generalized trust[13] have focused heavily on "stability and path dependency in the realm of civil society."[14] Some point to aspects of the historical state that continue to influence current patterns of social connectedness.[15] Others concentrate on relatively static characteristics of the modern political state,[16] such as levels of democracy[17] and vertical versus horizontal political relations,[18] as significant in determining the quality of social life.[19] As a result, despite their strengths, these studies often fail to pinpoint the particular public policies or processes that construct or break down social ties; as Dietlind Stolle rightly surmises, "[F]ollowing the institution-centered approach, we do not really know which aspects of government and which characteristics of political institutions might be particularly beneficial in fostering trust, related cooperative values and social participation."[20] How might dynamic and specific features of the modern state, such as the design of prisons and other public institutions, shape citizens' social orientations and behavior?

In this chapter, I argue that the increasingly punitive nature of the nation's prisons has substantial consequences for the individuals who pass through them, serving to propagate a particular form of community among both inmates and officers. This highly atomized form of social organization is marked by a collection of discrete, *densely knit* but *tightly bounded* social groups. They are densely knit in that individuals within each group are directly and closely tied to one another. However, these groups are tightly bounded in that there are few ties between different social groups. The result is that social networks and social trust work at cross-purposes. Networks within this fragmented community create meaningful solidarities between individuals and within delimited groups. Simultaneously, however, these closed communities actually serve to reduce generalized trust and ultimately promulgate countercultural norms of cynicism and aggression.

Ultimately, I contend that the organizational culture of the modern prison can play a pivotal role in whether crime control institutions either accomplish or undermine their most basic task: controlling crime. The experience of prison is influenced by characteristics of the individuals confined there, but also by the particular institutional context in which social relationships are created and maintained. As I will argue here, understanding the everyday culture of prison institutions is therefore central to understanding how criminal justice policies have shaped social communities in the United States over the past half-century.

The Changing Social Context of the American Prison

As I described in some detail in the preceding chapter, broad changes have occurred in the administration of American criminal justice. The end result of these relatively recent reforms was that American prisons became substantially harsher places in which to do time, offering fewer resources and services to inmates. This transition reflected a changing conception of the purpose of corrections; according to the modern ethos of punishment, prison conditions should be austere, not reformative and criminals should be punished, not educated.[21] In addition, a renewed focus on efficient management prioritized the classification of offenders and their assignment to appropriate levels of custody. This resulted in wider and more systematic variation in the formal culture of prison institutions within state correctional systems.

During this period of carceral transformation, changes were concurrently emerging in the *informal* culture of prison. In mapping the contours of the prison environment, scholars have described the formal organization of the administrative regime and the informal culture of inmate society as two related but distinct dimensions.[22] The formal prison regime includes a wide variety of institutional factors, ranging from the programs offered to inmates, to disciplinary procedures, to the security design of the physical structure in which inmates are housed.[23] In contrast, informal culture describes the unofficial but often strictly enforced rules of inmate behavior around such things as trading property, interracial relationships, and interactions with officers and other prison staff. It also governs the functioning of an internal inmate hierarchy, from the powerful "shot callers" to the lowly "new fish."

It is the informal culture of prisons that has historically dominated prison memoirs[24] and sociological studies of prisons.[25] In the 1940s and 1950s, a rich tradition of prison sociology was concerned with defining and describing the contours of inmate society. Classic inquiries of the period, most notably Gresham Sykes's 1958 *Society of Captives* and Donald Clemmer's 1940 *The Prison Community*, took seriously the social organization of prison life. Throughout the 1960s and 1970s, too, inmate culture was regularly explored as a central subject of scholarly interest, spawning a robust literature.[26] These studies examined inmate society from a variety of perspectives: as a microcosm of power relationships that could provide generalizable insights into hierarchy, authority, and role-taking; as a primary source of order maintenance within the prison, with which prison administrators must grapple in order to secure the safety and functioning of the institution; and as a central socializing force that shapes individual inmate outcomes, particularly with respect to recidivism.[27]

A variety of forces led to a precipitous decline in research focused on prison culture and inmate social life. While a complete accounting is beyond the scope of this discussion, several specific historical developments are worthy of note. The first is that ethnographic prison research of the kind pursued by Clemmer and Sykes became increasingly difficult to conduct. Perhaps in response to changes in inmate organization and demographics, and also as a result of shifting orientations in correctional management that delegitimized certain types of professional knowledge, prisons became less hospitable to the "soaking and poking" that characterized these early studies. The resultant obscuring of inmate culture was exacerbated further by restrictions placed on the publication of writing by inmates themselves. In particular, so-called Son of Sam laws introduced by many states starting in the late 1970s prohibited inmates from receiving royalties on stories of their crimes.[28] This precipitated a substantial decline in "portraits of life inside from the inmates' perspective."[29]

At the same time that both ethnographic and autobiographical work declined, quantitative data about prison institutions also became less available, even on a permission basis. Some prison administrators became more hesitant to freely distribute information on inmate activities to "liberal" researchers, many of whom might be inclined to criticize the expanding carceral system and its increasingly punitive character. In addition, as prison systems became progressively more budget-strapped and administratively burdened, many scaled back on collecting and distributing all but the most basic facts. For example, the California Department of Corrections and Rehabilitation – the largest of the U.S. state prison systems – dissolved its internal research organization in the mid-1990s, reinstating it only as recently as July 2005. At the start of the 21st century, the data collected by that state's correctional system was kept in more than 80 separate databases, many of which could not be linked.[30]

Partly as a response to these practical difficulties, there have been substantial shifts in the foci of the sociology of crime in general and of prison sociology in particular. Jonathan Simon identifies three topics that have emerged over the past few decades to displace prison social organization as the "central site for research and theory building in the US": the incarceration rate, both as a historical trend of interest and as it relates to shifts in objective crime rates over time; sentencing research; and the "fear of crime," both its decoupling from real rates of crime and its consequences for the punitive tendencies of the American public.[31] All three of these topics are of clear scholarly and policy importance. However, the growth of research on these topics has come at the expense of an earlier strain of prison sociology, one that focused attention on individual patterns of adaptation to prison life and the consequences of prison socialization for correctional outcomes.

The result is a dearth of detailed knowledge concerning day-to-day life in the modern American prison. In focusing on the "managerial needs of prison governors" rather than the informal "society of captives," the 1980s witnessed a new lens on the study and practice of prison administration, one that privileged "staff over inmates, formally authorized acts of authority over informal arrangements, and formal definitions of behavior over less measurable ways of collecting knowledge."[32] The result, as Simon aptly describes, was a "disappearance of inmate social life as an object of knowledge outside the precincts of the prison."[33] This is not to say that there have been no important works on modern inmate culture. In particular, a number of excellent studies have documented informal organization in women's prisons, in maximum-security prisons, and in the United Kingdom.[34] I mean only to suggest that Jonathan Simon's assertion that "in the 1990s the whole question of the prison social order appears distant from the concerns of both social science and prison management"[35] rings nearly as true two decades later.

What we do know is that prisons have undergone a great many changes since the era of Sykes and Clemmer, "changes that are embedded in the broader context of late-modernity that has, likewise, transformed the world outside the prison in which its inhabitants are socialized."[36] The 1960s witnessed the rise of a robust prisoners' rights movement, bolstered by inmates' newly won ability to bring claims about prison conditions under the Civil Rights Act. During this period, black prisoners such as Eldridge Cleaver and George Jackson became well-known political figures, authoring "revolutionary manifestos" about civil rights and the prison crisis. Most important, inmates built powerful alliances with legal and civil rights organizations, from targeted outfits like the People's Law Office and Prison Legal Services of Illinois to national organizations such as the American Bar Association, the American Civil Liberties Union, and the National Association for the Advancement of Colored People.

As they initiated legal battles, fought for legislation, and engaged in violent demonstrations, the "world behind bars became a site for political struggle and action in ways it had not been before."[37] From 1960 into the 1980s, prisoners and their defenders launched countless legal fights, including class action suits concerning the totality of prison conditions, at every level of the courts.[38] Indeed, James Jacobs describes this period as one in which "the courts [became] a battlefield where prisoners and prison administrators, led by their respective legal champions, engage[d] in mortal combat."[39] Throughout this period, prison reformers celebrated their successes and heralded the court's newfound commitment to halting torture, segregation, and maltreatment of people in police and prison custody. Led by the Black Muslims, inmates and their allies waged a "broadscale effort to redefine the status (moral, political, economic, as well as legal) of prisoners in a democratic society.... The success of the Muslims on the constitutional issue of free exercise of religious rights brought the federal courts into the prisons. The abominable conditions in American prisons kept them there."[40]

The tide began to turn in the years that followed, though, as funding for prisoner litigation became more difficult to come by and restrictions were placed on government grants prohibiting their use for class action and civil rights suits.[41] In addition, although prison activists and oorganizations continued to work toward reform, these groups failed to grow commensurately with the skyrocketing number of prisons and prisoners. This left relatively "fewer prison reformers to monitor far more institutions and inmates."[42] At the same time, a series of high-profile prison riots, while shedding light on abysmal prison conditions, served to undercut public sympathy for the cause of prison reform. The "image of the prisoner as hero, revolutionary, and victim" began to quickly wane.[43] By 2004, James Jacobs, who had written so optimistically in 1980 about the promise and success of the prisoners' rights movement, noted that "penal institutions [now] have no political constituency, except perhaps for the prison officers' unions in some states.... Forward momentum has been halted."[44]

The movement also mobilized countervailing forces. Some were skeptical that activist inmates were engaged in anything more than self-interested swagger; what was being passed off as a political movement was really just a bunch of criminals looking for plusher prisons, shorter sentences, or personal notoriety. In some quarters, rioting and other forms of violent protest in particular were touted as evidence that inmates were "screwballs" at best and "psychopaths" at worst.[45] Others were concerned that the prisoners' rights movement would itself motivate further violence, by urging hunger strikes, prison riots, and even revolution.[46] Still others maintained the normative position that inmates did not deserve rights, given their status as violators of the legal and moral code, or expressed fear that extending rights to inmates would undermine the authority of prison workers.[47]

Thus, as the civil rights movement waned, so did the movement for inmates' rights.[48] Throughout the 1980s and 1990s, the inmate hierarchies and informal self-government associations that had typified the prisons of the 1950s and 1960s began to break down. In their absence, gangs began to play an ever more important role in structuring prison social life. In sum, prison social dynamics came to reflect the segregation and complexity that increasingly characterized the parallel world outside.[49]

In particular, modern prisons - like contemporary urban spaces - have been increasingly marked by gangs and gang-related violence. Reliable national estimates of the prevalence of prison gangs are difficult to obtain for a variety of reasons,[50] not the least of which is that there is extensive debate about how best to define a gang and identify its members.[51] However, all available estimates suggest that prison gangs are rife in facilities across the country and few would disagree that the growth of prison gangs has become a serious concern for the management of modern American prisons. For instance, Camp and Camp's 1985 study found roughly 114 gangs, composed of about 13,000 inmates, spread across 33 of the 49 state systems they surveyed.[52] More recently, Knox and Tromanhauser have suggested that there may be as many as 100,000 or more prison gang members in the country.[53] Some have claimed that this is an overestimate,[54] while others have put the current population of gang-affiliated inmates at two times that number;[55] in fact, data from the FBI's National Gang Intelligence Center estimates 230,000 gang members incarcerated nationwide.[56] Despite this wide variance, though, there is a general consensus that the population of gang-affiliated inmates has grown over time. A study by the American Correctional Association found that the number of inmates with ties to prison gangs more than doubled between 1985 and 1992, increasing from about 12,624 to 46,190.[57] Similarly, a survey by the National Gang Crime Research Center found that gang membership in adult prisons increased from 9.4 percent to 24.7 percent between 1991 and 1999.[58]

In addition, gangs now account for a substantial proportion of prison violence.[59] In one study, gang-affiliated and non-affiliated inmates were found to have similar socioeconomic backgrounds and educational levels, but gang members were more likely to have a juvenile crime record, to have had more previous arrests, and to have used a weapon. During incarceration, gang members were also less likely to participate in rehabilitation programs and were more than twice as likely to repeatedly violate institutional rules and to engage in physical confrontations with other inmates.[60] Another study found that prison gang members accounted for roughly 3 percent of the prison population, but were responsible for 50 percent or more of prison violence.[61]

Through its increasingly central role in the organization of prisons' informal social life, the emergence of gangs and violence contributed to a tectonic shift in inmate culture. As David Skarbek describes:

Prior to the late 1950s, inmates relied on decentralized norms to govern the inmate social system. However, norms became ineffective at providing governance because of three demographic shifts. First, the inmate population increased dramatically during this period.... Decentralized governance is less effective in larger, more anonymous communities because keeping track of people's past behavior is more difficult. Second, correctional facilities began to experience severe overcrowding, reflecting increasing scarcity of inmate resources and a greater need to protect them. Third, an increase in the number and percentage of inmates incarcerated for narcotics-related crimes led to a thriving demand for illicit drugs. This created profit opportunities for groups that had a credible threat of violence.[62]

Thus, just as the formal culture of prison became harsher and more punitive, the social order of prison became substantially more aggressive. In a 1993 study, Geoffrey Hunt and colleagues conclude that the prison in the age of the "Pepsi Generation" is "an increasingly unpredictable world in which prior loyalties, allegiances and friendships [are] disrupted."[63] Likewise, in describing the contemporary prison, criminologist John Irwin portrays it as "not chaos, but a dangerous and tentative order" marked by racial violence, gangs, and a warehousing model of correctional administration that does little to address inmate needs.[64] Echoing this description, Loïc Wacquant suggests that a new culture of "increased levels of interpersonal and group brutality" has arisen, making the modern prison an "often unsafe and violent social jungle," structured by a "deadly symbiosis" between the prison and the ghetto.[65]

Social Ties and Public Institutions

In the preceding section, I described changes in the informal culture of American prisons. These transformations are not unrelated to changes in the formal administration of corrections, however. Rather, the two are interrelated and one has important consequences for the other.

There are three primary ways that the formal rules and culture of prisons can influence the social networks and social norms of citizens:

by altering the composition of social networks, by creating and reifying social identities, and by structuring the context of social interaction. In the following sections, I briefly describe how prison institutions can shape individual social connections through each of these general processes.

The Composition of Social Networks

Contact with others is the starting point for social organization. Most basically, as David Halpern points out, "it is clear that some forms of social engagement necessarily rely on there being other people to engage with – if you've got no one to play with, then you'll just have to play alone."[66] Through policies of incarceration, the state can affect the number and types of people with whom an individual interacts. That is, prisons place individuals within a physically delimited space that *alters the size and composition of social networks*. Inmates are located at a prison that makes it more or less easy to receive visits from friends and family. For instance, according to one report, the average male inmate is housed about 100 miles away from his children – for women, the average distance is about 160 miles – and incarcerated parents in state prison are sentenced on average to serve 80 months in state prison.[67] The ability of family members and friends to make this long trip, as well as to afford the relatively high cost of placing telephone calls to people in prison,[68] influences the likelihood that relationships will wane during incarceration. One study suggests that partners of the incarcerated may develop a new independence and self-sufficiency while their partner is away, whether out of desire or necessity, which can substantially change the dynamics of the relationship.[69] More generally, inmates often find that they and their families "drift apart" during the lengthy separation of imprisonment, as life on the outside moves on without them.[70]

Notably, the proportion of state prisoners serving time for non-violent crimes, as well as those serving their first term in prison, has increased substantially over the past several decades. In 1979, about 5.7 percent of inmates were admitted to prison for a drug offense and had no prior convictions for violent crimes. By 1991 the proportion of the inmate population with these characteristics was roughly 17.8 percent.[71] To the extent that non-violent, first time offenders are actually more likely than violent and repeat offenders to be integrated into social networks and communities before going to prison, the effects of incarceration on relationships with friends and family on the outside may be particularly severe. As James Lynch and William Sabol note, "Removing more such people, who were integrated into social groups prior to imprisonment, increases the likelihood that those groups will be disrupted."[72]

At the same time, people in prison encounter other inmates, who become their rivals, peers, or friends. Thus, through their ongoing interactions, inmates are likely to affect one another in important ways. For example, in their study of juvenile prisons, Bayer, Hjalmarsson, and Pozen examine whether the composition of prisoners in a given correctional institution significantly affects rates and types of recidivism. Using data on 8,216 youthful offenders who served time in 169 juvenile correctional facilities in Florida, the authors show that the composition of the group with whom a youth is concurrently incarcerated serves to reinforce existing criminal tendencies: "[E]xposure to peers with a history of committing a *particular* crime increases the probability that an individual who has already committed *the same type of crime* recidivates with that crime."[73] Their analysis suggests that incarceration's effects are influenced at least in part by characteristics of the peers with whom an inmate is imprisoned; different peers yield different outcomes. In sum, incarceration exposes individuals to a set of peers with criminal propensities, at the same time that it restricts contact with outsiders who might provide them with a countervailing or stabilizing pro-social influence.

As with inmates, the prison environment influences the likelihood that certain groups of correctional officers will have contact with one another (and not with others). Like inmates, new correctional officers also enter a social community with a particular set of characteristics. Officers join the ranks of correctional staff, developing workplace collegialities, friendships, and hostilities. For example, a female or Latino officer may be the only woman or minority employed at a particular prison, or may enter a facility where the staff is fairly heterogeneous by gender and race. The characteristics of others who are similarly situated within their institution will likely shape how officers experience their work, and the values and lessons they glean.[74] Officers also have interactions with inmates, and the type of inmates with whom they most commonly interact affects the quality of those interactions. An officer working with female inmates relative to males, or violent inmates relative to predominantly non-violent, may perceive his or her charges in systematically different ways.

The Creation of Social Identities

It is not only the ways that they enable or constrain social interactions, however, that make prisons a significant source of social organization; these institutions also help to *define social identities and confer status*. Through their direct contact with criminal justice authorities and through the social provisions the state provides (or withholds) within criminal justice institutions, citizens gain an understanding of how others value (or devalue) people like them[75] and receive signals regarding how they should value (or devalue) others. As Helen Ingram and Anne Schneider note, public policies can be the "primary means of legitimating, extending, and even creating distinctive populations – some of whom are extolled as deserving and entitled and others who are demonized as undeserving and ineligible.... Public policy is the primary tool through which government acts to exploit, inscribe, entrench, institutionalize, perpetuate, or change social constructions."[76] Through participation in government programs and contact with political institutions, citizens "acquire a sense of their own status in the polity."[77]

Individuals receive and respond to these messages concerning the construction of social groups to which they and others belong. For instance, welfare policies may serve to stigmatize the poor, by portraying recipients as "scamming" the system and as "lazy" and unwilling to work.[78] In the United States, welfare and other means-tested social programs have increasingly required recipients to show evidence of "personal responsibility" through mandatory drug testing, fingerprinting, and documented evidence of "sufficient" job search activities. This "criminalization of poverty" has consequences for levels of social connectivity with and among the nation's poor,[79] breeding distrust and heightening inter-racial (and potentially inter-class) animosity.[80] More generally, selective or conservative welfare states, which employ complicated rules for eligibility that separate out the "deserving" from the "undeserving," are likely to "create or manifest societal divisions" and undermine generalized trust.[81]

Like welfare policies, criminal justice activities can encourage the establishment of social roles. In ways both subtle and overt, prisons and other institutions of crime control teach people that certain attitudes and behaviors, rather than others, are normal and "role-appropriate";[82] the operational logics of the institution "provide individuals with vocabularies of motives and with a sense of self."[83] As Jonathan Simon writes:

> Crime is a genre, in the dramaturgical sense. It comes with certain kinds of roles; vulnerable victims, willing offenders, vigilant prosecutors, and harsh but fair judges (and all the deviant variations those set up). When we govern through crime we pass out these scripts to hundreds if not thousands of real people with little in the way of an audition and no accountability for the consequences.[84]

In America's more punitive prisons, the social role proscribed for inmates is a deeply dishonorable one. As inmates are classified, processed, and put "into the system," they are defined by the state as being part of a separate and distinct social category: the inmate, the gang member, the deviant, the criminal. Having one's hair cut a certain way, being issued certain clothes to wear, and seeing a sea of others with a similar appearance all serve to reinforce this new sense of outsider belonging. Significantly, this social identity may stay with an individual long after he or she leaves prison; the collateral consequences of a criminal conviction have been described as "civil death",[85] and long after finishing a sentence, an individual remains both formally and informally defined by it as an "ex-offender," "ex-felon," or "ex-con."

This stigma is both reinforced and personified by the relationships between inmates and officers. For inmates, prisons can provide a nearly totalizing experience of powerlessness and dehumanization. While confined in prison, individuals must cede nearly complete authority over their bodies and choices. In most prison systems, an individual's property or person may be searched at any time, without notice and without cause. In addition, freedom of movement is most often restricted or almost completely denied, and the state must be relied upon to meet the totality of one's physical needs. "For state prisoners, eating, sleeping, dressing, washing, working and playing are all done under the watchful eye of the State.... What for a private citizen would be a dispute with his landlord, with his employer, with his tailor, with his neighbor, or with his banker becomes, for the prisoner, a dispute with the state."[86] This type of profound disempowerment and loss of control may have especially destructive effects on one's sense of efficacy and power, "work[ing] to destroy the inmate's conception of him or herself as an autonomous being worthy of respect and self-respect."[87]

In this regard, prisons can powerfully reshape social identity and orientations toward the broader social world. By identifying inmates as "offenders" and isolating them along with others defined by this negative valence, prisons may inadvertently create or reinforce an oppositional group identity. This profound stigma may lead inmates to reject the norms and values associated with the dominant culture from which they have been so wholly excluded.[88]

A similar process of social marking and identity formation plays out for officers within the prison environment. They, too, are clothed uniformly and required to maintain standards of haircut and grooming. In this way, they are also visibly identifiable to one another as belonging to a particular group. And they, too, may come to conform to the expectations of their new social role, one that is defined both by solidarity with other officers and in opposition to inmates. Some officers surely feel valued in their professional role, as members of law enforcement who work in an especially dangerous setting. However, like inmates, many correctional officers report feeling that they are vilified by segments of the general public. As a recent report of the American Correctional Association commented, "[A]gencies will need to realize that they are appealing to a new generation of applicants who do not hold corrections in high esteem." The report cites evidence from one correctional workforce study that finds negative public perceptions are now a significant challenge to recruitment. "Both television and movies expose and magnify accounts of corruption among a small percentage of correctional officers as well as portray images of dark, dank hallways inhabited by fierce correctional officers who abuse and exploit the inmates they supervise."[89] In this way, officers, too, may come to feel that they occupy a stigmatized identity.

The Context of Social Interaction

Finally, government helps shape the nature of social contact through the resources, structures, and supports it provides (or fails to provide). In many prison institutions, the institutional culture that predominates is marked by the real or perceived threat of violence, as well as a pervasive sense that formal authorities either cannot or will not intercede to reduce conflict. In this context, where formal control is lacking and where resources are in scarce supply, gangs and other criminal networks may be perceived as providing the only means of protection from physical harm.[90] This helps to explain why the presence of gangs is posited to increase when violence increases. Criminal networks also rise up in order to help structure informal interactions – regulating commerce, enforcing codes of conduct, doling out punishment – in the face of feeble formal institutions and in the absence of other means of social coordination.[91] For instance, David Skarbek notes that "[o]rganized crime provides extralegal governance to protect property rights and enforce contracts in power vacuums where legitimate governments cannot or will not do so, and a genuine, long-term demand for governance exists."[92] Just as it does in the urban core, the "crumbling" of formal power in prison fuels an underground economy dominated by the retail and trade of drugs, where individuals serve as "entrepreneurs in violent predation."[93]

It is not only violence that matters, however, but also the availability of structured forms of interaction between diverse groups of inmates. For instance, when prisons offer education classes, church groups, and prison unions, they do more than provide inmates with literacy skills, religious teachings, and a living wage. They also provide them with classmates, fellow parishioners, and co-workers. Inside these programs, groups can be encouraged to mentor one another, communicate, and engage in cooperative behavior. In these circumstances, it is possible for people to get to know one another across diverse backgrounds, creating bonds predicated on the "perception of common interests and common humanity between members of the two groups."[94] Well-designed and executed programs might therefore exert a powerful influence on social relationships between inmates, helping to reduce existing intergroup conflicts; through structured contact, programs like vocational and educational training might help reduce out-group bias.[95] Such encounters may serve to build trust and interpersonal respect between otherwise hostile groups. Indeed, "if social and ethnic groups do not come into contact at all, there is no possibility of the formation of bridging social capital across groups to break down these [racial and ethnic] divides."[96]

In addition, the extent to which inmates feel that they are being treated fairly and humanely by prison staff can have significant consequences for the way they adjust and respond to imprisonment. When inmates encounter correctional officers whom they perceive to be efficient and compassionate, they are likely to gain confidence in the system as a whole[97] and come to believe that others in their community can be trusted.[98] When officers are instead experienced as unjust, incompetent, or even malfeasant, these observations may likewise be generalized to the broader social system.[99] Expressing this idea, Staffan Kumlin and Bo Rothstein suggest that citizens develop a generalized sense of trust when they feel services, laws, and sanctions are provided equally across society: "[People] draw inferences about others' trustworthiness from how they perceive public-service bureaucrats. If social workers, local policemen, public-health workers, and so on act in such a way that they cannot be trusted, why should people in general be trusted?"[100]

Officers vary widely in how they conduct themselves and in the orientations they adopt toward inmates.[101] Some officers, perhaps most, maintain a wary but professional style of interaction with inmates.[102] In the words of one prison administrator, however, prison culture and the contours of the professional role can make it difficult for officers to humanize their charges. "'You have to understand,' he urged, 'that much of the job is treating prisoners in a mass. When you have to deal with a large group of people it is easy to see them as a big bunch without any individuality. I think that is the biggest problem for the correctional officer. He tends to define everybody in terms of the lowest common denominator and that causes a lot of problems.'"[103] Stories of officers calling inmates derogatory names, mocking them, or even physically harassing them emerge regularly in inmates' formal administrative complaints and in informal accounts of imprisonment. As John May describes, modern prisons too "often resort to isolation, power, manipulation, and force to keep the prison orderly. Inmates soon adopt these same tools."[104]

Less frequently, far more damning stories of officer misconduct also emerge. For example, a decade ago, at a prison in California's Central Valley, officers were indicted for ostensibly setting up "gladiator-style" fights between groups of rival inmates. The officers involved were ultimately acquitted, but the state agreed to a large settlement for the family of an inmate who was fatally shot by guards during a melee on the prison yard, and the prison subsequently changed its policies governing which groups of inmates were forced to exercise together each day.[105] In the highly charged environment of prison, however, even far smaller departures from the everyday moral code of civilized society may be devastating to the institution's ability to build legitimacy and respect. Commenting specifically on the social and political meaning of the prison, Bert Useem and Anne Piehl write: "What legal institutions do (and how they do it) may signal society's underlying attitudes and established norms. If prisons themselves are lawless, their expressive value in asserting the rule of law is lost or even in the negative."[106]

Conversely, the types of programs and supports that the prison institution provides can also send important signals to inmates concerning their status vis-à-vis society and the state. For instance, in writing of the value of prison rehabilitation programs, one practitioner argues that high-quality prison programs "announce to prisoners, to their families and to their communities that the institution supports the individual prisoner in his or her effort to build a safe, healthy life, and that the State is committed to allowing prisoners to grow as human beings, rather than to 'keeping them down.'"[107] In more punitive facilities where these types of programs are largely absent, inmates receive a far different signal. Implicitly, such institutions communicate to inmates that they are incorrigible, undeserving of aid, or beyond repair.

Again, these dynamics are not specific to inmates. In her account of prison officers in England, Elaine Crawley describes the inordinate pressure individuals face to conform to the prevailing social norms, which in many prisons include harsh attitudes and aggressive behavior toward inmates. She writes:

In the prison setting it is not only prisoners who form cliques, gangs and loosely knit groups to meet the need for social approval. Prison officers also coalesce into exclusive social groupings with shared interests, values and beliefs.... As one senior officer commented: "I never cease to be amazed at how quickly the culture can grab somebody.... It's cause you're working in a very small, tight-knit community. And if you are seen to do something extraordinary, you will be excluded. And nobody likes to be excluded, do they?"[108]

Some scholarship suggests that officers' face-to-face interactions are limited by the solitary nature of their work, resulting in an absence of the type of strong solidarities evident among police officers or members of the military.[109] However, particularly when officers experience concerns about safety, they are likely to form alliances with one another for the purposes of protection. They may also unite for collective advocacy.[110] In California, for example, the correctional officers' union touts its members' commitment to "walking the toughest beat in the state" as a way of describing and encouraging a sense of camaraderie from shared experience.

At the same time, prison violence and disorder may strain officers' relationships with direct supervisors and management. When violence is persistent, prison administrators may be perceived by officers as unable to respond effectively or to prevent violence in the first place. However, the responsiveness of correctional institutions to incidents of violence may also have symbolic import for correctional officers. Taking disciplinary action against inmates who commit acts of violence implicitly conveys to officers that the institution values their safety, that someone is looking out for them, and that administrators are responsive to their concerns. Conversely, the feeling that assaults against staff are not dealt with, or are not dealt with sufficiently, may increase officers' feelings of isolation and decrease feelings of safety.

Many correctional officers also report feeling that they will be "hung out" by their direct supervisors; essentially, they will be held responsible for what happens while they are on duty, even when they were doing their best or were faced with situations outside their control. In one account, written by an experienced officer at Stateville Correctional Center in Illinois, the author describes quickly discovering that he could not rely on his direct superiors for guidance or support. He writes of "weird phenomena" in the workplace, including "convenient temporary amnesia.... This phenomenon would occur when a supervisor ... would give an officer some instructions to carry out. If the slightest thing went wrong with the order while it was in progress, the whiteshirt that gave the original order would have a real hard time recalling that he had in fact given the order in the first place. This situation happened routinely and the officer was left holding the bag."[111]

The Social Effects of the Punitive Prison

Through each of the processes I have just described, prison culture matters for the creation of social communities. In violent and resource-poor prisons, social networks among both inmates and officers come to be defined in opposition to and in conflict with others, what Ioannis Evrigenis refers to as "negative association." Among inmates, distrust of officers and fear of incarcerated peer groups result in a balkanized social structure, consisting of multiple groups with few interconnecting ties. In the same way, officers' frustration with administrators and their fear of inmate violence result in strong horizontal ties with weak vertical attachments. These features of the prison social landscape can be paramount for individual social orientations. As Evrigenis notes, "[N]egative association due to the fear of enemies constitutes a fundamental element of self-definition ..., which is itself constitutive of community rather than its product."[112]

Thus, to the extent that prison social groups are formed and maintained in the context of violence, insecurity, and stigma, they can be expected to have two key features: they are simultaneously both *tightly bounded* and *densely knit*. Putnam makes reference to these features of social groupings when he differentiates between bridging and bonding. Bonding, or exclusive social capital, ties together similar groups of people. By comparison, bridging, or inclusive social capital, builds connections across disparate networks or social groups. "Bonding social capital constitutes a kind of sociological superglue, whereas bridging social capital provides a sociological WD-40."[113]

Both types of social connection can produce social goods such as companionship and reciprocity. For example, as Frederic Thrasher's early work on gangs points out, much of the behavior of gangs, including "meeting face to face, milling, movement through space as a unit, conflict, and planning," is social in nature. "The result of this collective behavior is the development of tradition, unreflective internal structure, esprit de corps, solidarity, morale, group awareness, and attachment to a local territory."[114] In fact, gangs and other social organizations of this kind may be attractive to potential members precisely *because* they provide a meaningful sense of social belonging. This is likely to be particularly important to those who otherwise lack interpersonal connections with family or community members. This interpretation is supported by Thornberry et al.'s examination of juvenile gang involvement, which posits that the "perceived social benefits of gang membership 'will be viewed as a viable means of adjustment to the adolescent's somewhat bleak world.'"[115] The same is true in prison, where gangs create norms of trust and provide protection within the bounded social group.[116]

However, bonding groups like gangs are often simultaneously oppositional in nature, systematically excluding those who fall outside the defined boundaries of group membership,[117] displaying preferential treatment to those who are part of the in-group,[118] and discriminating against those in the out-group.[119] In fact, especially when groups are formed in the context of fear, persecution, or threat, so-called negative association may itself be critical to the cohesion of the group: "As the in-group forms its identity, both the situation to be avoided and the various out-groups serve as focal points. Contradistinction from [out-groups] is one of the most important – in some cases the most important – clearly identifiable determinants of the in-group's identity."[120] To the extent, then, that bonding occurs primarily through this process of purposeful differentiation and out-group distrust, social connectivity may have potential downsides, such as increased inter-group competition, or even factional violence.[121] Such groups become defined by distinction from others who are perceived to be the source of competition and threat, as well as against formal authorities who are considered weak, uncaring, and/or untrustworthy.

The result is that, while negative associations may provide protective, social, and even economic benefits to their members, the internal group cohesion built within these organizations is unlikely to translate into generalized trust. A classic case of this phenomenon is the close-knit ties of the mafia. In this "backward society," there are high levels of trust within the social unit; yet this does not translate into broader trust toward society. Instead, an "amoral familialism" develops, wherein individuals engage in mutual defection to advance the interests of their immediate families, without regard to others.[122] In contrast, generalized trust is actually created *outside* of social groups and associations, through the process of projection.[123] It is through the *generalization* of trust that the private social good is translated into a public social good; thus, critical to the positive role of associations is that membership not only foster trust between participants, but also help to build "sturdy norms"[124] of more generalized trust, reciprocity, and inter-group cooperation.[125] If such generalization does not occur, then strong social ties instead produce only a more limited form of "bounded solidarity"[126] or "communal" trust.[127]

Indeed, the norms and values of the type of social group likely to be formed in the context of violence and competition may actively foster *dis*trust of those outside the delimited inner circle, as well as antipathy toward the norms of the dominant culture. When individuals form groups for the purpose of attaining "safety in numbers," united in pursuit of mutual protection, they must secure themselves against the possible defection of individual members or collusion with outsiders. For instance, gangs may enforce codes of conduct by which individual gang members must abide, including restrictions on fraternization with nonmembers and rivals. Likewise, when the security of the group is seen as dependent on the loyalty and commitment of each member and his or her willingness to participate in preemptive or retaliatory aggression, leaders may choose to foster a kind of xenophobia, contempt, or hostility of others in order to deter exit from the group.[128]

Likewise, in this context, anti-social norms may be employed as a form of social currency. Describing the emergence of this phenomenon in the urban ghetto, Elijah Anderson suggests that aggression and violence become a form of clout in settings where other forms of power and markers of status are largely unavailable. In poor communities, where youth have little access to money or education that might otherwise define their sense of self, they may turn to violence as a way of proving to others that they have value. In these neighborhoods, "despair is pervasive enough to have spawned an oppositional culture, that of 'the streets,' whose norms are often consciously opposed to those of mainstream society.... [S]treet culture has evolved what may be called a code of the streets, which amounts to a set of informal rules governing interpersonal public behavior, including violence."[129] In a similar vein, Douglas Massey and Nancy Denton point to segregated disadvantage as creating a "bleak social work" in which "oppositional states are normative."[130]

In prison, particularly in facilities where resources are scarce and violence is pervasive, tight-knit social groups can similarly "anchor and reinforce oppositional cultures,"[131] asserting specific norms that individuals are expected to follow.[132] Of particular concern are shared norms that encourage "subcultural values" by rewarding displays of dominance or aggression.[133] For inmates, codes of conduct may emerge inside harsher prison settings that frown on "snitching" or other types of cooperation with prison staff and that condone or even encourage violence and retaliation. For officers, social norms may encourage a hostile attitude toward prison administrators, an aggressive or overly harsh orientation toward inmates, and a "code of silence" that prioritizes the protection of other officers over the well-being of inmates or the functioning of the prison as a whole.

In many respects, then, the particular forms of social organization that develop inside harsher prisons – even those that seem difficult to understand in another context – can be conceptualized as a rational response to features of the environment. In this, I echo Hans Toch and others who argue that "[d]isplayed elsewhere, much prison conduct would suggest twisted personalities or strained psyches. But inmate acts fit the prison situation. They may be no more than extreme, evanescent adjustments to extreme, temporary trials.... It is easy to find objectively undesirable conduct among inmates – but it is hard to find dysfunctional acts."[134] For inmates in more punitive prisons, even social bonds that spur violence against others provide both companionship and safety to their members.

The same logic holds for correctional officers. Prison workers, like inmates, display a set of social dynamics that are readily understood as a practical response to an often unreasonable set of pressures and constraints. Indeed, even the most grievous injuries (both physical and psychological) suffered by inmates at the hands of overly aggressive prison staff might be comprehended, if not forgiven, within the context that they occur. One of the most disturbing aspects of the "siege mentality"[135] is that it can motivate and justify the infliction of intentional harms on others. Under sustained duress, the injudicious use of violence can come to seem like an acceptable and even righteous response to perceived threat. In this context, what might reasonably appear to an onlooker to be aggressions carried out without cause may be perceived by the perpetrator as merely preemptive self-defense.

In sum, I suggest that when state institutions fail to provide for the basic safety needs of citizens, individuals will be more likely to turn to informal associations to resolve conflict and distribute social goods.[136] The social ties forged within these pockets of "bounded solidarity"[137] can provide individuals with a sense of social belonging and enable intra-group cooperation.[138] However, they may simultaneously serve to reinforce the authority of existing homogeneous ties, undermine respect for those outside one's own social network, and promote norms of interpersonal hostility and violence. The state is thus not exogenous to civil society; it plays a critical role in determining not only the extent of associational life, but also its quality.

In the American prison, social connections and identities are built within a particular context. The specific attributes of this institutional context determine the nature of the resulting social groups. But neither the social group nor its influence on individuals is solely confined to the prison institution. As I have already noted, nearly all individuals eventually leave prison, either on a regular basis (as with correctional officers) or following the completion of their sentence (as with inmates). Ultimately, as I will show, the social identities that are formed in the punitive prison have downstream effects for American communities and important consequences for efforts toward controlling crime.

4

The Culture and Consequence of Prison

Paranoia is an illness I contracted in institutions.
It is not the reason for my sentences to reform school and prison.
It is the effect, not the cause.

Jack Henry Abbott, *In the Belly of the Beast* (1981)

In the previous chapters, I have provided a wide-ranging overview of the changing landscape of corrections in the United States. This is important, I have argued, because variation in the culture of institutions can play a significant role in shaping the way individuals interact, both within and beyond the prison walls. In the remainder of this book, I turn from this broad historical and theoretical background toward a narrower empirical investigation of the book's central premise.

My aim in this chapter is twofold. First, I outline the case of California corrections. In the United States, nearly half of all prisoners are released to just five states, and California alone accounts for about a quarter of all people released from prison.[1] As in the nation as a whole, California's incarceration rates steadily increased over past decades, with the number of prison inmates growing from 22,632 in 1979 to 168,350 as of 2006. In that year, there was about one state prison inmate for roughly every 168 adult Californians.[2] Using three sources of data, in this chapter I examine the culture of California's state prison institutions, with an emphasis on systematic variation in formal and informal dimensions of prison culture across different security levels.

Having established the ways in which the prison environment varies across California's security levels, I then explicate the specific issues involved in estimating the effects of prison culture on individual outcomes. Most basically, assignment to a security level is not random, but is predicated on specific, pre-existing features of the individual. I therefore rely on two quasi-experiments, which I outline here in some detail.

California Corrections

California is frequently considered to have been in the vanguard of the prison rehabilitation movement. As Joshua Page points out, the Golden State vigorously pursued the rehabilitative ideal in its approach to corrections following the Second World War. "State officials and penologists reasoned that if the Allies could defeat Fascism abroad, surely California could transform socially and psychologically afflicted offenders into well-adjusted, law abiding citizens."[3] It is therefore particularly remarkable that California was also on the forefront of the move toward a more punitive approach to corrections. California's inmate population is not without significant needs. For instance, about 15 percent of inmates in the California prison system have less than an eighth-grade education.[4] Yet, while some of California's prisons still offer basic education, most correctional facilities in the state have significantly decreased the number of rehabilitation programs they provide, largely embracing the new ideological regime. In fact, in her comprehensive *Understanding California Corrections*, Joan Petersilia points out that California now enrolls a significantly lower percentage of inmates in vocational and educational programs than the national average: 31 percent of inmates nationwide participate in vocational programs and 38 percent in educational programs, compared with only 13.8 percent in California for the two types of programs combined. Petersilia suggests that California's comparative lack of educational and vocational programming is due both to the growth of the state's prison population, which has strained the capacity of existing programs, and to the defunding of programs as a result of political pressure and perceived inefficacy. Of the $9.77 billion CDCR budget for the 2007–2008 fiscal year, about $456.87 million, or just 4.7 percent, was allocated to offender programs.[5]

Part of this punitive transition can be explained by the broader context in which criminal justice policies are crafted in California, which is highly politicized relative to that of other states.[6] Beginning in the 1970s with the passage of determinate sentencing, California's political climate of crime control has been marked by intense and heated political debate. Several high-profile ballot initiatives have been proposed and passed by voters that established particularly draconian sentencing policies, and the state's political parties have consistently staked out fairly punitive positions on criminal justice policies in their public platforms.[7] In addition, the public sector union representing correctional officers in the state, the California Correctional Peace Officers' Association (CCPOA), has been a powerful and well-financed fixture in California politics throughout the recent period. Along with other major interests, including the California District Attorneys Association and victims' rights organizations, the union in the 1990s pushed a policy agenda that unequivocally called for a punitive approach to crime control. In a 1995 policy paper, the union argued that rehabilitation is a "political philosophy that absolves [convicts] of responsibility for their actions, makes excuses for behavior, and assumes [that the government has] responsibility to change them."[8] And against the argument that "we need to rehabilitate criminals," the CCPOA reasoned:

The unspoken assumption in this argument is the criminal *can* be changed by someone else. The premise of this statement is incorrect. No set of factors, sociological, psychological or biological, is sufficient to explain the mind of a criminal.... Unless a person *wants* to change, you cannot make them change. In this regard prison ministry programs are probably the *only* worthwhile rehab type programs because they go to the heart and motivation of a person. The rest is expensive window dressing.

The political activities of CCPOA and its allies helped raise the stakes of criminal justice policy, increasing the importance of the issue and heightening political conflict.[9] Through its powerful political action committee, the union made large contributions to public awareness campaigns that moved penal policy in a punitive direction; it employed professional public relations experts to campaign for stricter enforcement of drug laws and increased prison terms; and through both financing and mobilization activities, the union supported candidates it considered to be supportive of its positions.[10]

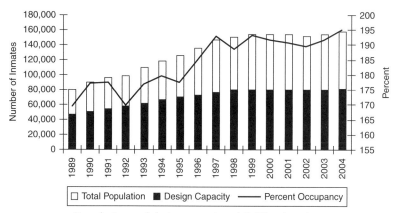

FIGURE 4.1. Population and design capacity of California prisons, 1989–2004. *Source*: Offender Information Services Branch, Estimates and Statistical Analysis Section, Data Analysis Unit, California Department of Corrections.

In addition, the politics of crime control in California have increasingly centered around issues of overcrowding. Crowding has long been a problem in the state's prisons, but it has become a critical source of strain on the system in the recent period. While the total design capacity of California prisons was almost doubled between 1989 and 2004, increasing from 47,210 to 80,890, it has been outpaced by increases in the state's inmate population (see Figure 4.1).

In October 2006, Governor Schwarzenegger declared a state of emergency in response to the situation of overcrowding in California prisons. By the time of the governor's announcement, almost 10 percent of California inmates, or roughly 17,000 men and women, were being housed in "bad beds," defined by Corrections Secretary James Tilton as "bunks in areas not designed as living spaces ... converted gyms, hallways and lounges ... [and] roughly 1,500 sleep in triple-decker bunks."[11] These high levels of overcrowding severely affected all areas of prison capacity, from infrastructure to administration. "Crowding is so severe, the governor's emergency decree [stated], that it has overwhelmed water, sewer and electrical systems at some prisons and fueled hundreds of prison riots, melees and smaller disturbances in the last year."[12]

Thus, despite the significant costs of criminal justice to the state,[13] the modern California prison system is critically dysfunctional. A report of the Little Hoover Commission described the system as "a billion dollar failure," and evidence of the system's problems abounds: California has one of the highest recidivism rates in the country; rates of assault, homicide, and suicide are higher in the state's prisons than the national average; and California prisons are home to some of the most notorious gangs in the nation.[14] (Indeed, California battles one of the highest per capita rates of gang association in the country.)[15] In addition, despite the $1.1 billion a year spent on prison health care, in 2005 U.S. District Judge Thelton Henderson ordered the prison health care system into court receivership, citing the needless deaths of inmates due to substandard care and "outright depravity."[16]

Measuring Variation in California State Prisons

As in other states, California's prisons operate with a combination of centralized state authority and institutional discretion. Thus, while some of the issues I have just described are constant across prisons, there is substantial variation across the state's 33 adult state prison facilities (Figure 4.2). In addition, California's adult institutions vary systematically according to a classification system that seeks to match groups of inmates with appropriate institutional settings commensurate with their perceived risks and needs. (Appendix A details each of California's prison facilities.)[17] State prisons are organized into four security levels, ranging from the least (Level I) to the most (Level IV) restrictive, and higher-security facilities differ from lower-security prisons in terms of both formal and informal culture.

Three available sources of information help paint a more detailed picture of California's prison security levels. The first is the *California Code of Regulations, Title 15: Crime Prevention and Corrections*, colloquially called the "Director's Rules." This document lays out the rules and regulations that govern adult operations and programs for the Department of Corrections and Rehabilitation. The second dataset is from the COMPSTAT Branch of the Office of Audits and Compliance, produced as part of a series of statistical reports that provide "localized management reviews" of individual institutions, parole regions, and administrative program areas. COMPSTAT reports from the Division of Adult Institutions offer data on a wide variety of facility-level characteristics for adult prisons. Many institutions house more than one security level, and these reports do not provide sub-institutional breakdowns. I therefore classify each institution by security level

FIGURE 4.2. California correctional facilities.
Source: "California's Correctional Facilities," California Department of Corrections and Rehabilitation, 2008.

according to the security-level designation of the majority of its inmates. Institutions with less than 50 percent of inmates in a single security level are excluded. Finally, where administrative data are not available, I turn to the California Correctional Officer Survey, an original data collection effort to gather the thoughts, attitudes, and experiences of correctional officers working in the California state prison system.

I conducted the California Correctional Officer Survey (CCOS) from April to October 2006. The survey asked officers a series of closed-ended questions about a variety of topics, including job satisfaction, work stress, personal safety and security, attitudes toward inmates, and professional orientation. Surveys were sent to each correctional officer through the mail, to his or her home address, rather than distributed at either union meetings or the workplace. This was intended to ensure

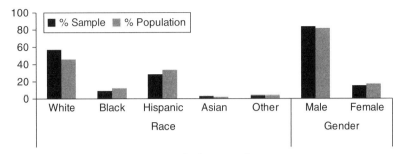

FIGURE 4.3. CCOS response sample demographics.
Note: Population data are taken from the Department of Corrections and Rehabilitation Office of Personnel Services for October 12, 2006. Sample race sums to more than 100% because some respondents selected more than one racial category. Sample *N* = 5,775; population *N* = 21,243.

that officers felt they could be honest about their work experiences. Respondents were also assured that surveys would be completely anonymous and that no one outside the research team would have access to individual surveys. (The survey instrument and additional details of survey administration are included in Appendix B.)

The survey ultimately yielded 5,775 completed and returned surveys, for a response rate of about 33 percent.[18] The large size of the survey sample provides a fairly representative cross section of officers by race and gender (Figure 4.3). Moreover, though response rates varied by institution, no facilities had to be excluded from analysis due to a paucity of respondents. (A breakdown of the survey sample by institution is provided in Appendix C.)

Comparing the Culture of Confinement

Using these data, it is possible to compare the culture of confinement across security levels. In California, the most immediate feature of variation across security levels is related to physical infrastructure. Facilities are designated to house a particular security level or levels according to the "physical security and housing capability" they can offer. As specified in Article 10, Section 3377, of the Director's Rules:

Level I facilities and camps consist primarily of open dormitories with a low security perimeter; Level II facilities consist primarily of open dormitories with a secure perimeter, which may include armed coverage; Level III facilities primarily have a secure perimeter with armed coverage and housing units with cells adjacent to exterior walls; Level IV facilities have a secure perimeter with internal and external armed coverage and housing units … or cell block housing with cells non-adjacent to exterior walls.[19]

According to COMPSTAT reports, Level IV facilities are also the only security-level institutions that make use of "supermax" units, supermaximum secure housing units designed to segregate inmates thought to pose the highest risk to institutional security.

Inmates classified at different security levels also receive different levels of oversight, with security procedures and freedom of movement becoming progressively more stringent as custody status increases. Minimum-security inmates (Level I) can attend work assignments or activities "located either on or off institutional grounds" and supervision must be sufficient to "ensure the inmate is present."[20] In contrast, maximum-custody inmates (Level IV) may attend programs only within a segregated area of the prison and are required to be "under the direct supervision and control of custody staff" at all times.[21] Security procedures for inmates classified as either Level II or Level III custody fall somewhere in between.[22] Commensurate with these stipulations, higher-security facilities employ a greater number of custody staff per inmate. Data from COMPSTAT show Level II facilities (defined here as prisons housing more than 50 percent of inmates at this designation) reporting an average of 15 custody staff per 100 inmates. By comparison, the number of custody staff for every 100 inmates is 18 at Level III and 22 at Level IV (see Table 4.1; note that reliable data for Level I are not available).

In addition to offering greater oversight, higher-security prisons are differentiated from lower-security prisons by the number of programs and services they provide. Specifically, higher-security prisons offer fewer vocational training programs, work assignments, and opportunities for substance abuse counseling. Consequently, smaller proportions of inmates at higher-custody facilities complete vocational training programs or substance abuse programs, or become certified within a professional industry. Higher-security institutions also provide fewer opportunities for participation in inmate "leisure" groups, which include Alcoholics Anonymous and Narcotics Anonymous, as well as veterans groups and other social organizations, although the difference falls just short of statistical significance. Again, participation rates in each of these

TABLE 4.1. *Variation across California Facilities by Security Level, Monthly Average*

	Level II	Level III	Level IV
Safety			
Disciplinary reports/100 inmates**	3.9	6.3	7.7
Violent disciplinary reports/100 inmates***	5.1	11.25	25.8
In-cell incidents, same race/100 inmates	0.002	0.016	0.036
In-cell incidents, different race/100 inmates#	0.000	0.005	0.013
Incidents/100 inmates**	0.48	0.95	1.7
Order			
Use of force/100 inmates***	0.20	0.36	0.90
In special housing units/100 inmates	0.000	0.000	0.64
Number of lockdowns**	2.13	1.56	5.13
Programs			
Education			
Capacity/100 inmates	16.8	17.8	16.9
Enrollment/100 inmates	13.1	12.0	12.4
GED completed/100 inmates	2.9	2.5	1.9
Vocational			
Capacity/100 inmates**	5.9	4.8	2.1
Enrollment/100 inmates**	4.7	4.0	1.8
Training completed/100 inmates***	2.1	1.1	0.18
Industry certification/100 inmates**	5.3	3.9	0.72
Substance abuse			
Capacity/100 inmates***	3.34	0.30	0.00
Enrollment/100 inmates***	2.93	0.26	0.00
Completed/100 inmates***	0.65	0.08	0.00
Work assignment			
Available/100 inmates**	75.8	62.7	49.5
Assigned/100 inmates***	68.4	55.6	42.3
Inmate groups			
Number/100 inmates	0.63	0.57	0.37
Attendance/100 inmates#	47.2	50.6	18.5
AA contact hours/100 inmates	129.8	221.6	348.1
NA contact hours/100 inmates	78.5	222.5	111.4
Veterans groups contact hours/100 inmates	4.7	6.4	2.3
Personnel			
Total/100 inmates	26.1	30.4	36.7
Custody/100 inmates#	15.2	18.4	22.1
Education/100 inmates	0.84	0.79	0.77
Ratio education to custody#	.05	.04	.04
N	4	7	5

Note: Includes only facilities housing male inmates in which more than 50 percent are a single security level.
#$p < .1$, *$p < .05$, **$p < .01$, ***$p < .001$.
Source: COMPSTAT Division of Adult Institutions.

groups, where they are offered, are significantly lower at higher-security facilities, as measured by the overall number of inmate contact hours. Finally, higher-security facilities appear to proffer somewhat fewer education staff per inmate than lower-security facilities (0.84 at Level II, 0.79 at Level III, and 0.77 at Level IV) though this difference also does not reach statistical significance.

These data make clear that higher-security facilities operate with a different formal culture than lower-security settings. In particular, they offer fewer opportunities for inmates to interact through programs, informal organizations, and prison-based employment. At the same time, additional data show that higher-custody settings are marked by substantially more violence and disorder. Clearly there is no "objective" measure of the number of violent incidents against which to compare the prevalence of filed disciplinary reports or recorded incidents; different reported rates of violence are likely to be a reflection of true disparities in prison disorder, but they also may reflect differences in the extent to which violence is noticed and officially documented by staff. However, the available data suggest that higher-security prisons experience more disciplinary infractions each month – on average, there are 4 per 100 inmates at Level II, compared with 6 and 8 per 100 at Levels III and IV, respectively. Even larger disparities appear in the rate of *violent* disciplinary infractions, such as assault or battery on staff, inmate assaults on other inmates, riots and disturbances, the presence of weapons, and murder or attempted murder. Level II facilities report 5 such incidents per 100 inmates, in comparison with 11 at Level III and 26 at Level IV. Likewise, serious events including violence and drug-related incidents are highest at Level IV and decrease in frequency at lower custody levels. Finally, in-cell incidents also vary across security levels, but only for incidents between inmates of different races, which are more frequent at higher-security prisons.

Unfortunately, administrative data detailing the proportion of inmates affiliated with gangs at each security level are not available. However, according to estimates from the CCOS, the proportion of inmates involved in gangs or gang activity ranges from 66 percent participation at Level I to 69 percent at Level II, 71 percent at Level III, and fully 80 percent at Level IV ($p < .001$). Moreover, officers attribute significant amounts of violence to these organizations. Fully a quarter of officers across all prisons in the state reported that gang-related violence occurs in their prison a few times a week, with an additional 10 percent reporting that gang violence is an everyday occurrence. However, officers working at higher-security facilities report that gang violence is substantially more frequent on average ($p < .001$). The majority of officers, 74 percent, also feel that gang-related activity, even when it arises as a response to inmates' problems with staff or prison conditions, makes the prison less safe. Again, however, this is more so the case at higher-level custody ($p < .001$).

Finally, COMPSTAT data show that institutional responses to violence are more frequent at institutions where disorder is more prevalent. These data help to paint (at least in broad strokes) a picture of the inmate–staff relationship. At higher-security prisons, there is a greater average monthly incidence of the documented use of force by staff against inmates (0.20 per 100 inmates at Level II, 0.36 at Level III, 0.90 at Level IV). Maximum-security prisons also report a higher frequency of lockdowns, in which programs for all or part of the facility are canceled for at least 24 hours due to concerns about security. During these periods, inmates may be confined to cells for most or all of the day. On average, Level IV prisons experience 61.6 lockdowns per year, compared with 18.7 at Level III and 25.2 at Level II. In addition to being a reflection of overall violence within the prison, the frequency of lockdowns reduces the actual availability of programming for inmates within the institution.

Estimating Prison Effects

Taken together, these data suggest that higher-security prisons are marked by a formal and informal culture that is substantially different from that of lower-security institutions. How might these myriad differences across prison institutions affect the socialization of those who pass through them? Do different kinds of prisons yield different outcomes? Or are the details of institutional design largely irrelevant to the subjective experience of the prison?

In the coming chapters, I test the idea that these substantial variations in prison culture have important consequences for the social adaptation processes of both inmates and officers. One of the challenges of this analysis, however, is to sufficiently parse out cause and effect. That is, if inmates and officers in higher-security prisons have different social orientations from those in lower-security prisons, this may be evidence of the causal effect of institutional culture. Alternatively, any descriptive differences between those at higher- and lower-security may simply be a function of dissimilarities between groups that pre-date exposure to a particular prison environment. A simple comparison across security levels cannot distinguish between these competing interpretations.

To illustrate the causal effect of the prison environment, what we would like to do is compare the outcomes for a given individual were he or she to be placed in one type of prison, relative to what *would have happened* to that same individual had he or she been placed in a different type of prison. Clearly, this is not possible; the counterfactual condition is unobservable. Thus, we are stuck with a "fundamental problem of causal inference."[23] That is, if a particular individual is assigned to Higher-Security Level A, we are unable to directly observe the outcome for that same individual if he or she had instead been assigned to Lower-Security Level B.

More formally, in estimating the effect of different types of prisons on individuals, we are interested in the potential outcome for a given individual (i) if he or she is "treated" by being assigned to a higher-security prison ($T = 1$) relative to *what would have happened* to that same individual under the "control" condition of a lower-security setting ($T = 0$). We would thus like to evaluate the treatment effect for that individual by comparing his or her outcome – for instance, features of his or her social network– under the treatment condition, Y_{i1}, to his or her outcome under the control condition, Y_{i0}:[24]

$$P_i = Y_{i1} - Y_{i0}$$

The obvious difficulty is that we cannot directly observe both outcomes; a single person cannot simultaneously experience both conditions, and so we are stuck with a missing-data problem.[25]

Random assignment is the "gold standard" solution to this problem. If inmates or correctional officers are randomly assigned to different types of prison, then with a large enough sample we can estimate the average effect by comparing the first group's average outcome with that of the second. In other words, one group simulates the hypothetical condition for the other. In the case of perfect random assignment and with a large enough sample, treatment is independent of all covariates, both observed and unobserved. The average outcome for the

treated group in the experiment serves as the counterfactual for the
control group, and the average treatment effect (*ATE*) can be estimated by comparing the expected outcome of the treated group (the
group mean) to the expected outcome of the control group:

$$ATE = E(Y_{i_1} \mid T_i = 1) - E(Y_{i_0} \mid T_i = 0)$$

It is difficult to imagine getting permission to implement this type
of fully experimental design inside prisons, however, nor would it be
ethical to do so. A great deal of attention and administrative oversight
is devoted to ensuring the appropriate placement of inmates, and randomly assigning inmates might risk increasing prison violence, riots,
or even death to the subjects under study. Similarly, correctional officers' work assignments are dictated by a variety of factors, not the
least of which is their personal preferences. Outside of slavery, we cannot mandate that individuals work in a particular setting, and officers
would surely be resistant to being located at random prisons purely
for the purpose of research.

In the empirical chapters that follow, I therefore rely on two quasi-
experiments. The first estimates the causal effects of imprisonment,
and the second estimates the causal effects of prison work. For both
correctional officers and inmates, assignment to a particular security
level is not strictly random, so we cannot assume that the treatment
and control groups in these cases are truly equivalent. We must therefore make additional identifying assumptions in order to estimate the
treatment effect. Specifically, we must assume that assignment to the
higher-security prison depends on some set of observable covariates, X.
This strong ignorability of assignment[26] allows us to estimate the average treatment effect for the treated (*ATT*), the quantity of interest, by

$$ATT = E\{E(Y_i \mid X_i, T_i = 1) - E(Y_i \mid X_i, T_i = 0)\}$$

Using these dual quasi-experiments, I am able to estimate the causal
effect of the prison environment on individual social outcomes.

Estimating the Effects of Imprisonment

For inmates, assignment to a particular prison is based on a classification score. This makes it difficult to figure out if differences
across inmates are the result of assignment to a particular security

level or whether it is simply that inmates assigned to higher-security prisons are already different from those assigned to lower-security prisons. However, a subset of inmates – those whose classification scores fall very close to the cutoff point determining assignment to a higher- or lower-security prison – can be treated "as if" randomly assigned. Among this subgroup of inmates, observable and unobservable characteristics that pre-date incarceration are comparable, but one group is assigned to a higher-security prison and the other to a lower-security prison.

The particular setup can be thought of as follows. Say that we are interested in the effect of a scholarship on how well students do in college. The scholarship is given to high school students who receive a 1400 or above on the SAT. What we would really like to know is what would have happened to a given individual who received the scholarship if instead she had not received it. However, we can obviously never directly observe this counterfactual. Simply comparing those who received the scholarship with those who did not is confounded by other differences between the two groups. For example, we know that SAT takers who get higher scores are more likely to have attended high-performing high schools and are less likely to have parents who did not attend college. These factors predict both SAT scores and how well students do in college.

The SAT is an imprecise measure of academic ability, though; it contains some amount of randomness, or "noise." For instance, on any particular day, one student may have a cold and do worse than she otherwise would, while another eats her Wheaties and does particularly well. This means that students who scored a 1390 are likely to have characteristics that are, on average, statistically indistinguishable from students who get a 1400. However, the latter group will be "treated" with the scholarship and the former will not. Comparing only these subgroups of comparable students who have scores right near the cutoff helps eliminate potential confounders, such that the 1390 scorers who do not receive a scholarship provide the counterfactual condition for the 1400 scorers who do.

The classification score that assigns inmates to higher and lower security levels functions somewhat like the SAT. Individuals entering the prison system are assigned a classification score, which is a composite of a set of individual items related to both background characteristics and prior incarceration behavior, just as the final SAT score is a composite of correct and incorrect answers on a set of individual questions. Background factors taken into consideration and scored include age at first arrest; age at reception; term in years; gang involvement, as well as type of gang and method of verification (e.g., self-admission, tattoos and symbols); prior jail or county juvenile sentence of 31+ days; and prior incarceration(s). Factors related to prior incarceration behavior include any serious disciplinary history; battery or attempted battery on a non-prisoner; battery or attempted battery on an inmate; distribution of drugs; possession of a deadly weapon (double weighted if within the past five years); inciting a disturbance; and battery causing serious injury. Inmates are then placed into a security level according to the range in which their score falls.[27] A score of 0–18 designates Level I, 19–27 Level II, 28–51 Level III, and 52 or above Level IV. (A sample of the CDCR classification score sheet is available in Appendix D.)

This classification score is clearly imprecise, but it provides a relative measure of how dangerous or risky a particular individual is considered to be. Thus, inmates who have classification scores between 19 and 27 have different average characteristics from those with scores between 28 and 51. For example, we would expect the former to have fewer previous arrests than the latter on average and to be incarcerated for less violent crimes. However, just as SAT 1390 scorers are similar in expectation to 1400 scorers, inmates with a 26 or 27 should look fairly indistinguishable in the aggregate from inmates with a 28 or 29. Because the 26 and 27 scorers happen to fall just below the classification cutoff point, though, and the 28 and 29 scorers fall just above it, the two groups will be sent to distinct types of prison facilities.

Thus, the 28 and 29 scorers can be considered the "treatment" group who experience incarceration in a higher-security prison, while the 26 and 27 scorers can be considered the "control group" who experience incarceration in a lower-security prison. If we then find a gap between the treatment and control groups in our outcomes of interest, such as the extent and character of their social ties, we can have great confidence that it is the result of the two groups having been assigned to different types of prisons. This estimation strategy is illustrated in Figure 4.4.

In addition, it is important to note that there is very little subjectivity in the individual items used to calculate the classification score;

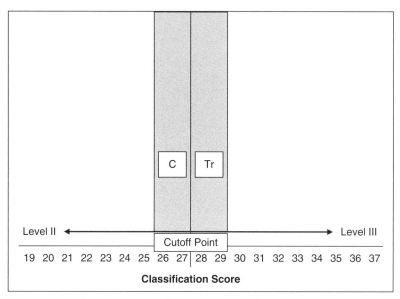

Level II ←   → Level III

Cutoff Point

19 20 21 22 23 24 25 26 27 | 28 29 30 31 32 33 34 35 36 37

Classification Score

FIGURE 4.4. The inmate natural experiment: an illustration.

most are objective measures, such as the number of previous arrests or whether an individual was ever suspended or expelled from school. This means that classification officers tasked with compiling information on each inmate have very little discretion in how scores are calculated, so will not be able to easily "game the system" by pushing scores just above or below the cutoff.[28] (Additional features of the security-level assignment process are detailed in Appendix E.)

This setup can be thought of as a classic "regression discontinuity design." Regression discontinuity was introduced by Thistlethwaite and Campbell in the *Journal of Educational Psychology*[29] and has since been applied to a wide variety of issues in education research.[30] A number of recent studies have also made use of these methods in criminal justice research.[31] Formally, the regression discontinuity model is estimated as

$$Y_i = b_0 + b_1 X_i + b_2 Z_i + e_i$$

where Y_i is the outcome for individual i, and X_i is a continuous index, such as the SAT score in the example described earlier. The variable Z_i is a binary variable that denotes whether an individual is in the treatment or control group, such that

$$Z_i = 1 \, if \, X_i \geq x_{Tr}$$

$$Z_i = 0 \, if \, X_i < x_{Tr}$$

where x_{Tr} is some fixed value of X. The decision rule for assignment is known and can be observed; no unobservable variables affect assignment to treatment. In the case of the SAT score scholarship, X_{Tr} is set at 1400. In a sharp regression discontinuity, treatment is deterministic given X_i, and the treatment effect can be estimated directly from the regression coefficient, b_2. In the "fuzzy" case, where the continuous score is not a perfect predictor of assignment, estimating a discontinuity at x_{Tr} depends on the *probability* of treatment given X_i:

$$E\left[Z_i|X_i = x\right] = \Pr\left[Z_i = 1|X_i = x\right]$$

In the inmate classification system, those with scores equal to or above each cutoff ($X_i \geq x_{Tr}$) are assigned to the higher-security "treatment" group ($Z_i = 1$), and those with scores below the cutoff ($X_i < x_{Tr}$) are assigned to the lower-security control condition ($Z_i = 0$).

To verify that inmates who have classification scores that fall just below (a score of either 26 or 27) and just above (a score of either 28 or 29) the cutoff point for assignment into Levels II and III are in fact comparable, I start by comparing their average demographic, criminal history, and personal history traits (Table 4.2). On most relevant covariates, the groups do not significantly differ. In their levels of education, scores on a Current Violence Scale (measuring the "degree of violence in the present offense"), and length of prison sentence, those above and below the cutoff are on average statistically indistinguishable. There is some difference in the distribution of controlling offenses between the two groups, as those below the cutoff are more likely to be incarcerated for drug possession. There is also a slight difference between the two groups in terms of their number of current charges at conviction. However, it is actually inmates who have classification scores that fall just *below* the cutoff that have the higher number of charges. The average age of the two groups of inmates also differs slightly between those with scores just above and below the

TABLE 4.2. *Balance Above and Below Classification Cutoff Points*

| | Level II to Level III | | | |
	Below	Above	Chi Sq.	F-Statistic
Age 16–30 (%)	80.6	83.4	1.693	
GED (%)	78.7	80.6	0.510	
Highest grade completed	10.69	10.69		0.001
Current charge (%)				
Homicide	0.4	0.7	0.324	
Sex offense	0.9	1.2	0.290	
Assault	15.7	15.3	0.025	
Robbery	10	7.5	2.529	
Property	32.8	36.8	2.228	
Drug possession	25.3	18.6	8.158**	
Drug trafficking	14	11.4	1.929	
Domestic violence	5.8	5.8	0.001	
No. of current charges or offenses	1.73	1.59		4.344*
Violence of current charge (scale)	4.2	4.37		0.488
Term in years	5.25	5.28		0.043

Data are for all offenders in the COMPAS database with an 839 placement score less than 2 points from the cutoff points for classification: 26 or 27 and 28 or 29. Individuals placed through administrative determinants or classified prior to 2003 are omitted. $N = 1,264$ (677 below the cutoff and 587 above).

cutoff, though the difference is confined to the upper two age groups: those 31–40 years of age and those older than 41.

On measures of substance abuse, financial problems and poverty, and vocational and educational problems, the two groups are also equivalent. There is likewise no apparent difference between those just above and just below the cutoff on three scales measuring past criminality: the history of non-compliance (measuring number of failures when previously placed in community corrections), history of violence, and family criminality. Though there is some difference between the two groups on the Early Socialization Failure Scale, individual items in the scale are largely comparable: on average, those with classification scores just below and just above the cutoff are equally likely to have been charged with a violent felony as a juvenile and they have equivalent numbers of juvenile felony charges. The disparity in socialization scale scores is due primarily to differences between the two groups in the probability of having been incarcerated while a juvenile and in histories of educational failure, including skipping classes and suspensions or expulsions. In both cases, the magnitude of difference on these variables is small and only marginally statistically significant (p < .1).[32] In sum, descriptive statistics comparing the two groups of inmates suggest that they provide a reasonable simulation of random assignment. The quasi-experimental design therefore helps to rule out the possibility that pre-existing characteristics of the individual account for any evidenced effects.

Estimating the Effects of Prison Work

Empirical assessments of correctional officers' beliefs have progressed from relying on simple regressions to employing more sophisticated multi-level models.[33] However, surprisingly little is known about how the norms of rehabilitation or retribution are learned by correctional staff and whether changes in the formal culture of prison policy are reflected in the attitudes of those who administer them. Despite a significant increase in the amount and quality of research on the subject of correctional officers' professional norms,[34] extant research has offered inconsistent findings. This has led some researchers to surmise that the "nuances of the correctional officers' job may not be amenable to survey research."[35]

One persistent problem in this literature is that methodological hurdles have continued to stymie attempts to establish causality. In particular, as in most professions, several layers of self-selection are at work in determining an officer's occupational context. First, individuals choose employment that fits with their personality, preferences, and interest. In corrections, officers are tasked primarily with maintaining safety and order, while counselors and program staff focus more directly on rehabilitation and prisoner assistance. We should therefore expect individuals who hold different attitudes toward crime causation, punishment, and rehabilitation to be attracted to these different occupational roles. For example, community and institutional case management officers are more supportive of rehabilitation than correctional officers.[36]

A second layer of selection occurs as officers sort themselves into particular types of penal facilities that reflect their existing orientation toward corrections. For example, officers with less punitive attitudes are more likely to be found working in a treatment facility or with younger offenders.[37] By the same token, correctional officers choose to work with inmates at a particular security level. Officers who are less supportive of rehabilitation programs may prefer to work in a higher-security environment where fewer such programs are offered. More punitive-minded officers may also prefer more restrictive or punitive prison settings because they believe them to be the "right" type of prison or because they are comfortable with the more contentious nature of the inmate–staff relationship that might typify such prisons. Some may also like the feeling of power associated with overseeing inmates who are confined to their cells more of the time or who have fewer privileges. Conversely, officers who are more rehabilitation-oriented may select into a lower-security prison that offers more or higher-quality rehabilitation programs. In order to estimate the effect of prison culture, it is necessary to address these selection issues.

In this regard, CDCR procedures for placing new correctional officers into particular work assignments provide an excellent quasi-experiment. The CDCR relies on its website, unemployment offices, and active recruitment on military bases, as well as other traditional recruitment outlets like job fairs, in order to attract potential job candidates. The minimum requirements to become a California correctional officer are that individuals be U.S. citizens, be more than 21 years of age, have a high school diploma or equivalency, have no felony convictions, be in good physical condition, and be eligible to own or possess a firearm. Prospective officers who fit the hiring criteria undergo an extensive screening process, which includes a standard civil service written exam, a background check, a physical fitness test, vision and medical exams, drug screening, and a psychological evaluation.[38]

Candidates who successfully complete the screening process are then eligible for placement on the certification list, from which the incoming class of cadets at the Basic Correctional Officer Academy (BCOA) is chosen. Once at BCOA, cadets are provided with an inventory of all adult prison facilities in the state and are instructed to specify up to 10 prisons (about a third of the state's adult correctional institutions) where they would be willing to serve a twenty-four-month apprenticeship. Apprenticeship is the final, on-the-job training component of cadets' mandated peace officer training, during which they must acquire a minimum of 3,600 hours of professional experience.[39] Once assigned to an institution, apprentice officers are not allowed to transfer to another facility for the full twenty-four months. If a cadet has no preference, he or she can note "statewide" in the paperwork, indicating a willingness to accept placement at any state facility.

The Peace Officer Selection Office matches officers' preferences to available positions and provides cadets with placement offers. These allocations fluctuate depending on the critical staffing needs of the department. Thus, it is difficult to predict trends in staffing needs at any given time. CDCR therefore makes clear in its hiring materials that positions are offered according to departmental needs, noting that "[o]fficers are offered employment at locations with the greatest hiring need at the time of hire."[40] When a cadet receives an offer, he or she can either accept it or choose to decline, in which case a waiver is issued and a new offer is generated. Cadets are allowed only three waivers before losing status as available-for-hire, at which time they must reapply for candidacy.

According to official policy, officers are, "whenever possible," assigned to institutions close to where they live.[41] However, although the allocation of available positions fluctuates for a variety of reasons, some facilities are consistently considered "hard to fill." These facilities either are located in remote areas, making them difficult to travel to, or are in counties where the cost of living is relatively high. Consequently, these facilities are among those with the highest transfer request rates, leaving positions frequently open. These facilities are therefore nearly always on a list of critical need for apprenticeship placements.

In an interview with staff at the Peace Officer Selection Office, one senior staff member noted that the recent downturn of the economy has had a significant impact on apprenticeship placement, in the sense that apprentices are now more likely to indicate they are willing to work anywhere in the state, in addition to being more likely to accept the first offer from the hiring office rather than opting for waivers. Placement officers encourage cadets to think of apprenticeship as "paying your dues" and remind cadets that, though they may not serve their apprenticeship in an ideal situation, after completing the required hours, officers who are working at an institution that is not their first choice may submit a transfer packet. Institutional reassignments are then made as positions become available and according to seniority. (Transfer requests can be submitted annually until an officer is reassigned. However, the department receives between 80 and 100 transfer requests statewide each day, so transfer out of a "hard to fill" facility is never guaranteed.)[42]

Given these procedures, it is likely that correctional officers sort into their preferred security level and facility as they gain seniority within the CDCR. However, apprentice officers have little control over their placement, and so are not able to select with much precision into a particular prison based on their preference. In addition, even when CDCR is able to meet officers' geographic preferences, self-sorting by security level does not necessarily follow, as the location of facilities is largely uncorrelated with the security level(s) they house; analysis reveals no correlation between the security level at a particular prison and the region in which the prison is located.[43] Thus, the result of the apprentice assignment protocol is that, among new recruits who are still in their probationary period, the institution and security level to which an apprentice is assigned are likely to be uncorrelated with individual-level characteristics, including his or her pre-existing social attitudes. That is to say, it is reasonable to treat correctional officers in their first two years of work "as if" random assignment to security levels had occurred.

The California Correctional Officer Survey (CCOS) contains a sample of 310 correctional officers who are in their period of apprenticeship (defined as being in their first two years of employment), 265 of whom are in their first year with CDCR. Among this group, the large majority work at security Level III ($N = 65$) or IV ($N = 167$).[44] If apprentices have indeed been arbitrarily assigned to a particular security level, then the "treatment" of assignment to a maximum- rather than lower-security post should be independent of all observable characteristics.

As Figure 4.5 shows, this appears to be the case. Apprentice officers who are assigned to work with Level III and IV inmates are statistically comparable in terms of their gender, age, level of education, current educational status, and race. The only discrepancy between apprentice officers assigned to Level III and Level IV is their partisan identification: the proportion of self-identified Republicans at Level IV is somewhat higher than at Level III. However, as on other observables, the difference between the two groups is not statistically significant ($p = .29$).

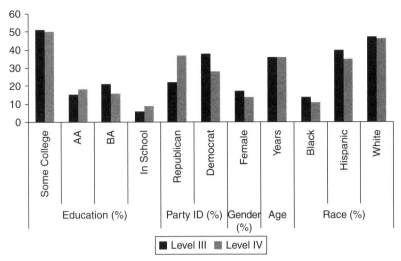

FIGURE 4.5. Demographics of apprentice correctional officers.
Note: Includes only officers that began employment in 2005 or 2006.
Source: CCOS.

These equivalencies support the claim that new officers in the CDCR are assigned to posts arbitrarily; the data suggest that apprentice officers are not sorting themselves or being sorted into different security levels conditional on their observable characteristics. To the extent that we then see differences between apprentice officers across security levels, this is likely to be explained by the effect of correctional work. In sum, while we cannot directly observe what would have happened to officers assigned to higher-security prisons if they had instead been assigned to lower-security prisons, the group of apprentice officers assigned to the lower-security setting simulates the counterfactual outcome for the group of apprentice officers assigned to the higher-security prison.

Additional Issues: Generalizability and Specification of Mechanisms

There are two important caveats to these research designs. The first is that the effects I estimate among subsets of inmates and correctional officers may not generalize to the entire populations of each group, respectively. Among inmates, the research design offers only "local independence"; that is, it is only individuals who have classification scores in a small window around the cutoff who can be treated as if randomly assigned. The farther away from the cutoff point the "window" is opened, the less comparable the higher-security and lower-security inmates become. I therefore cannot say anything about whether the effects I find in this subgroup of inmates are similar to the effects of incarceration among the total inmate population.

This is particularly true given that, in this case, the other inmates (both those who have higher classification scores than the higher-security inmates in my subsample and those who have lower classification scores than the lower-security inmates in my sample) are themselves part of the "treatment" that the inmates I consider have undergone. That is to say, inmates who have classification scores that fall just above the cutoff, in addition to being assigned to a higher-security prison, are also the "least criminal" of the inmates similarly assigned, at least insofar as their relatively higher classification score is a measure of some true underlying tendency. Conversely, inmates who have classification scores that fall just below the cutoff, in addition to being assigned to a lower-security prison, are the "most criminal" of the inmates similarly assigned. We must therefore consider the overall culture of the institution, as well as inmates' particular position within the social organization of prison life, to be components of the treatment.

Generalizability is likewise a potential issue among correctional officers. Apprentice officers might be unlike the total population of officers in a number of ways, given that what attracts individuals to correctional work may change over time. Differences may be particularly apparent when apprentice officers are compared with those officers who are nearing retirement, as at least some of these more senior individuals may have entered the system before the punitive turn had fully taken hold. In addition, apprentice officers are, by definition, just starting out in correctional employment. If the effects I find in this study are either heightened or mitigated over the years, as individuals accumulate work experience, I may under- or overestimate the average effects for correctional workers over the course of their careers.

A second limitation of these research designs is that they do not allow for adjudication between the different dimensions of prison culture, or the specific mechanisms, that may account for the evident effects of incarceration and prison work. This is important, given that there is some disagreement among scholars and practitioners about whether the formal or informal environment matters most for the way individuals experience prison.[45] However, as I have already described, these institutional features do not vary independently across security levels in the state; rather, higher rates of institutional violence and gang activity covary with the lesser provision of rehabilitation programming.

In fact, it is arguably impossible to separate out the myriad, highly correlated attributes of prison culture that shape the experience of prison and account for its psychological effects. Instead, there is reason to think of these dimensions as theoretically linked, such that the functioning of each has direct consequences for the other. First, even if rehabilitation programs serve no truly rehabilitative purpose, they keep inmates busy in ways that mitigate tensions. Thus, keeping "inmates busy as bees in meaningful activities" might reduce the chances of rioting and other disturbances.[46] As Pennsylvania Superior Court Judge Robert Freedberg suggested, "[F]ew conditions compromise safety and security in prisons more than idle prisoners."[47] Even correctional officers and others who are generally skeptical of making rehabilitation a primary purpose of incarceration[48] are therefore often supportive of rehabilitation programs because they see them as contributing to the maintenance of order within the institution.[49]

Conversely, the elimination of programs and harsher prison conditions can breed resentment among inmates, leading to more violence: "Even dogs confined to cages for long periods of time go berserk.... Brutality breeds hate, and hate breeds violence."[50] As I have argued extensively in the preceding chapter, when prisons are experienced as harsh and unpredictable, inmates may band together in gangs or other groups in order to obtain the safety that the institution is perceived as unable or unwilling to provide; in violent prisons as in unstable communities, inmate solidarities are often perceived as one of the only means of protection from physical harm.

The result is that informal and administrative cultures are likely to be mutually reinforcing. As John DiIulio illustrated in his study of prison administration, correctional facilities that maintain order are able to provide more effective programming.[51] When instead violence is pervasive, it is more difficult for prison administrators to justify the risks associated with allowing inmates to congregate and converse.

Higher-security prisons thus have the dual consequence of placing individuals with more extensive criminal histories in sustained contact with each other and at odds with staff, while at the same time reducing opportunities for inmates to engage in activities that have the potential to build (pro-)social connections.

The limitations I have just described are not insignificant. However, these drawbacks are heavily outweighed by the advantages these research designs can offer. Namely, by relying on these two quasi-experiments, I am able to separate the pre-existing characteristics of correctional officers and inmates from the causal effect of prison institutions, identifying the ways in which the prison environment actively shapes the social ties and collective norms of individuals.

5

The Social Effects of Incarceration

Tell me thy company, and I'll tell thee what thou art.
Miguel de Cervantes, *Don Quixote* (1605–1615)

Existing scholarship presents competing theories of the effects harsher prison environments might have on inmates' social attitudes and propensities for crime. By one reasoning, incarceration of any kind will have little effect.[1] Indeed, underlying the modern concept of incapacitation is the implicit assumption that prison time is a holding pattern, during which individuals are removed from society and placed in institutions whose primary function is simply to contain them. Those who espouse this view of imprisonment argue that most inmates enter prison with an existing set of characteristics that have been shaped by formative experiences within families, school systems, and communities. The time that most inmates spend in prison is likely to be inconsequential relative to these other more salient sources of socialization, doing little to alter already deeply rooted predispositions. If this is the case, inmates exiting prison should be expected to be essentially no different than they were when they entered.

A rival school of thought argues that prisons can effectively discourage crime, changing attitudes in ways that decrease the likelihood of recidivism. Emerging from an economic theory of rationality, deterrence theory argues that when deciding whether or not to commit a crime, individuals will weigh the possibility of being caught and sentenced to a term of incarceration. The higher the "costs" associated with punishment and the greater the perceived probability of receiving it, the less motivated individuals will be to engage in criminal activity. T he specific deterrent effect might be particularly robust for first-time offenders, who learn the harsh realities of prison and update their perceived utility of re-offending accordingly. As Michael Windzio writes:

When committing first offences, adolescent men have no clear idea of the "pains of imprisonment". Juvenile male offenders incarcerated for the first time must learn how to arrange their everyday social interactions with inmates and prison staff. They have to deal with the process of finding their position within the inmate hierarchy and have to cope with severe restrictions of autonomy. Moreover, being incarcerated means that friendships and social interactions with persons outside are extremely restricted and sometimes grievously missed. Under the assumption that both social integration and autonomy are basic needs, painful experiences with respect to both dimensions could be deterrent effects of imprisonment and might have an impact on criminal behaviour in the future.[2]

Those who challenge this view, however, argue that imprisonment, particularly in harsher prisons, can actually have a criminogenic effect. Theories of "institutionalization" or "prisonization" posit that the prison environment socializes inmates toward heightened criminality. Either through peer learning in so-called schools for crime or through the "hardening" required to survive in a prison environment that is often violent and unpredictable, incarceration can make inmates less trusting, more violent, and more likely to internalize the stigma associated with being a criminal.[3] Again, these effects may be particularly strong for individuals who are entering prison for the first time, and as a result are particularly susceptible to the socialization processes that result from entering into an unfamiliar institutional environment.

These three frameworks provide conflicting expectations about the effects of incarceration. Likewise, while theories concerning the deterrent or criminogenic effects of incarceration have been much debated, empirical studies examining the effects of incarceration relative to other types of sanctions have revealed decidedly mixed results.[4] In a meta-analysis of studies estimating the effects of custodial versus non-custodial punishment, Villettaz et al. found only a handful that employed experimental or quasi-experimental methods. Of these, 2 revealed lower re-offending rates among those with custodial sanctions, while 11 were more favorable to non-custodial sanctions. An additional 4 results were favorable to non-custodial sanctions but were not statistically significant. The remaining 10 results detailed in the meta-analysis revealed no difference between custodial and non-custodial sentences.[5] Other review articles have reported similarly inconclusive results. For instance, Lin Song and Roxanne Lieb described four studies comparing incarceration and probation and found that while two showed probation to be more effective in reducing recidivism, one demonstrated the reverse and the other evidenced no significant difference.[6]

Both the deterrent and prisonization models of prison effects also provide reason to believe that different *types* of prisons will yield different modes of acculturation. However, their expectations point in opposite directions. To the extent that harsher prisons are seen as a higher price to pay for committing a crime, they should serve as a greater deterrent than less punitive prisons; as specific deterrence theory suggests, individuals who spend time in them will be especially loath to return. Conversely, in harsher prisons, where there is more violence, peers with more extensive criminal histories, and fewer opportunities to participate in rehabilitation programs, individuals may be more likely to internalize the norms of hostility and aggression that prevail. This should be expected to increase recidivism following release.[7]

Again, there exist only a small number of experimental or quasi-experimental studies that estimate the effects of prison type on prison misconduct and recidivism.[8] However, the quasi-experimental studies that focus on recidivism generally concur that incarceration in a harsher prison environment increases rates of post-release offending. For instance, Keith Chen and Jesse Shapiro examined the effect of assignment to a higher-security prison on the recidivism rates of 949 federal inmates released in the first half of 1987. As the authors point out, the small size of their sample precludes a definitive finding, and statistical significance varies across their estimates. However, they found no evidence to suggest that harsher prison conditions deter crime. Instead, they estimated that inmates assigned to above-minimum custody are 10–13 percent more likely to be rearrested within one to three years of release than demographically equivalent inmates assigned to minimum security.[9]

In a second study, Gerald Gaes and Scott Camp used data[10] on a set of inmates who were randomly assigned to either an old or a new classification system. While most inmates were designated for the same security level by each system, a subset of about 561 inmates who would have been placed in a lower-security prison under the old system were instead placed in a higher-security prison by the new system. Gaes and Camp found that assignment to the higher-security facility had a criminogenic effect on these inmates, increasing rates of recidivism relative to those assigned to the lower-security setting.[11]

These are well-designed examinations of imprisonment's criminogenic effect. However, recidivism is not the only outcome of interest; incarceration in a higher-security prison may have other measurable effects worthy of inquiry. In particular, by limiting the outcomes we are interested in to re-offending behavior only, we have likely missed a wide array of incarceration's social and psychological impacts. In addition, because they focus only on a single behavioral outcome, existing experimental studies give us little purchase on the *mechanism* through which serving a prison sentence in a higher-security prison might alter propensities for crime. In this chapter, I argue that the type of prison institution in which an individual is incarcerated has important consequences for his social ties and social norms in ways that help to explain changes in the likelihood of subsequent criminal behavior.

Socialization and the Institutional Environment

Data compiled by Bert Useem and Anne Piehl suggest that many of the most serious markers of prison violence have in fact declined over the past few decades. For instance, the number of inmate homicides decreased substantially from 1984 to 2000, from 90 per year to 49. The number of staff killed by inmates and riots has also declined; nine prison workers were murdered in 1982, compared with two individuals killed in the line of duty in 2000. There were seven riots in 1982, compared with four in 2000. On all of these measures, however, the ratio of mortalities to the total population has always been very small. For instance, even the 90 individuals killed while incarcerated in 1984 constituted only 23.6 per 100,000 people in prison in that year.

Non-lethal forms of violence and disorder, however, are substantially more common, and on these measures, downward trends are less compelling (though still sometimes present). In particular, assaults on inmates declined in the 1980s and early 1990s, from a high of 41.1 per 1,000 inmates in 1984 to 30.9 in 1990 and 25.5 in 1995. Assault rates then increased slightly again in the following period, returning to 29.2 per 1,000 inmates by 2000. (Assaults on staff changed little over this period, remaining fairly stable at about 15 assaults per 1,000 inmates.)[12] These rates of violence are extraordinarily high. As a point of comparison, consider that in the neighborhood of Los Angeles with the highest per capita violent crime, the total rate is just 12.2 incidents per 1,000 residents.[13] This measure includes homicide, rape, aggravated assault, and robbery.

When sentenced to a term of incarceration, prisoners thus frequently find themselves thrust into an unpredictable and violent social world. It is not surprising, then, that the prison environment can invoke feelings of extreme fear, depression, and helplessness in inmates.[14] For example, in his testimony before the Senate Judiciary Subcommittee on Corrections and Rehabilitation, a former member of the California State Assembly who served 29 months in federal prison described being imprisoned as feeling

… like an amputee. I was cut off from my family, my friends, my work, my church and my community. Then, with my stumps still bleeding, I was tossed into a roiling cauldron of anger, bitterness, despair and often violence. In prison, inmates are completely defenseless. They are deprived of the usual ways we protect ourselves. They do not choose where to live and sleep, they have no choice in their companions, they cannot avoid going in dark places, and they are prohibited from arming themselves for self-defense.[15]

Some inmates may turn to imagined or actual attempts at escape in order to cope with these inordinate stresses. Others may choose to turn within themselves, "withdraw[ing] into fantasy based on fondled memories of the past or imaginary dramas of life after release"[16] rather than engaging with those around them. Indeed, a variety of forces may preclude a prisoner from seeking the company of peers. An inmate may see him- or herself as different from other prisoners, less prone to violence or criminality.[17] Alternatively, internalization of the stigma associated with being labeled a "felon" or "offender" may cause an inmate to maintain distance from others with similar social standing.[18] In one study, for example, many ex-inmates within a community, despite their high concentration, chose not to speak of their prison experience with neighbors who had also served time behind bars because of the shame associated with the experience.[19]

Yet, despite the urge some prisoners may have to avoid social interaction, ethnographic explorations of the prison social order suggest that most inmates do engage with others to at least some degree while incarcerated.[20] As Gresham Sykes suggested in his classic study of social organization in a maximum-security prison, the callow inmate encounters a choice between two paths: "On the one hand, he can attempt to bind himself to his fellow captives with ties of mutual aid, loyalty, affection, and respect, firmly standing in opposition to the officials. On the other hand, he can enter into a war of all against all in which he seeks his own advantage without reference to the claims or needs of other prisoners."[21] He concludes:

However strange it may appear that society has chosen to reduce the criminality of the offender by forcing him to associate with more than a thousand other criminals for years on end, there is one meaning of this involuntary union which is obvious – the individual prisoner is thrown into prolonged intimacy with other men who in many cases have a long history of violent, aggressive behavior. It is a situation which can prove to be anxiety-provoking even for the hardened recidivist and it is in this light that we can understand the comment of an inmate of the New Jersey State Prison who said, "The worst thing about prison is you have to live with other prisoners."[22]

In this chapter, I suggest that incarceration reshapes individual social ties and ways of interacting in complex and important ways. To counter the "pains of imprisonment," inmates band together for the purposes of companionship and mutual protection.[23] And because inmates are isolated from the outside world and often come to see administrators and staff as responsible for their suffering (or at least as unable or unwilling to prevent it), peer relationships play a prominent role in shaping the experience of imprisonment.[24]

Moreover, I show that both the criminal history of the individual *and the relative culture of the prison* matter for whether and how socialization occurs. Specifically, I provide evidence that assignment to a higher-security prison shapes individuals' attitudes and behavior in criminogenic ways and that it does this most significantly for inmates with the lowest levels of prior criminality. In conclusion, I suggest that individual social networks adopted in higher-security prisons do not result in productive norms of mutual benefit. Rather, harsher prisons produce a different kind of social network, one that yields far more anti-social results.

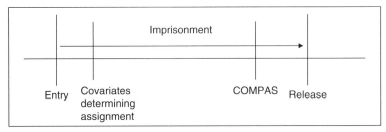

FIGURE 5.1. Timing of inmate data collection.

Measuring Inmate Outcomes

To measure inmates' social networks and social attitudes, I rely on data from the Correctional Offender Management Profiling for Alternative Sanctions (COMPAS), a risk and needs assessment tool employed by the California Department of Corrections and Rehabilitation. COMPAS was designed by Northpointe Institute for Public Management, Inc., a private correctional research consulting firm, for use in the supervision and case management of individuals in the state's correctional system. Surveys were conducted with inmates roughly 120 days before release from prison and gathered information on 141 separate items, combining official records, a self-report survey, and a semi-structured interview (Figure 5.1). The COMPAS system then uses these individual items to automatically calculate scores on 22 separate scales. Four of these scales are predictive, assessing the likely risk of post-release violence, recidivism, failure to appear, and community non-compliance. In addition, 7 scales describe criminal and anti-social behavior; 8 describe social and personal adjustment; and 3 describe social and criminal psychometrics. (A full list and description of the COMPAS scales are given in Appendix F.)

As with any survey that touches on sensitive topics, there are valid concerns about the veracity of responses to questions on the COMPAS survey. This is a particularly important issue when surveys are administered under some degree of duress, as might be expected with a risk assessment conducted on individuals about to parole from prison. While it is impossible to definitively confirm the honesty of subjective responses, the COMPAS system does include two separate validity tests: a "lie test" that checks for "defensiveness in responding" and a test for randomness and inconsistency.

The lie test is designed to flag individuals who may be lying in order to "look good," by identifying extreme answers to eight questions that would be expected to elicit moderate responses. For example, strongly agreeing with the statement "I have never felt sad about things in my life" is considered suspect, in that most individuals have felt sad at some point. Likewise, most people would not strongly disagree with the statement "I feel unhappy at times," as most people feel unhappy at least some of the time. Anyone who gives extreme responses to three or more of these statements is automatically flagged as potentially distorting answers.[25]

The second validity test seeks out inconsistencies that may indicate a careless or random responder. The test is modeled after the Variable Response Inconsistency (VRIN) test in the Minnesota Multiphasic Personality Inventory (MMPI-2), a well-known empirical assessment tool for the identification of psychological disorders. Like the VRIN, the COMPAS test matches responses to pairs of statements that are expected to be highly correlated. For example, most of those who respond with "agree" or "strongly agree" to the statement "If someone insults my friends, family or group they are asking for trouble" would be expected to also agree or strongly agree with the statement "I won't hesitate to hit or threaten people if they have done something to hurt my friends or family." The COMPAS test matches 37 such pairs of statements and records the proportion of mismatches between paired responses. As with the lie test, respondents who give a particularly high proportion of suspect responses (those in the highest 5 percent of the distribution) are flagged for closer scrutiny.

Effects on Inmate Isolation

To estimate the effects of imprisonment, I start by examining individuals' self-reported descriptions of their social networks. COMPAS contains a Social Isolation Scale, which describes "feelings of social isolation and loneliness ... feeling close to friends, feeling left out of things, the presence of companionship, having a close best friend, feeling lonely, etc." (Table 5.1). The scale is an additive linear index of eight separate items. For each statement, respondents are asked to

TABLE 5.1. *Items in the COMPAS Social Isolation Scale*

Statement Wording	Mean	Std. Dev.	Factor	Factor Description
I have friends who help me when I have troubles.	2.43	1.16	1	Supporting networks
I have friends who enjoy doing things with me.	2.14	0.97	1	Supporting networks
I feel very close to some of my friends.	2.29	1.08	1	Supporting networks
I can find companionship when I want.	2.08	0.88	1	Supporting networks
I have a best friend I can talk with about everything.	2.26	1.15	1	Supporting networks
I feel lonely.	2.40	1.17	2	Belonging
No one really knows me very well.	2.49	1.18	2	Belonging
I often feel left out of things.	2.25	1.04	2	Belonging
SCALE (Possible range 8–40)	18.32	5.53	–	–

Note: Data are from completed offender assessments in the COMPAS database through October 2006. Those placed with an administrative determinant or classified prior to 2003 are excluded. A variable is considered part of a particular dimension if it loads higher than 0.40. N = 9,331.

indicate whether they "strongly agree," "agree," are "not sure/neutral," "disagree," or "strongly disagree." Responses are coded 1–5, with a 5 indicating a high degree of social isolation.

Raw scores on the scale are then converted to decile scores, ranking individuals relative to the appropriate gender-specific norm group: either male incarcerated or female incarcerated. A decile score of 1 means that the score falls in the lowest 10 percent of the corresponding population; a 2 indicates a score that is above 10 percent but below 20 percent relative to the norm group; a 3 that the score is above 20 but below 30 percent; and so on up to a score of 10. In this way, the decile score provides an easily interpretable measure of individual scores as compared with the total relevant group.

The Social Isolation Scale has high internal reliability (Cronbach's alpha of .797), making it appropriate to combine the items into a single scale. However, a factor analysis reveals that the items are best described as two separate dimensions.[26] The first dimension evaluates connections to supporting networks, probing the extent to which an individual maintains meaningful social connections. Five items load high on this factor, including "I have friends who help me when I have troubles"; "I have friends who enjoy doing things with me"; "I feel very close to some of my friends"; "I can find companionship when I want"; and "I have a best friend I can talk with about everything." The remaining three variables load high on the second dimension, measuring feelings of social belonging. These items include "I feel lonely"; "No one really knows me very well"; and "I often feel left out of things."

To estimate the causal effect of custody assignment on individual social isolation, I rely on the regression discontinuity approach detailed in the preceding chapter. In the sample of inmates as a whole, there appears to be no significant difference in social isolation between those with classification scores just below and just above the cutoff between Levels II and III. On average, the two groups describe having the same supporting networks and feelings of belonging. However, a significant effect of assignment to a higher-security prison appears when the sample is divided into subgroups by criminal history. For those in the bottom three deciles of criminal involvement – those with relatively low prior contact with the criminal justice system as measured by previous jail, conviction, arrest, or probation – there is a significant difference between the two groups. Specifically, among inmates with a low criminal history, those with classification scores that fall just above the cutoff for higher-security assignment have an average Social Isolation Scale score that is about 1.28 points lower than those with scores just below the cutoff ($p < .05$). This suggests that those with higher scores, who are more likely to be placed in a higher-security prison, actually report *less* social isolation (Table 5.2). This gap cannot be explained by pre-existing differences; as in the sample as a whole, the subgroup of inmates with low criminal histories that fall above and below the cutoff for classification are statistically equivalent in their pre-existing characteristics. (Details on balance within the low criminal history subgroup are provided in Appendix G.)

How do we interpret the magnitude of this effect on social isolation scores? For a more intuitive sense of this between-group difference, it is helpful to consider the corresponding gap in social isolation decile scores. As already described, COMPAS deciles provide a relative,

TABLE 5.2. *Effect of Classification on Social Isolation, by Criminal History*

	Social Isolation		Social Isolation Subscales	
	Scale	Decile	Networks	Belonging
Low criminal history				
Mean difference	−1.28	−0.88	−0.83	−0.46
F	4.49*	7.18**	3.74*	2.30
Medium criminal history				
Mean difference	0.79	0.51	0.50	0.31
F	2.17	3.25	2.02	1.66
High criminal history				
Mean difference	−1.11	−0.55	−0.72	−0.40
F	2.66	2.34	2.08	1.55

***p < .001, **p < .01, *p < .05.

Note: Low criminal history inmates are those with a decile score of 1, 2, or 3 on the Criminal History Scale; medium inmates are those with a decile score of 4, 5, 6, or 7; and high inmates are those with a decile score of 8, 9, or 10. Those placed with an administrative determinant are excluded. Low N = 278 (134 cases below cutoff and 144 above).

rather than absolute, measure of social connection; they describe where an individual's score falls among the total population of gender-corresponding inmates.

For those with low criminal history, the gap of 1.28 points on the Social Isolation Scale translates into almost a full decile difference. Those with classification scores just below the cutoff have a median decile score between 4 and 5, and a mean score of 5.12. That implies that this group is, on average, more socially isolated than about 51.2 percent of other inmates. By comparison, those with classification scores that fall just above the cutoff have a median decile between 2 and 3, and a mean decile score of 4.24. This group, on average, is more socially isolated than only about 42.4 percent of inmates. The difference in means of 0.88 deciles is statistically significant (p < .01).

It is also possible to consider the two dimensions of the Social Isolation Scale separately – the extent of social networks and one's reported feelings of social belonging. Comparing the two groups on each set of indicators shows that the effect is driven primarily by changes in an individual's social networks rather than feelings of belonging. Inmates with scores just above the cutoff are more likely to report having friends who provide support and companionship; those just below the cutoff have an average social network score of 11.39, while those just above the cutoff have an average of 10.56, for a gap of −0.83 ($p < .05$). By comparison, there is no significant difference between the two groups in feelings of belonging.

Concern may still remain that the effects evident here are the result of other factors that differ between the two groups. As a further test of these between-group differences, I therefore examine the relationship between the Social Isolation Scale and having a classification score that falls just above or below the cutoff, controlling for other factors. I do this by regressing the Social Isolation Scale on the classification score, a dummy variable for having a score above and below the cutoff (coded 0 for scores between 19 and 27 and 1 for scores between 28 and 51), and the full set of demographic, criminal history, socialization, and personal history controls detailed in Appendix G.[27] In this multivariate model, the estimated effect on social isolation of having a score above the cutoff rather than below is −1.2 ($p < .05$). When I examine the same model but instead estimate the effect on the social isolation decile score, the gap corresponds to a decline of more than two-thirds of a decile at the cutoff (−0.71 deciles, $p < .01$). These results are shown in Figure 5.2.[28]

Finally, I conduct a set of placebo tests to further assess the meaning of these results. If the difference in social isolation I have uncovered is truly the effect of being assigned to a higher-security prison, we should expect the cutoff point for assignment to Level III to be the only value of the classification score between 19 and 51 where a significant discontinuity appears. To test this postulation, I simulate cutoffs between each set of points along the classification score. For example, instead of the true cutoff point between 27 and 28, I designate a simulated cutoff point between 19 and 20. I then run the same regression analysis, substituting the simulated cutoff point for the true value. I do this at each pair of consecutive points and I expect to find no significant effect at any cutoff value except in the "true" regression, which uses the actual cutoff point. The placebo tests confirm expectations. As anticipated, the only statistically significant gap in social isolation scores is at the true cutoff point; compared with the significant discontinuity found at the true cutoff ($p < .01$), none of the simulations yields a discontinuity with a p value of less than 0.1.

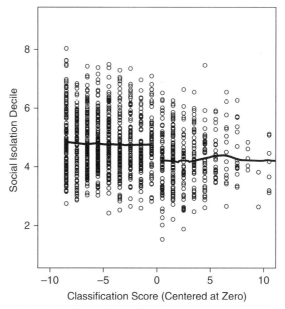

FIGURE 5.2. Predicted effect of classification score on social isolation decile scores.

Note: Sample includes only those in the lowest three deciles of the Criminal History Scale. Inmates placed with an administrative determinant or classified before 2003 are excluded. N = 1,207.

"Criminal" Peers and the Prison Effect

The data presented here suggest that assignment to a higher-security setting decreases social isolation among inmates with a low criminal history. Inmates assigned to higher-security prisons are more likely to agree with sentiments such as "I feel very close to some of my friends" and "I can find companionship when I want." However, there are at least two possible explanations for this effect. It may be that individuals form more extensive or salient attachments to peers inside harsher prisons. Alternatively, it may be that assignment to a higher-security prison strengthens an inmate's relationships with his family and/or friends on the outside.

This latter interpretation of the results seems unlikely. Maintaining close ties to loved ones outside prison is likely to be especially hard for individuals incarcerated in higher-security prisons, where visitation is generally more controlled. In some cases, physical contact with visitors is restricted or entirely prohibited. In other higher-security settings,

TABLE 5.3. *Effect of Classification on Social Network Composition*

	Mean Below Cutoff	Mean Above Cutoff	Difference
Family contact	1.47	1.50	0.03
Criminal associates (index)	7.67	8.55	0.88*
Friends arrested	2.02	2.27	0.25*
Friends jailed	1.89	2.12	0.23*
Friends do drugs	1.94	2.09	0.15
Friends in gangs	1.82	2.07	0.25***

***$p < .001$, **$p < .01$, *$p < .05$.

Note: Sample includes those in the lowest three deciles of criminal history who have a classification score of 26 or 27 (below the cutoff) and 28 or 29 (above the cutoff). Those placed with an administrative determinant or classified prior to 2003 are excluded. $N = 278$ (134 cases below cutoff and 144 above).

inmates and their visitors are completely separated by a wall of glass. In addition, the available data show no evidence of an effect of security assignment on family ties. The COMPAS survey asks respondents how often they have contact with family, either in person, on the phone, or by mail. Among low criminal history inmates, a comparison of means shows no significant difference between the two groups in terms of the extent of family contact; inmates with classification scores that fall just above the cutoff report the same average frequency of contact with family as those with scores that fall just below the cutoff.

A more likely explanation is that individuals assigned to higher-security prisons adopt new or strengthened social bonds with concurrently incarcerated peers. COMPAS asks several questions that probe the characteristics of friendship networks, including how many of a respondent's friends have ever been arrested, have served time in jail or prison, are taking drugs regularly (more than a couple times a month), or are gang members. As Table 5.3 shows, inmates with classification scores just above the cutoff have significantly more friends who have been arrested, friends who have been jailed, and friends involved in gangs. A multiple regression model similar to the one described in the preceding section confirms these differences, particularly with respect to gang associations; all else equal, inmates assigned to a higher- rather than lower-security prison report significantly more friends or acquaintances who are gang members ($p < .001$). The size of the effect suggests a jump of about 10 percent of the scale ranging from "none" to "most" of one's friends who are involved in gangs.[29]

These results bolster the contention that, rather than isolating themselves or otherwise avoiding prison social life, many inmates choose (though some perhaps with reticence) to integrate into the social order of inmate society. Significantly, the institutional context in which inmates find themselves influences the extent and character of the social networks they adopt; those assigned to higher-security prisons report more extensive social networks and a higher proportion of criminal peers. Several questions naturally follow. In particular: Are these changes in inmates' social networks consequential for the attitudes inmates develop while incarcerated? And do inmates who gain more criminal associates while in prison evidence an increased propensity for recidivism following release?

We can consider at least three potential ways that the social networks adopted in prison might encourage subsequent offending.[30] First, incarceration provides individuals with peers who can reinforce problems with addiction, encouraging the continuation of (or return to) substance use and abuse. Addiction, in turn, has been shown to be highly correlated with the commission of crime.[31] Second, prisons confine individuals together who can share information and resources related to criminal activity, facilitating the creation of social networks among inmates that translate into subsequent co-offending partnerships. Finally, peers can exert a significant social pressure, encouraging or reinforcing the adoption of aggressive, violent, or otherwise anti-social attitudes. In each of these ways, social interactions with high-risk peers can make prisons "schools for crime" that ultimately result in higher rates of subsequent illegal behavior. It is this final explanation related to social norms that I explore in more detail in the following section.

Effects on Criminal Cognitions

In addition to measuring the composition of individual social networks, COMPAS includes a set of 10 psychometrics designed to measure "cognitions that justify, support, or provide rationalizations for the person's criminal behavior. These include moral justification, refusal to accept responsibility, blaming the victim, and rationalizations (excuses) that minimize the seriousness of crime."[32] Like the Social

Isolation Scale, the variables that make up the Criminal Cognitions Scale actually measure multiple dimensions of this concept. The first dimension measures norms of violence and interpersonal aggression. Four variables in the scale measure this underlying dimension. These items include "Some people just don't deserve any respect and should be treated like animals"; "Some people must be treated roughly or beaten up just to send them a clear message"; "If someone insults my friends, family or group they are asking for trouble"; and "I won't hesitate to hit or threaten people if they have done something to hurt my friends or family."[33]

The second dimension is composed of four other variables that measure the perceived legitimacy of the law (Table 5.4). These items include "When people get into trouble with the law it's because they have no chance to get a decent job"; "Some people get into trouble or use drugs because society has given them no education, jobs or future"; "When people do minor offenses or use drugs they don't hurt anyone except themselves"; and "The law doesn't help average people." Two additional items, "A hungry person has a right to steal" and "When things are stolen from rich people they won't miss the stuff because insurance will cover the loss," load on both dimensions.

Table 5.5 compares average criminal cognition scores of inmates with classification scores that fall just below the cutoff (a score of either 26 or 27) with those who have scores just above the cutoff (a score of either 28 or 29). As with effects on criminal networks, the data show no difference in the total sample. Again, it is only among those in the lowest tercile of criminal history that placement in a higher-security prison has an attitudinal effect, predicting an increase of 1.8 points on the Criminal Cognitions Scale. The corresponding mean cognition decile score is 5.98 below the cutoff and 6.7 above, a statistically significant gap of 0.72, or roughly three-quarters of a decile ($p < .05$).

As with the Social Isolation Scale, it appears that one dimension of the Criminal Cognitions Scale is primarily driving the results. The effects of higher-security prison assignment on criminal cognitions appear to be attributable primarily to changes in the cognitive dimension related to norms of aggression rather than changes in perceptions about the legitimacy of the law. When the two dimensions are estimated separately, there is no significant difference between the two

TABLE 5.4. *Items in the COMPAS Criminal Cognitions Scale*

Statement Wording	Mean	Std. Dev.	Factor	Factor Description
Some people just don't deserve any respect and should be treated like animals.	1.77	0.80	1	Norms of violence
Some people must be treated roughly or beaten up just to send them a clear message.	1.96	0.87	1	Norms of violence
If someone insults my friends, family or group they are asking for trouble.	2.67	1.09	1	Norms of violence
I won't hesitate to hit or threaten people if they have done something to hurt my friends or family.	2.32	1.06	1	Norms of violence
The law doesn't help average people.	2.38	1.03	2	Legitimacy of law
When people get into trouble with the law it's because they have no chance to get a decent job.	2.15	0.99	2	Legitimacy of law
Some people get into trouble or use drugs because society has given them no education, jobs or future.	2.37	1.08	2	Legitimacy of law
When people do minor offenses or use drugs they don't hurt anyone except themselves.	2.51	1.22	2	Legitimacy of law
A hungry person has a right to steal.	2.12	0.93	1 [2]	Norms of violence Legitimacy of law
When things are stolen from rich people they won't miss the stuff because insurance will cover the loss.	1.97	0.85	1 2	Norms of violence Legitimacy of law
Scale (possible range 10–50)	22.23	5.92	–	–

Note: Data are for all completed offender assessments in the COMPAS database through October 2006. A variable is considered part of a particular dimension if it loads greater than 0.40. A factor is in brackets if the loading for that variable is higher than 0.30 but lower than 0.40. N = 16,043.

TABLE 5.5. *Effect of Classification on Criminal Cognitions Scale, by Criminal History*

	Mean Below Cutoff	Mean Above Cutoff	Difference
Total (all deciles)	23.4	23.8	0.4
Criminal history deciles			
Low (1–3)	22.9	24.7	1.8***
Medium (4–7)	23.5	23.5	0.0
High (8–10)	23.7	23.4	−0.3

***$p < .001$, **$p < .01$, *$p < .05$.
Sample includes those with a classification score of 26 or 27 (below the cutoff) and 28 or 29 (above the cutoff). Those placed with an administrative determinant or classified prior to 2003 are excluded.
Low criminal involvement, $N = 278$ (134 cases below cutoff and 144 above); medium criminal involvement, $N = 375$ (206 cases below cutoff and 169 above); high criminal involvement, $N = 229$ (122 cases below cutoff and 107 above).

groups in regard to the legitimacy of law. Rather, it is in the degree to which people espouse justifications for harming others, such as "Some people just don't deserve any respect and should be treated like animals," that a statistically significant effect appears; when combined into an additive linear index, group differences on this subscale are highly significant ($F = 9.123$, $p = .003$).

The effect of assignment on criminal cognitions remains significant even when potential confounders are accounted for. Estimating criminal cognitions in a multiple regression again shows a significant discontinuity at the cutoff point between security levels. The slope coefficient for the assignment variable is 1.85 ($p < .001$), and regressing criminal cognition decile scores on the full set of predictors shows a jump of more than two-thirds of a decile (0.72, $p < .01$) at the cutoff point for classification (see Figure 5.3).[34]

Criminal Cognitions as Peer Effect

It is clear from these data that assigning inmates to higher-security prisons significantly increases the prevalence of anti-social attitudes. The question remains, however: What accounts for these effects? Do these attitudinal changes result from changes in inmates' social networks?

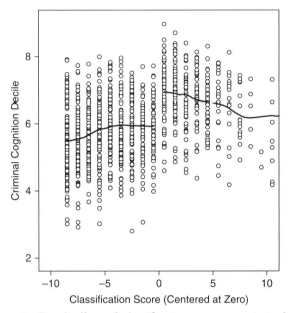

FIGURE 5.3. Predicted effect of classification score on criminal cognition decile scores.

Note: Sample includes only those in the lowest three deciles of the Criminal History Scale. Inmates placed with an administrative determinant or classified prior to 2003 are excluded. Line is subgroup LOESS fit. $N = 1,207$.

Or are these social and attitudinal outcomes two independent results of assignment to a particular institutional environment?

As I have already shown, there is no significant difference between inmates with classification scores just above the cutoff and those with scores just below in terms of their frequency of family contact. Thus, it is unlikely that this accounts for the attitudinal changes experienced by inmates assigned to higher-security prisons. These effects could also be explained if inmates assigned to higher-security prisons are more likely to retain or attract criminal associates outside prison. Such pre-existing social ties, if strengthened during incarceration, might explain increases in anti-social attitudes. However, given that inmates in higher-security prisons most often have their contact with the outside world more strictly controlled than do those in lower-security settings, this also seems implausible. A more likely explanation is that the changes in social attitudes that result from incarceration in a higher-security prison can be explained by characteristics of the prison environment itself. In particular, criminogenic attitudes may be communicated and reinforced through the newly acquired social networks formed between concurrently incarcerated peers.

Existing work provides substantial evidence that peer delinquency is highly correlated with individual criminal attitudes.[35] However, there are a variety of potential explanations for this type of group homogeneity. Conformity is one explanation (that individuals change their attitudes, adopting the prevailing norms of their peers), but alternative explanations include self-selection (that individuals choose peers whose attitudes are congruent with their own) or selective elimination (that the least conforming members of a peer group are purged or choose to leave voluntarily).[36] In addition, it may be the case that the social group itself has little influence and that instead all of the individual members of the group are affected by the same outside influence (e.g., poverty or inadequate educational opportunity). Each of these explanations would help account for shared norms (and behaviors) among members of a social group. A key distinction is that only the first and last explanations, conformity and equivalent outside influences, involve a *change* of attitudes. If instead self-selection or selective elimination is at work, the characteristics of peers do not actually shape an individual's social norms, but instead only reflect them. As Robert Putnam writes, describing the difficulties of sorting out cause and effect: "These studies have been at the center of a rigorous debate, mostly over whether they have actually proven anything besides the tendency of like-minded people to congregate in the same places.... Critics rightly note that the most sophisticated statistical analysis has trouble identifying the invisible forces that might cause 'birds of a feather' to flock together."[37]

Additional evidence from the COMPAS survey provides further context in which to consider prisons' attitudinal effects. First, comparing the attitudes of inmates with classification scores that fall just above or just below the classification cutoff with the average scores of all inmates within their respective security level suggests that the effect of higher-security assignment on social norms could plausibly be a peer effect. As Table 5.6 shows, inmates within the small window around the cutoff value appear to converge in their attitudes

TABLE 5.6. *Criminal Cognitions Relative to Incarcerated Peers*

	Criminal Cognition Decile Scores	
	Full COMPAS Sample	Classification Scores Just Above and Below Cutoff
Level I	5.3 (N = 4,309)	
Level II	5.5 (N = 1,868)	5.9 (N = 134)
Level III	6.5 (N = 985)	6.7 (N = 144)
Level IV	6.7 (N = 35)	

Note: Inmates assigned administrative determinants or classified prior to 2003 are excluded. Inmates with classification scores above or below cutoff include low criminal history only.

with those around them, socializing in the direction of their peers. The total sample of COMPAS inmates in Level II custody has an average decile score of 5.5 on the Criminal Cognitions Scale. The subsample of inmates with classification scores just below the cutoff, which designates them for assignment to Level II, has an average decile score of 5.9. By comparison, inmates in the COMPAS sample as a whole who are assigned to Level III custody have an average decile score of 6.5, and those with classification scores just above the cutoff have an average score of 6.7.

Further analyses show that the effects of assignment to a higher-security prison on criminal cognitions vary in important ways according to the gang status of inmates when they enter and exit prison. For the purposes of analysis, I categorize individuals into four broad categories of gang affiliation: an inmate enters and exits prison without gang affiliation (abstainers), enters without gang affiliation and leaves with gang affiliation (joiners), enters with gang affiliation and leaves without gang affiliation (renouncers), or enters and exits prison with gang affiliation (maintainers). In the data, gang affiliation is designated either by an inmate's self-admission or by a staff member who can support such a claim with "at least three independent source items," including at least one that provides a "direct link to a current or former validated member or associate of a gang." Source items can include evidence of a gang-related offense, tattoos or symbols, written materials, such as training materials or constitutions of particular gangs, photographs with gang connotations, or other kinds of information coming from staff or other agencies, including testimony from informants or information about known gang-affiliated associates.[38] (A sample of the CDCR gang designation form is included in Appendix H.)

Unfortunately, creating these four subsamples within the already limited subgroup of inmates whose classification scores fall just above or below the cutoff significantly diminishes the sample size, leaving both joiners and renouncers with fewer than 20 cases. However, the available data do suggest that those who abstain from gang membership or renounce membership during incarceration show no significant effects of assignment to a higher-security prison. It is only among joiners and maintainers that a significant effect of security-level assignment on social norms appears. In fact, among those who join a gang while in prison, having a classification score above the cutoff predicts an increase of about 2.63 deciles on the Criminal Cognitions Scale ($p < .1$). There are substantially more data on those who maintain gang membership ($n = 290$), and for this group a score above the cutoff predicts an increase of 0.73 deciles in criminal cognitions ($p < .05$), with particularly significant effects on the dimension related to norms of violence ($p < .05$). This suggests that both the acquisition of a gang affiliation during incarceration and the maintenance or strengthening of gang ties during a period of incarceration may facilitate the adoption of anti-social norms.

Attitudinal effects among those who maintain gang ties remain significant when demographic and personal history variables are controlled for. Figure 5.4 shows the results of a regression model estimating the effect of having a score above or below the classification cutoff on criminal cognition decile scores, all else equal. The sample here is limited to "maintainers" – those inmates who enter and exit prison as gang members. For this group, even when other potentially relevant factors are controlled for, having a classification score above the cutoff predicts an increase of almost a full decile in criminal cognitions (0.88) and the effect is statistically significant at conventional levels ($p < .05$).

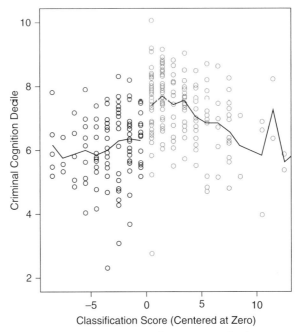

FIGURE 5.4. Discontinuity in criminal cognition decile scores for gang maintainers.
Note: Sample includes only those in the lowest three deciles of the Criminal History Scale and only those inmates who enter and exit prison as gang members. Inmates placed with an administrative determinant or classified before 2003 are excluded. Line is subgroup LOESS fit. $N = 290$.

Effects on Recidivism

I have provided substantial evidence here that higher-security prisons actually promote potentially criminogenic social norms. However, it is still possible that the anti-social attitudes measured by these scales represent only posturing by inmates, a pretense taken on by individuals seeking to assert themselves in an environment where heightened criminality is the norm. It is also possible that these attitudes do not persist beyond imprisonment, but are specific to the environment in which they are adopted. If this is the case, then the attitudinal changes I have just described are unlikely to predict subsequent behavior.

The data do not allow me to directly analyze the durability of attitudinal effects. However, previous research provides evidence that criminal attitudes are strong indicators of the likelihood of future criminal behavior. In fact, meta-analyses have consistently identified criminal psychology as one of the strongest predictors of prison misconduct, as well as of criminal conduct and recidivism; criminal cognitions are one of the "big five" risk factors in predicting criminal behavior.[39] In addition, criminal associates are among the most critical predictors of criminality, particularly for gang members.[40]

In addition, the Criminal Cognitions and Social Isolation Scales I have employed here were specifically designed to predict the risk of future offending. In a study by Northpointe Institute for Public Management, the firm that developed the COMPAS tool, the predictive validity of COMPAS measures was assessed using data on 2,328 probationers across 18 county-level probation agencies in an "eastern state."[41] The authors found that both the Social Isolation and Criminal Cognitions Scales are highly significant predictors of felony recidivism. In another preliminary validation study of the COMPAS scales in use for California inmates, David Farabee and Sheldon Zhang examined data on 515 state inmates and found a significant and positive correlation between the Criminal Cognitions Scale and two indicators of recidivism: return to custody and non-technical parole violation within a year of parole. The strength of these correlations was equivalent to the relationship between recidivism and having a history of non-compliance (the number of times in the past an individual was arrested or charged while on parole or probation). In a follow-up study, the same authors (along with Robert Roberts and Joy Yang) showed that COMPAS measures are quite comparable to equivalent variables in the Level of Service Inventory–Revised (LSI-R), which is among the most well-known commercial risk and needs assessment tools currently in use. They found that the California COMPAS tool does an acceptable job of predicting general risk of recidivism, though it falls just short of the conventional threshold for acceptability in predicting future violence.[42]

Additionally, I am able to directly examine the critical question: Do individuals assigned to higher-security prisons evidence behavioral differences following parole in the form of increased recidivism? In line with previous studies, I find a significant effect of assignment to a higher-security prison on the likelihood of recidivism following release (see Figure 5.5). Among inmates with a score that falls just below the cutoff for assignment to a higher-security prison, the rate of recidivism in the first three years following release is about 61 percent.

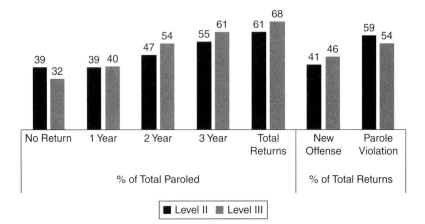

FIGURE 5.5. Effect of classification score on recidivism.
Note: N paroled = 134 (Level II), 144 (Level III). Inmates assigned administrative determinants or classified prior to 2003 are excluded. Only inmates with classification scores above or below cutoff and lowest three deciles of criminal history are included.

By comparison, about 68 percent of those with classification scores that fall just above the cutoff return to prison within this time period ($p < .01$). Even more significantly, the percentage of those returning to custody for new offenses, as opposed to returning only for violation of parole, is also different across the two groups. Among those with classification scores that fall above the cutoff, the percentage of those returning for new offenses is 5 percent higher relative to those with scores below the cutoff ($p < .05$).

The effect size, though seemingly small, is substantively quite significant when placed in broader context. A quick back-of-the-envelope calculation helps to make this clear. According to the COMPAS data, roughly 11 percent of those who are released from prison had an initial classification score that is comparable to the population I have focused on here – a score that falls just above (28 or 29) or below (26 or 27) the assignment cutoff. By construction, a third of these individuals are in the low criminal history group, among whom there was a significant effect of incarceration. We can estimate, then, that about 47,400 individuals have been paroled in California over the past decade who can be considered directly comparable to the subsample I have examined. This is an extremely conservative estimate, as it assumes that only those with classification scores that fall in this small window around the classification cutoff experience these criminogenic effects.

If all of these inmates had been assigned to a Level III facility, we would expect about 32,232 of them (68 percent) to return to custody. In total, those individuals would be responsible for the commission of 14,827 (46 percent) new crimes. Now let us assume instead that all of these individuals had been incarcerated in Level II prison settings. In this case, we would expect that 28,914 of them (61 percent) would recidivate, 11,855 (41 percent) for the commission of new crimes. The difference even under this very conservative assumption is nearly 3,000 additional crimes.

It is also useful to briefly consider an upper bound on this estimate, calculating a much less conservative (but still quite plausible) number of additional crimes that can be attributed to the more punitive environments of California's higher-security prisons. To do this, I relax the assumption that the recidivism effects of incarceration hold only in the small sample of individuals who fall just above or below the classification cutoff. Instead, let us assume that there is some effect for all low criminal history inmates of having been assigned to a more punitive, more violent, less rehabilitation-focused higher-security prison environment, as compared with a less punitive, less violent, and more rehabilitation-focused lower-security prison environment. Let us again assume that, on average, individuals assigned to Level II are 5 percent less likely to commit new crimes following release than individuals assigned to Level III.

In 2007, there were 129,261 individuals released from prison in California.[43] Given average rates of recidivism, a 5 percent reduction in new crime commissions, even among just those parolees who entered prison with criminal histories in the lowest tercile, would amount to a decline of about 64,630 crimes over a 10-year period. Assuming a distribution of crime categories that is equivalent to those among recidivists in the COMPAS data, this would be expected to include nearly 2,000 murders, as well as 3,000 rapes and roughly 8,400 assaults.

Punitive Prisons and the Production of Crime

California's large prison population, as well as its relatively high recidivism rate (see Figure 5.6), makes it something of an outlier. However,

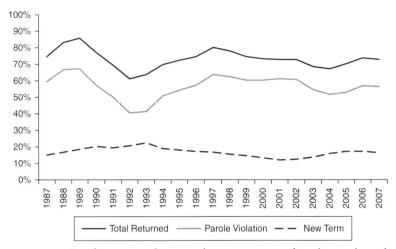

FIGURE 5.6. Parolees returned to custody as percentage of total annual parole population.
Source: Data Analysis Unit, Department of Corrections and Rehabilitation, *Historical Trends*.

in its general patterns it is certainly not alone. The vast majority of inmates who spend time in prison will eventually return to their communities, and subsequent rates of recidivism are consistently high across the country. The Bureau of Justice Statistics estimates that roughly a third of prisoners are incarcerated more than once, and among those who go to prison twice, four-fifths will return.[44]

In this chapter, I have shown that prisons are important sites for the transmission of collective norms and values, shaping individuals' attitudes and behavior; a prison is not a "behavioral deep freeze"[45] and incarceration is not merely a period of incapacitation. Rather, confining people in more punitive prisons increases the extent of their social ties, while simultaneously exacerbating alienation from law-abiding society and lowering the probability that they will successfully reintegrate into the community. Indeed, as early as 1973, just as the nation's "punitive turn" had begun to take hold, the National Advisory Commission on Criminal Justice Standards warned that "[t]he prison, the reformatory, and the jail have achieved only a shocking record of failure. There is overwhelming evidence that these institutions create crime rather than prevent it."[46] The growing punitiveness of America's prisons is likely only to have exacerbated these undesirable effects.

The results presented here locate prison social context front and center within the important debate over specific deterrence. According to the deterrence theory of criminal behavior, people obey the law out of fear that they will be punished if they are caught breaking it. Thus, people should be increasingly likely to obey the law the more they believe they will be caught and the harsher they perceive the resulting punishment.[47] There is significant debate, however, about whether and under what circumstances people actually make the kind of rational calculations on which deterrence theory relies.[48]

In addition, deterrence is a costly form of social control, as it requires constant oversight and a significant investment of resources. For instance, it is extremely difficult for societies to deter drunk driving through the threat of punishment alone, as through their own experience people will discover that the true likelihood of discovery is low.[49] As Tom Tyler notes, "Given that the regulation of behavior through social control is inefficient and may not be effective enough to allow a complex democratic society to survive, it is encouraging that social theorists have recognized other potential bases for securing public compliance with the law."[50] These "potential bases" include both external social pressures and internalized social norms that foster respect for and compliance with the law.[51] For instance, in the public at large, breaking the law constitutes a shared social taboo. This helps to explain why people are less likely to jaywalk when in the presence of others who are waiting at a light.[52] More broadly, an individual's perception of the social desirability of obeying the law is highly predictive of whether or not that individual will be law-abiding.[53]

Social groups may also foster an intrinsic form of social control. That is, to the extent that social group members internalize the norms of the group, external controls are no longer needed to maintain individual compliance; people will effectively police their own behaviors. For example, though it is highly unlikely that people will be caught if they cheat on their taxes, most people report their income accurately every year.[54] This suggests that the likelihood of compliance with a norm might be dictated as much by internal mechanisms as by external threats of punishment or promises of reward.

Conversely, social groups that promote norms of lawlessness or aggression may promulgate competing "oppositional norms."[55] Like norms of compliance, when these anti-social collective mores are internalized, social groups can shape the behavior of their members even when direct peer pressure is no longer present. In the case of incarceration, social ties built in prison may contribute to the perpetuation of criminal activity following parole, resulting in higher rates of crime and recidivism.

6

The Social Effects of Prison Work

You shall have joy, or you shall have power, said God;
you shall not have both.

Ralph Waldo Emerson, *Journals* (1842)

In the preceding chapter, I presented evidence that incarceration can create communities of inmates that are best described not as relations of "mutual aid, loyalty, affection, and respect" or as a "war of all against all," but instead as a precarious combination of the two. As Gresham Sykes pointed out, describing the social dynamics of inmate life: "In actuality, the patterns of social interaction among inmates are to be found scattered between these two theoretical extremes. The population of prisoners does not exhibit a perfect solidarity yet neither is the population of prisoners a warring aggregate. Rather, it is a mixture of both and the society of captives lies balanced in an uneasy compromise."[1] The social effects of higher-security prisons, in particular, are marked by both solidarity and strife; inmates form strong social ties, but these groups serve as the basis for development of contentious and sometimes even violent inter-group norms. Thus, life for inmates within the prison setting may be experienced simultaneously as "predominantly cohesive" and as "a jungle-like existence."[2]

Inmates are not the only group of people who spend substantial periods of time within these institutions, however. In addition, correctional officers and other prison staff can and do accumulate years of work in the prison environment. Like inmates, officers interact with others on a regular basis while inside the prison, and the character of these interactions is intricately tied to the context in which they occur.

In this chapter, I turn my attention to the effects of different prison regimes on correctional officers' professional orientations and personal relationships. I argue here that, as with inmates, the culture of prison institutions can have powerful consequences for officers' social ties and attitudes, both within and beyond the prison. Specifically, I show that prison custody level matters for the social orientations officers develop toward others within the prison (i.e., inmates, peers, and supervisors), as well as the relationships they have with family members and friends outside the prison walls. The pattern of effects I find among officers mirrors those I uncover among inmates: for those who work within more punitive prisons, daily experiences can be conducive to the construction of strong social solidarities with peers, while simultaneously incubating a broader sense of social distrust.

The Effects of Prison Work

Officers' most fundamental workplace interactions occur with inmates, and these encounters are necessarily complex. In one sense, officers are tasked with securing the safety and health of the incarcerated. Thus, one primary role they carry out within the institution is addressing potential violence between inmates. At the same time, though, officers are charged with administering the "pains of imprisonment," by restricting freedom of movement and preventing escape. Some officers may see these two sets of tasks as overlapping. For instance, even among officers who believe that inmates should be punished and that prisons should not try to rehabilitate, levels of support for specific rehabilitation programs are often quite high because such programs are seen as keeping inmates busy and reducing levels of violence.[3] Others, though, may regard these dual roles as being in fundamental tension with one another.[4]

There are at least three ways that features of prison work might shape officers' attitudes toward inmates and correctional work – formal training, direct experience, and informal socialization – and these pathways are not mutually exclusive. First, prison systems spend a great deal of time and money on officer training. In California, for instance, correctional officers attend a 16-week training academy prior to their first work assignment, during which time they complete 640 hours of academic, physical, and weapons curriculum. This intensive training period "seeks to instill the skills and experience needed to function in a prison setting and to build esprit de corps among the cadets."[5] By communicating explicitly to trainees how correctional administrators view the nature of prison and the correctional officers' role within the system, the Department of Corrections and Rehabilitation seeks to indoctrinate new officers into the norms and culture of state prison work. Yet while training is the most direct way for prison systems to communicate particular responsibilities and roles to correctional staff, the efficacy of formal curricula may be conditional on other factors such as structural incentives, organizational capacity, and commitment to the training regime.[6]

A second way that professional work can shape officers' orientations is through their occupational experience. What officers learn in training may sometimes be at odds with the informal rules that govern prisons in practice,[7] and, over time, day-to-day experiences in the prison setting may lead to the development of a more individualized philosophy that guides how individual officers conduct themselves. For instance, in describing his field training as a Baltimore city police officer, Peter Moskos writes that "on the street, as the trainee becomes a police officer, the desire to help or 'serve' the public lessens as part of a greater shift from a public-centered ideal to more police-centered ideals: minimizing unpleasant dealings, avoiding paperwork, and getting home safely."[8]

Like police, correctional officers may adopt particular perspectives in response to the resource constraints and contextual cues that they face in their work environment. For officers, their formal role within the prison is increasingly a paramilitary one, which emphasizes hierarchical ranks (officers, corporals and sergeants, lieutenants and wardens), military-style discipline, and the maintenance of order and security through the use of force when necessary. However, officers also are encouraged to use their discretion to resolve issues within the confines of the law. As one correctional officer described it, "We were told to follow orders, but cross reference the orders to legal interpretations. We were taught laws, regulations, and post orders and told to interpret them and use our best judgment. Less 'Take the hill!' and more 'Take a look at the hill, report on the hill, try to talk to the hill, and maybe take a stroll over the hill.'"[9]

Third, new officers' attitudes might be shaped by those around them. This process of informal socialization can be both vertical (supervisor–subordinate) and horizontal (peer–peer)[10] and can be transmitted through both the explicit and implicit cues provided by other officers. For example, as I have already described in detail, new officers participate in an apprenticeship program following their formal training, which includes on-the-job training at their assigned prison. During this time, officers are expected to absorb the practical details of their posts, as well as the nuances of prison organizational culture, in large part through observation of and guidance from more experienced officers. They also receive more formal training during this time, including ongoing professional curricula and mandated supervision. Horizontal and vertical influences can be mutually reinforcing.[11] Alternatively, lessons gleaned from peers may run counter to the official organizational mission, as officers grasp "the gap between how things must be done (the formal rules) and how things should be done the informal rules that develop over time... [and discover that] some violations of the book of general orders are so ingrained as to be standard operating procedure."[12]

These processes shape how officers relate to inmates, supervisors and also peers in prison. However, unlike inmates, officers leave the prison at the end of every shift and return to their homes, where they may be expected to interact with friends and families. Like other professionals who work long and irregular hours, employment can place significant strain on personal relationships.[13] Compounding this are overnight shifts, mandated holdovers, and significant amounts of overtime that can regularly intrude on family and social life. Even more difficult, though, is that filling their professional role may require officers to develop a certain amount of rigidity, aloofness, or even aggression. This hardened workplace persona, which is particularly likely to develop for those working in violent or otherwise threatening institutions, may be difficult to shed at the end of the day.[14] When they bring home the wariness and strain of the workday role, officers' feelings and behavior may conflict with loved ones' expectations of what is desirable or appropriate in the role of partner, father, mother, or child. For example, in her qualitative study of prison workers, Elaine Crawley quotes one officer's description of how correctional work affected his family life:

I thought I'd seen everything when I joined [the correctional workforce], but I knew nothing. My family thought I'd changed; I'd got a lot more confidence.

But the change resulted in my divorce. My wife said I'd become more methodical … [I'm] much more suspicious. And I think that's what made us split up.[15]

Though limited, extant empirical evidence suggests this officer's experience may not be unique; a 2004 study found that many correctional officers report at least some degree of work–family conflict to be a significant personal and professional issue.[16] Another study found divorce rates among correctional officers to be twice the national average.[17]

Experiences with Violence and Feelings of Safety

The experiences many officers have on the job are distinct from those of workers in other sectors of employment. In particular, incidents of non-fatal workplace violence are higher for correctional officers than for workers in any other profession, with the exception of police officers.[18] Relatively few California correctional officers have been killed in the line of duty; only 20 state correctional employees have been fatally wounded on the job since 1952. Fifteen of those killed were stabbed to death, two were bludgeoned, two shot, and one thrown to his death from a tier. Of those killed, the majority (17 of 20) were custody staff, including 14 correctional officers.[19] Yet, despite the relative rarity of *fatal* violence against correctional staff in the California system, the rate of non-fatal violence against correctional staff is high. Figure 6.1 charts the number and rate of assaults and batteries against staff in California prisons for each year from 1989 to 2004.[20] As the bars show, the annual rate of assault or battery incidents against staff increased by more than 340 percent in just a decade and a half. As indicated by the lines in Figure 6.1, the rising number of assaults against staff is not merely a function of a growing population of inmates. Rather, levels of violence against staff when considered as a rate per population of inmates have almost doubled.

The frequency with which individual officers report having personally been the target of violence is therefore quite high. Roughly 16 percent of respondents to the CCOS reported having been assaulted personally at least once over the past six months, and 12 percent reported having been personally injured in a direct assault during that

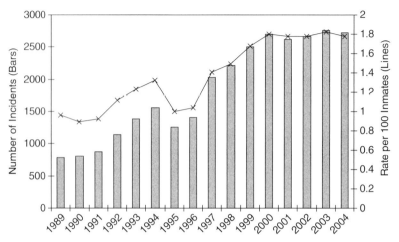

FIGURE 6.1. Number and rate of assault/battery incidents on correctional staff.
Source: Inmate Incidents in Institutions and *Historical Trends, 1984–2004* Data Analysis Unit, California Department of Corrections and Rehabilitation. Rate is relative to the total inmate population on December 31 of that year.

time period. Among those who had been assaulted, fully 40 percent reported having had this experience more than once. Similarly, among those who reported having been injured in a recent attack, 42 percent were injured multiple times. Nor are physical assaults against staff the only type of violence that correctional officers experience, or even the type experienced most frequently. For instance, fully 79 percent of officers reported having responded to inmate-on-inmate violence at least once in the past six months. Of these, 17 percent had been injured at least once.

These occupational experiences vary systematically across California's prisons, in ways that are likely to shape officers' attitudes toward the purpose and goals of corrections, as well as their orientations toward inmates. In particular, as shown in Table 6.1, although rates of experience with violence are high overall, a larger proportion of officers at higher-security prisons reported having had personal experiences with violence than did officers at lower-security prisons. Likewise, assaults and injuries were reported to be more frequent. As might therefore be expected, officers' perceptions of their personal safety while at work also differ across security levels. Overall, about

TABLE 6.1. *Personal Assaults, Injuries, and Perceptions of Safety by Security Level*

	At Least One Assault (%)	At Least One Injury (%)	Mean Assaults	Mean Injuries	Perceptions of Safety Index
Level I	5	5	0.06 (0.31)	0.10 (0.65)	0.63 (0.20)
Level II	9	7	0.12 (0.43)	0.12 (0.54)	0.55 (0.19)
Level III	14	11	0.18 (0.51)	0.21 (0.89)	0.53 (0.20)
Level IV	18	15	0.24 (0.60)	0.32 (0.36)	0.50 (0.20)

Data exclude officers who have worked primarily with more than one security level over the past six months, as well as officers working with female inmates. For mean scores, standard deviation is shown in parentheses. Perceptions of safety is an index combining two statements – "I rarely feel safe when I am at work" and "I feel safe when working among the inmates" (reverse coded). N = 317 at Level I; 783 at Level II, 1,519 at Level III, and 1,864 at Level IV.

half of correctional officers (53 percent) report that they do not feel safe when on the job. When asked specifically about working with inmates, the percentage of those indicating concern about safety is even higher: almost 60 percent report feeling unsafe when working among inmates. However, officers working in lower-security prisons are significantly more likely to disagree that they "rarely feel safe when I am at work" and more likely to agree that they "feel safe when working among the inmates."

Attitudes toward Inmates and Corrections

Do officers' varying experiences at work affect their attitudes toward inmates and their orientations toward corrections? Previous studies provide conflicting evidence on whether security level is significantly related to officers' attitudes toward correctional work. One study found that minimum-security staff are more optimistic about inmates.[21] By comparison, another study of six Midwestern prisons suggested that officers in minimum-security prisons are more punitive,[22] and a third study found no relationship between security level and support for either custody or rehabilitation.[23]

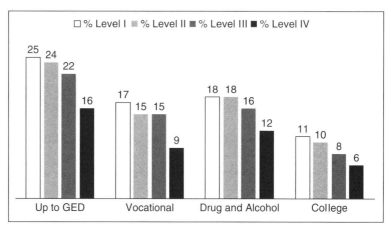

FIGURE 6.2. Support for rehabilitation programs by security level.
Note: Data are for all respondents to the CCOS. Indicates percentage of those who strongly agree that each program type should be offered.

CCOS data help to adjudicate between these differing expectations. In a simple descriptive comparison, the data show that officers working in higher- and lower-security prisons hold distinct attitudes toward a variety of rehabilitation programs (Figure 6.2).[24] Specifically, officers working at higher security levels are significantly less likely than those at lower security levels to agree that inmates should be offered GED programs, college education, vocational training, or drug and alcohol treatment, and these differences across security levels are all statistically significant ($p < .001$). However, variation in attitudes is largely in the *strength* of support for each type of program rather than the percentage of officers at each level who agree that the provision of services is at all desirable. Officers in higher-security institutions are less likely to "strongly agree" that vocational, GED, and drug and alcohol programs should be offered to inmates who want them.

Attitudes toward rehabilitation as a correctional philosophy also vary somewhat by security level, though the differences are smaller. Officers at the lowest security level are more likely than those at the highest to say that the purpose of a prison is more rehabilitation than punishment (15 percent at Level I and 13 percent at Level IV), to agree that rehabilitation should be a central goal of prison (49 percent at Level I and 43 percent at Level IV), and to disagree that prisons are for public safety, not to help inmates (35 percent at Level I and

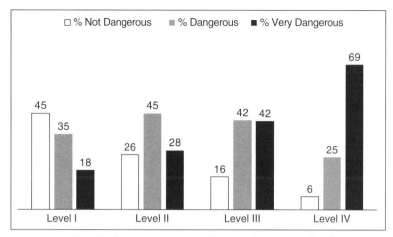

FIGURE 6.3. Perceived dangerousness of inmates by security level.
Note: Officers were first asked what security-level inmate they have worked with most often during the past six months. They were then asked the follow-up question "What percentage of the inmates at this security level do you think are: very dangerous, dangerous, not dangerous?" Security levels are for men's prisons only. Level 1 N = 309; Level 2 N = 784; Level 3 N = 1,916; Level 4 N = 1,864.

31 percent at Level IV). Again, differences between security levels are all statistically significant (p < .05 for all questions), despite being substantively small.

Additionally, officers differ in how they think of and relate to inmates. Not surprisingly, when asked to assess the dangerousness of the inmates with whom an officer has had the most contact over the past six months, there are significant differences across security levels (Figure 6.3). Officers working in Level I prisons consider almost half of the inmates with whom they work (45 percent) to be "not dangerous" and only a small percentage (18 percent) to be "very dangerous." At each successively higher security level, officers perceive a larger proportion of inmates to be dangerous and very dangerous, and a smaller proportion to be not dangerous. At Level IV, officers perceive the highest percentage of "very dangerous" inmates (69 percent) and the lowest percentage of inmates deemed to be "not dangerous" (6 percent).[25]

It is impossible from surveys alone to know the extent to which these varying attitudes toward inmates predict differing behavior in

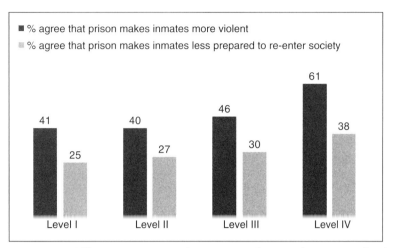

FIGURE 6.4. Officer assessments of prison socialization by security level. Security levels are for men's prisons only. Level 1 *N* = 309; Level 2 *N* = 784; Level 3 *N* = 1,916; Level 4 *N* = 1,864.

the workplace. However, the data do suggest that there is a strong correlation between working in a higher-security prison setting and the way that officers describe the quality of interactions with inmates. In the CCOS sample as a whole, officers at lower custody are more likely to characterize the relationship between officers and inmates at the prison where they work as generally pleasant. Compared with 57 percent of officers at Level I, substantially smaller proportions of officers at Levels II, III, and IV say this is the case – 52, 49, and 39 percent, respectively (*p* < .001). The same patterns hold in characterizations of officers' personal interactions with inmates. Compared with 34 percent of officers at Level I who describe their own interactions with inmates as "more pleasant than most other officers," this is true of 24 percent of Level II officers and 22 percent of officers at both Level III and Level IV (*p* < .001).

Finally, it is worth noting that officers at higher-security prisons are more likely to believe that incarceration in the prison where they work has a detrimental effect on inmates (see Figure 6.4). Data from the CCOS indicate that fully half of correctional officers believe that incarceration in the prison where they work causes inmates to become more violent. Roughly a third believe that when inmates leave prison they are less prepared to be law-abiding citizens than they were when they entered. A larger proportion of those working in higher-security settings believe that prison has these negative effects, though. Compared with 41 and 40 percent of officers at Level I and II prisons who believe that serving time at the prison where they work makes inmates more violent, 46 percent of officers at Level III and fully 61 percent of officers at Level IV prisons assert this belief ($p < .001$). Similarly, compared with 25 percent of officers at Level I facilities who believe that when inmates leave prison they are less prepared to be law-abiding citizens than they were when they entered, 27, 30, and 38 percent of officers voice this opinion in Level II, III, and IV prisons, respectively ($p < .001$).

Orientations toward Supervisors and Peers

In addition to concerns about safety, officers report a wide variety of work-related problems. First, officers' evaluations regarding both the consistency and adequacy of institutional responses to violence are mixed. Less than a third of officers (about 28 percent) report that disciplinary action is always taken in response to incidents of inmate violence against staff. By comparison, 27 percent of officers feel that action is rarely taken, and 8 percent report that disciplinary action when a staff member is assaulted is either very rarely or never taken. Moreover, even when some type of action is taken, many officers feel that it is too often insufficient; in the aggregate, only 8 percent of officers across the state say that disciplinary action taken in response to staff assaults is always adequate, whereas about 22 percent of officers report feeling that actions taken in response to inmate-on-staff violence are either very rarely or never adequate.

More generally, when presented with a series of work-related issues, a significant number of officers report having experienced at least some of them in the past six months: 31 percent report issues with an inmate or inmates; 28 percent report problems concerning performance feedback or recognition; 27 percent report a problem with another staff member; 23 percent report harassment by a supervisor or management; and 22 percent report issues concerning work schedule, attendance, leave, or pay.[26]

Despite the relative frequency of these varied and important issues, though, nearly half of officers (47 percent) report feeling that when they have a problem at work, there is no one they can talk to who will really help them solve it. The extent to which officers feel they can rely on horizontal relative to vertical sources of support to help resolve issues is substantially different, however. Compared with just half of officers (55 percent) who report that if a work-related problem arose in the future they would consider contacting a supervisor to resolve it, about 70 percent report that they would consider contacting CCPOA.

Many officers say that they would not reach out for help because they do not believe it would make a difference. A higher percentage cite the belief that contacting their supervisor (46 percent) would not help resolve their issues than say this is true of the union (38 percent), however. A larger proportion of officers express hesitation about reaching out to direct supervisors for other reasons, too, as compared with contacting the union: 38 percent of officers do not trust their supervisor, compared with only 14 percent of officers who do not trust the union; 44 percent would not contact a supervisor because they are concerned about a negative reaction from management, but this concern is only a factor for 29 percent who would not contact the union; and while 25 percent would not contact a supervisor because they are concerned about negative reactions from co-workers, only 14 percent cite this as a factor in their decision not to contact the union. The only exception to this pattern is that 14 percent of officers believe that contacting their supervisor would require too much time and effort, compared with a slightly larger percentage of officers (23 percent) who believe this to be the case with the union.

Again, there is a significant correlation between the security level at which officers work and their willingness to contact a supervisor for help. The difference is primarily confined to the lowest security level, though. Compared with 64 percent of officers at Level I, 57 percent of officers at Level II, 56 percent at Level III, and 54 percent at Level IV would consider doing so ($p = .01$). In contrast, there is no significant relationship between security level and officers' reported willingness to contact the union to help resolve work-related problems.

One explanation for this difference is the variation officers report in their concerns about violence. In the data, officers who feel safe at work are as likely as those who feel unsafe to consider using the union as a resource to solve problems. By contrast, officers' willingness to contact a supervisor is negatively correlated with their perceived personal safety in the workplace. Specifically, of those who report that

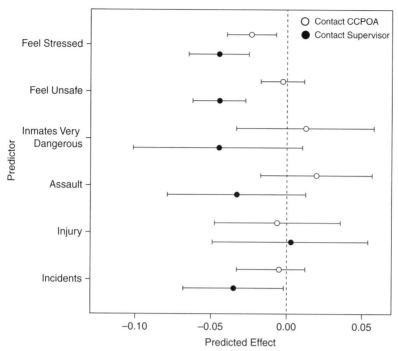

FIGURE 6.5. Predicting reliance on officers' union and supervisors. *Note:* CCOS total sample; $N = 5,468$. HLM coefficients with 95% CI. Controls include partisan identification, race, gender, age, education, tenure, gender of inmates, percent female officers, percent white officers, security level. Dependent variables range from 0 to 1.

they rarely feel safe at work, 49 percent say they would consider contacting a supervisor to resolve problems. By comparison, 64 percent of those who report feeling safe at work would think about contacting a supervisor ($p < .001$).

The relationship between perceptions of workplace safety and officers' preferred resources for problem solving remains significant when additional controls are introduced. In a set of hierarchical models, I estimate the likelihood that an officer will reach out for help to resolve a work-related problem (Figure 6.5). The nested structure of the models allows me to take into account that officers have more similar experiences within particular prisons than across different institutions. In the first model, I estimate the likelihood that an officer says he or she would contact the union. In the second model, I estimate the likelihood that an officer will contact a supervisor. In each model, the dependent variable is regressed on the extent to which officers report experiencing work-related stress, the extent to which they feel unsafe at work, the percentage of inmates at their institution whom they describe as "very dangerous," and three measures of experiences with violence in the past six months: whether they have been personally assaulted, personally injured in an assault, and the frequency with which they have responded to violent incidents. In addition, I include a set of individual-level controls (partisan identification, race, gender, age, education, tenure at CDCR) and controls at the institution level (gender of inmates, percentage of officers who are female, percentage of officers who are white, security levels housed).

As Figure 6.5 shows, concerns about and experiences with violence are negatively predictive of willingness to contact a supervisor. That is, officers who report responding to violent incidents with greater frequency are less likely to say that they would consider contacting a supervisor to help resolve a problem at work ($p < .05$). The same is true of those who feel unsafe in the work environment ($p < .001$) and those who feel more stressed or under greater pressure while on the job ($p < .001$). In comparison, only reported feelings of stress are associated with a decreased likelihood of contacting CCPOA to help resolve a work-related issue. In fact, recent experience with assault and the percentage of inmates considered to be "very dangerous" both appear *positively* correlated with the likelihood of contacting the union, although neither relationship is statistically significant at conventional levels.

Relationships Outside the Prison

The previous analyses suggested that features of the institutional context are related to officers' relationships within the prison bureaucracy. Does prison culture likewise matter for their relationships at home?

Simple cross-tabulations suggest that prison work takes a psychological toll on many officers that can carry over to personal relationships outside the prison (Table 6.2). A majority of officers (70 percent) report feeling tense or stressed while at work, and about two-thirds (65 percent) report that they usually feel they are under a lot of pressure at work.[27] Not surprisingly, these attitudes correlate with perceptions of violence. Of those who report feeling relatively safe at

TABLE 6.2. *Workplace Safety, Stress, and Work–Family Conflict*

	Total (%)	I rarely feel safe when I am at work.			Chi Sq.
		Disagree (%)	Undecided (%)	Agree (%)	
Work-related stress					
When I'm at work, I often feel tense or stressed.	70	56	64	83	527.80***
I usually feel that I am under a lot of pressure when I am at work.	65	50	60	77	527.13***
Work–family strain					
I have become harsher or less trusting toward family members since I took this job.	48	38	42	55	180.01***
What happens at work negatively affects my relationship with my spouse/partner or children.	50	39	45	59	249.69***

Percentages include those responding "somewhat agree," "agree," or "strongly agree."
N = 5,468.
***p < .001.

work, about half indicate some amount of work related psychological stress. Specifically, 56 percent of officers who feel safe report feeling tense or stressed while at work, and 50 percent report usually feeling under a lot of pressure when at work. By comparison, a much larger proportion of those who feel *unsafe* at work express these sentiments. Of this group, 83 and 77 percent experience high levels of psychological stress and pressure, respectively.

Many officers also report sizable difficulty in confining these work-related stresses to the workplace. About half of CCOS respondents (48 percent) report having become harsher or less trusting toward family members since taking a job as a correctional officer, and roughly the same proportion feel that what happens at work negatively affects family relationships (50 percent). Of those who report feeling relatively safe at work, however, the proportion is somewhat lower than the mean. In this group, 38 percent feel they have become harsher or less trusting since taking their job, and 39 percent believe that what happens at work negatively affects relationships with family. Conversely, a significantly larger proportion of those who report feeling *unsafe* at work express these sentiments. Of this group, a majority (55 and 59 percent) indicate that correctional work results in some degree of work–family strain and conflict.

Again, institutional context appears to play a significant role in how officers cope with prison work. In the CCOS sample as a whole, the security level at which officers work is highly correlated with measures of both psychological well-being and social ties. Compared with 60 percent of officers at Level I, 67 percent of officers at Level II and 72 percent at Levels III and IV report that they often feel tense or stressed at work ($p < .001$). Officers assigned to higher-security posts are similarly more likely to report that they usually feel they are under a lot of pressure while at work ($p < .001$).

This is not surprising, given the higher levels of violence at these facilities and the link between officers' concerns about workplace safety and levels of anxiety while at work. The relationship between security level and strained work–family relationships is somewhat less consistent, however. Officers at higher-security prisons are not more likely to report having become "harsher or less trusting" since they began correctional work. However, there is a marginally significant relationship ($p < .1$) between one's security level and the belief that workplace experiences negatively affect relationships at home. The relationship between security level and work–family strain becomes stronger when those who are "undecided" about the effects of their work-related stress on family life are included among those who agree. Here, perceptions of having become harsher toward one's family also look to be significantly related to prison context ($p < .1$) and the relationship between security level and the belief that "what happens at work negatively affects my relationship with spouse/partner or children" is fully significant at conventional levels ($p < .05$).

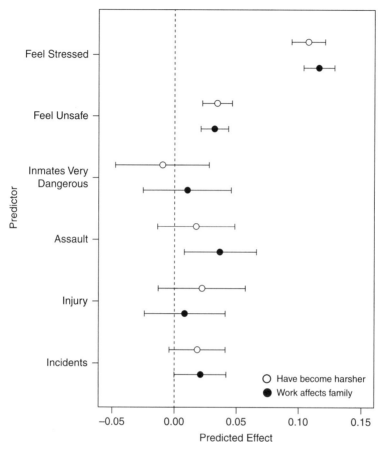

FIGURE 6.6. Predicting officers' personal social ties.

Note: CCOS total sample; N = 5,468. HLM coefficients with 95% CI. Controls include partisan identification, race, gender, age, education, tenure, gender of inmates, percent female officers, percent white officers, security level. Dependent variables range from 0 to 1.

These differences across security levels continue to obtain significance in hierarchical models (see Figure 6.6). The setup of these models is the same as those described in the preceding section, and the results show a strong relationship between levels of work-related stress and both measures of work–family conflict. Those who experience more stress and pressure at work are significantly more likely to report having become "harsher or less trusting" and are more likely to say that what happens at work negatively affects what happens at home ($p < .001$). The same is true of officers' perceptions of workplace safety. Those who feel less safe at work experience more issues in their personal social ties ($p < .001$).

The relationship between work–family strain and recent experiences with violence are somewhat more mixed. Officers who have been assaulted at work at least once in the past six months are more likely to report that work negatively affects relationships with family ($p = .01$), and the same is true of the frequency with which officers have responded to violence in the institution ($p = .05$). These variables do not appear likewise correlated with officers' reports concerning how prison work has shaped their social orientations, though. Finally, neither the percentage of inmates an officer deems "very dangerous" nor whether an officer has been injured in a direct assault is associated with either measure of work–family stress.

A Quasi-Experiment

These descriptive analyses suggest that officers working in higher-security prisons hold different attitudes and have different relationships with others than those working in lower-security prisons. However, it may be that officers working at different security levels differ on some other factor that explains this divergence. Existing research on the professional norms of custody staff posits two sets of variables that predict officers' attitudes toward correctional goals: institutional context, but also individual demographics.[28] These are referred to as the work/role model and the importation model, respectively. The importation model suggests that the professional norms of officers correlate with stable attributes of the individual that precede correctional employment. For example, studies focusing on the demographics of individual officers have examined whether characteristics like race,[29] education,[30] gender,[31] and tenure[32] are related to officer attitudes.

The work/role model, by comparison, argues that work-related experiences have a *causal* effect on officers' attitudes. Some studies suggest that work variables exert a stronger influence on attitudes than individual demographics, while others support a joint impact of imported and environmental factors.[33] As evidence, existing studies supporting a work/role model find strong correlations between officers' perceptions of correctional work and a variety of organizational characteristics. For instance, working a late shift[34] has been shown to correlate with support for rehabilitation programs, but also to predict a custodial orientation.[35] Likewise, both having a lower rank and being assigned to inside picket duty have been shown to predict positive attitudes toward some treatment programs.[36]

A simple comparison of how officer attitudes vary across security levels cannot adjudicate between these competing explanations. This is because, as described in Chapter 4, prison officers may choose to work at the particular security level that best conforms to their existing preferences and beliefs. Thus, while there may be a negative relationship between working at a higher security level and support for rehabilitation, this may be purely due to selection. This type of assignment process – according to individual preference – makes it difficult to assess the effects of occupational experience independent of pre-existing attitudes.

In order to address this concern, I leverage a feature of employment in the CDCR: in the California state prison system, correctional officers who are still in their first two years of work are assigned to a particular prison and security level through a largely arbitrary process, one over which they have limited control. (This estimation strategy is described in detail in Chapter 4.) By comparing a matched sample of apprentice officers who are assigned to higher and lower security levels, it is therefore possible to obtain an unbiased estimate of the effect of the prison environment on new officers' attitudes and relationships.

Inmates and Correctional Work

Do apprentice officers develop divergent attitudes toward rehabilitation? Like among officers as a whole, levels of support for rehabilitation programs are consistently high among new recruits. In fact, almost all apprentice officers (97 percent) agree that at least one of the four types of rehabilitation programs should be offered to inmates. However, among these new officers, those assigned to a higher-security prison support the provision of significantly fewer. Among apprentices assigned to Level III, about 70 percent believe all four types of programs should be offered to inmates who want them. By comparison, only 48 percent of new officers assigned to work at Level IV agree that all four programs should be offered ($p < .01$). In particular, officers assigned to the higher-security setting are less likely to support vocational training (94 percent of apprentices at Level III agree that this type of program should be offered, relative to 80 percent at Level IV; *p* < .001) and education at the college level (74 percent at Level III and 54 percent at Level IV; *p* < .001).

In contrast to attitudes toward specific rehabilitation programs, there are no significant differences between the ideological orientations of higher- and lower-security apprentice officers. On all of the rehabilitation ideology statements – "Rehabilitation should be a central goal of incarceration"; "The job of a prison is to keep the public safe, not to help inmates"; and "The purpose of a prison is rehabilitation, punishment, or both" – apprentice officers assigned to Level III and Level IV hold statistically equivalent attitudes. These comparisons suggest that the security level to which an officer is assigned plays a significant role in shaping his or her attitudes toward specific rehabilitation programs, but that security level has little or no causal effect on broader orientations toward rehabilitation as a correctional philosophy.

In order to reduce any biases that might stem from even minimal differences between these two groups, I also create a matched dataset of apprentices. Using a genetic matching algorithm,[37] I match officers assigned to Level IV with officers assigned to Level III on all observable covariates, as well as on a propensity score predicting the probability of assignment to a higher-security setting.[38] Essentially, I artificially create a comparable set of apprentice officers who have been assigned to higher and lower security levels, making sure that they are well balanced on all observable characteristics that might potentially confound my analysis. The matched sample of apprenticed officers improves the statistical balance between those who are assigned to Levels III and IV; after matching, no significant differences remain in the observed characteristics of the two groups (see Figure 6.7).

I then assess the effects of prison context on officers' attitudes toward rehabilitation using the matched sample. The results of these estimates confirm inferences from the unmatched data: prison context appears to have a significant effect on attitudes toward rehabilitation programs but no effect on attitudes toward rehabilitation as a professional ideology. On the question of whether "rehabilitation should be a central goal of incarceration," the effect of assignment to Level IV rather than Level III is 0.01, or a difference of less than 1 percent of the scale ranging from 1, "strongly disagree," to 6, "strongly agree." This effect is not statistically significant ($p = .96$). The same is true when

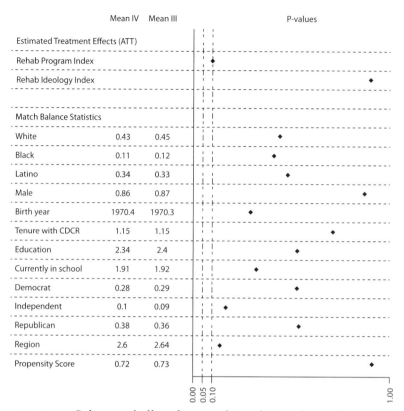

	Mean IV	Mean III	
Estimated Treatment Effects (ATT)			
Rehab Program Index			
Rehab Ideology Index			
Match Balance Statistics			
White	0.43	0.45	
Black	0.11	0.12	
Latino	0.34	0.33	
Male	0.86	0.87	
Birth year	1970.4	1970.3	
Tenure with CDCR	1.15	1.15	
Education	2.34	2.4	
Currently in school	1.91	1.92	
Democrat	0.28	0.29	
Independent	0.1	0.09	
Republican	0.38	0.36	
Region	2.6	2.64	
Propensity Score	0.72	0.73	

FIGURE 6.7. Balance and effects for treated (Level IV) and control (Level III) groups in matched sample.

Note: Sample includes only officers who are in their apprenticeship period of employment; $N = 169$ matched observations. Region is coded as a continuous variable, such that matching prefers the closest geographic area.

I consider support for rehabilitation relative to punishment. On this question officers assigned to Levels III and IV are statistically indistinguishable. On the Rehabilitation Ideology Index, which combines these two questions, those at the higher and lower security levels are statistically equivalent.

In contrast, the security level to which an apprentice is assigned has a significant effect on his or her attitudes toward the provision of specific rehabilitation programs; apprentice officers assigned to lower-security posts adopt more supportive attitudes toward programs. In the matched sample, being assigned to the higher-security prison predicts a decrease of about 4 percentage points on the Rehabilitation Program Index ($p < .1$), a measure that combines support for the four program types. In particular, assigning officers to work with higher-custody inmates makes them less likely to support offering either academic training at the college level or vocational training. The size of the effect of Level IV assignment on support for college education is a decline of about 7 percentage points, and the effect on support for vocational training is roughly equivalent. Both of these effects are significant at the 95 percent level.

Differences in officers' attitudes toward inmates are likewise significant when the CCOS sample is restricted to Level III and IV officers who are still in their period of apprenticeship. Among these officers, there is a marginally significant and negative effect of assignment to a higher-security prison on officers' evaluations of their own interactions with inmates ($p < .1$). The size of this effect is substantively small, however; 20 percent of new officers in Level IV prisons describe their relationship to inmates as more pleasant than that of most officers, compared with 22 percent of those at Level III, a difference of just 2 percentage points. The effect is more substantial where more general evaluations of the officer–inmate relationship are concerned. On this question, apprentices assigned to Level III are fully 18 percentage points more likely to describe the interactions between correctional officers and inmates where they work as generally pleasant than those assigned to Level IV ($p = .01$).

Among apprentice officers there is also an effect of assignment to Level IV rather than Level III on perceptions of how inmates socialize to prison. Among new officers assigned to a lower-security Level III setting, about 38 percent believe that time spent as an inmate in the prison where they work leads inmates to become more violent. The proportion believing this to be true is 53 percent among new officers assigned to the highest security level ($p < .05$). Similarly, 25 percent of apprentice officers at Level III and 30 percent of officers at Level IV believe that inmates actually leave the prison where they work less prepared to obey the law than they were when they entered ($p < .01$). These results remain significant in the matched sample.

Peers, Managers, and Family Ties

It is not only officers' attitudes toward inmates that are shaped by the correctional context, though; other relationships are likewise affected.

TABLE 6.3. *Work-Related Stress, Work–Family Conflict, and Officer Tenure*

	When I'm at work, I often feel tense or stressed.	What happens at work negatively affects my relationship with my spouse/partner or children.
Years at CDCR		
1–2	50	23
3–5	67	41
6–10	73	52
>10	72	56

Percentage includes those responding "somewhat agree," "agree," or "strongly agree." N = 5,468.

Among apprentice officers, there is a strongly significant relationship between being assigned to a higher-security post and the resources officers are likely to draw upon to help resolve work-related problems. Specifically, new officers assigned to Level IV facilities become less likely to consider contacting a supervisor than are those assigned to Level III, although the difference of roughly five percentage points is not statistically significant. New officers at higher-security prisons also become somewhat more likely to consider contacting CCPOA, and this difference is slightly larger (about eight percentage points) and somewhat more robust ($p < .1$). This effect remains statistically significant in the matched subsample of apprentices.

Security level does not appear to translate into work–family conflict early on in an officer's career, however. About a quarter of officers assigned to both Levels III and IV report that what happens at work negatively affects relationships with family. Of course, this does not mean that security level does not ultimately have an effect on officers' social ties outside the prison. Rather, it may be the case that the particular effect of prison context on personal relationships outside prison is not reflected among apprentice officers, because they have been on the job for a relatively short period of time.

Indeed, in the CCOS sample as a whole, those who have been employed with CDCR for longer report significantly more work-related stress and work–family conflict than do officers with less tenure (see Table 6.3). This remains true in HLM models predicting work–family conflict when other variables, including an officer's age, race, gender, and education, are accounted for. In these models, officers' tenure working for the CDCR is strongly correlated with both psychological stress and self-reported strain in relationships with family and friends. These significant relationships may reflect an accumulation of pressure over time. Alternatively, the larger proportion of older officers reporting stress and strain in personal relationships may be a response to aging while holding a physically demanding job. It may also be the case that officers who have seen a great deal of change in the prison environment experience more stress; for officers who undertook correctional work in the early 1980s, when California prisons were somewhat less crowded, more rehabilitation-oriented, and less violent, adjusting to substantial changes in the work environment may have proved difficult.

Conclusions

At the outset of this chapter, I discussed three ways that employment might shape the attitudes of correctional officers: formal training, occupational experience, and peer socialization. California correctional officers all receive the same training at the academy, irrespective of the institution and security level to which they will be subsequently assigned. If this foundational training fully accounted for officers' attitudes, we would expect to find little variation by security level. The effects found here therefore suggest that peer socialization and/ or occupational experience also play at least some role in determining officers' patterns of adaptation. In this regard, the findings presented here echo the supposition of others that, because of their relative intensity and duration, occupational experiences may have the most substantial effect. In 1974, David Duffee wrote:

It is likely that an hour or two of lecture on a particular subject has a miniscule effect on even the best students listening to the best professor in a good university. Such lectures are only effective as they counterpoint carefully selected readings and occur within the peculiar university atmosphere where foreign ideas, even in the least interested students, enjoy some prestige. Such is not the case in a correctional training academy where many officers hold little respect for "book learning," or for the men whose learning is from books rather than the real life of the cell block.[39]

While this quote is now somewhat dated, it remains true that simply offering better or different training may not, by itself, fully (re-) orient the views of correctional staff. If working norms are not only purposively inculcated by the prison administration but also acquired informally, officers' attitudes will come to reflect the prevailing norms associated with the particular prison setting in which they work. This process of professional socialization makes prison culture self-reinforcing, as new officers assimilate to the environments in which they are employed, rather than conforming solely to the formally stated mission of the correctional organization.[40]

In addition, how safe officers feel while on the job, and the significant levels of stress and strain that result, may have broader implications for officers' well-being that are worthy of consideration. One study of corrections employees found that about a quarter of those surveyed (nearly 26 percent) had symptoms suggesting a clinical diagnosis of post-traumatic stress disorder, rates comparable to those found in combat veterans, prisoners of war, and disaster survivors.[41] And a number of recent studies suggest that the work experiences of correctional employees may frequently result in depression or other serious psychological disorders. In one such study, 25 percent of correctional officers reported frequently experiencing a lack of emotional responsiveness, 20 percent an inability to find pleasure in anything, and 13 percent a feeling of hopelessness and/or worthlessness.[42] Another study found the relative risk of suicide to be 39 percent higher than that of the general working-age population.[43]

Though it is difficult to find rigorous studies of whether the psychological stresses associated with prison work are also detrimental to correctional officers' physical health, high rates of stress among prison workers appear to be associated with increased risk of stress-related illnesses, such as hypertension, heart disease, and ulcers.[44] In fact, one newspaper article cites insurance data that suggest correctional officers have a life expectancy of 59 years, compared with the 77 years that is the average for the U.S. population. That article, titled "Prison Horrors Haunt Guards' Private Lives," argues that many officers "harden themselves to survive inside prison.... Then they find they can't snap out of it at the end of the day. Some seethe to themselves. Others commit suicide."[45]

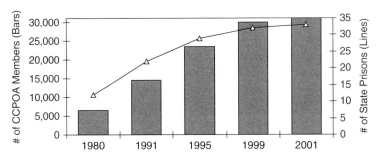

FIGURE 6.8. Growth in CCPOA membership and state prisons, 1980–2001. *Source*: Center on Juvenile and Criminal Justice; Data Analysis Unit, California Department of Corrections and Rehabilitation.

Finally, the data shown here suggest that the experiences officers have at work may affect the nature of criminal justice politics at the state level. Despite most unions across the country experiencing declining membership over the past few decades, the size of the CCPOA has grown significantly since its founding in 1957 (Figure 6.8). Formed originally as a small "pizza and beer" organization of fewer than 2,500 members, CCPOA has expanded to represent more than 31,000 members and, although CCPOA is an open shop, 97 percent of California correctional officers are members.[46] Under the leadership of Don Novey, and subsequently Mike Jimenez and Chuck Alexander, the union has successfully negotiated salaries for state correctional officers that are 58 percent higher than the national average,[47] and the union's political action committee has become one of the largest sources of campaign contributions in California, employing an aggressive lobbying and public relations strategy.[48] Thus, to observers of California politics, the union is now generally regarded as a political powerhouse that can make or break proposals for criminal justice reform and that has been instrumental in the election and removal of more than one state politician.[49] For instance, the Center on Juvenile Criminal Justice describes the union as "a powerful political machine that has had a dramatic effect on the state's correctional system.... When the CCPOA exerts power, more people are incarcerated."[50]

There are several plausible explanations for the extraordinary growth of CCPOA. In part, the increase in membership has been a simple function of the exponential growth in the number of officers employed by the state. As the number of prisons in California has grown, so has the number of correctional officers. The union has also increased its membership by actively organizing related groups of professionals, including parole officers, psychiatric and medical technicians, and correctional counselors.[51] In addition, the union likely also benefits from several characteristics that are associated with higher rates of unionization more generally. First, union declines have been heavily concentrated in the private sector.[52] As CCPOA represents public employees, it may not have been as susceptible to decline as unions representing market sector employees. Second, there has been more strength over time in female union membership relative to male,[53] and CCPOA has been particularly successful in helping to integrate the correctional ranks. In fact, about 18 percent of CCPOA's membership is female, making it one of the most gender-diverse law enforcement unions in the country.[54]

Perhaps the most compelling explanation for the high and persistent unionization rates of California correctional officers, though, may be the contentious relationship between officers and the CDCR. As the data I have presented here make clear, a large proportion of officers hesitate to contact their direct supervisors to resolve problems. In contrast, fewer say they would not go to the union if they needed help with work-related issues. This pattern is particularly stark among officers who experience the threat of violence in the workplace. These data suggest that the union's organizational strength is at least in part a response to the internal dynamics (and dysfunction) of the prison work environment itself.

CCPOA has been widely criticized for the substantial influence it has over criminal justice politics in California. Yet what often goes overlooked in discussions of the union is the considerable level of commitment the organization elicits from its members. To many of the rank and file, the union is the lone actor on the political landscape that regularly advocates for them, the men and women who put their safety at risk every day in the state's correctional facilities. If reliance on CCPOA to resolve grievances at work is indeed linked to perceptions of safety in the workplace, it is unlikely that – for better or for worse – the political power of the union will wane until the difficult problems of prison safety have been successfully addressed.

7

From Individuals to Communities

Your own safety is at stake when your neighbor's wall is ablaze.
Horace, *Epistles (20–c. 8 BC)*

In the preceding chapters, I have argued that the choices states make about institutions of punishment can play an important role in shaping how individuals perceive of and engage with one another. Specifically, I have shown that more violent and punitive correctional institutions create a disjointed form of social community; salient social ties are formed between some groups of individuals within these institutions, but such groups serve to bond rather than bridge. More important, these prison-based social groups foster attitudes among their members that discourage generalized trust and a broader sense of social connection. For inmates, social ties in a more violent and punitive prison can promote an aggressive response to resolving interpersonal conflict and may help to explain increased rates of recidivism. For correctional officers, social dynamics within the punitive prison may foster a wariness of others and a harsher orientation toward inmates, which can spill over to their personal lives.

The focus of these analyses has been the individual officer and inmate. However, I have suggested throughout the previous chapters that these individual-level effects may have wider consequences for American communities. In this chapter, I ask: To what types of communities do prisoners return?

As has already been well documented, concentrated surveillance in low-income and urban neighborhoods has led to wide geographic disparities in the prevalence of incarceration. For instance, in a study of incarceration in Chicago, Robert Sampson and Charles Loeffler note: "Large swaths of the city, especially in the southwest and northwest, remain relatively untouched by the imprisonment boom.... By contrast, there is a dense and spatially contiguous cluster of areas in near-west and south-central Chicago that have rates of incarceration some eight times higher (or more)."[1] These patterns, and the intensification of this spatial dynamic over time, could not be explained by crime rates alone. Instead, communities with similar levels of crime had very different levels of incarceration, a variation that was significantly predicted by concentrated disadvantage.

In the analyses that follow, I explore the geographic dispersion of individuals returning to communities from prison, examining the social characteristics of the neighborhoods that ex-prisoners call home. I argue here that the areas to which ex-inmates predominantly return are not only distinct in terms of race and poverty, as has been shown in extant research. In addition, these communities are distinguished by their patterns of social organization. Using data from Los Angeles County in California, as well as from a variety of other states, I find a strong relationship between the spatial concentration of parolees and the social attitudes and behavior of community residents. In particular, the evidence suggests that communities receiving large numbers of people returning from prison are marked by somewhat more informal social activities between families and friends, but lower levels of generalized trust. In this regard, these areas display social dynamics that echo the atomized social organization of America's more punitive and violent prisons.

These results, I suggest, mean that disadvantaged neighborhoods are caught in a negative feedback loop. Within these communities, social disorder translates into lower levels of community cooperation and informal control. This, in turn, increases rates of crime and predicts higher rates of incarceration.[2] The notion of "addition by subtraction" posits that removing criminals from a community will thereby remove the problems these individuals caused. As Todd Clear writes, "The hard-and-fast assumption of incarceration as a tool of public safety is that removing these people from their communities subtracts only (or primarily) the problems they represented for their places, and thereby leaves those places better."[3] Through policing and imprisonment, undesirables and delinquents are removed from the community, increasing the safety and security of neighborhoods and cities.[4]

However, when large groups of individuals return from prison to these concentrated areas of disadvantage, the receiving community has limited resources to help them resocialize into community life. In fact, I suggest that the concentration of returning parolees may actually reduce community cooperation and collective problem solving. In addition, to the extent that incarceration is itself a criminogenic experience, areas that receive a disproportionate number of returning prisoners will only begin the cycle again, as they welcome these residents back home.

Punishment and Concentrated Communities

As California's prison population has grown over the past few decades, so has its parole population. From 1995 to 2005 alone, the number of adult parolees in the state increased 21 percent.[5] California now has the largest population of parolees of any state in the country. Commensurate with the size of its prison population, nearly 15 percent of the nation's total parole population was incarcerated in a California prison.

With few exceptions, inmates released from prison in the state are returned to their county of commitment for supervision. For this reason, parolees are geographically concentrated in certain areas of the state, namely those areas that send the most individuals to prison. Almost two-thirds of parolees are returned to southern California, to areas like Los Angeles, San Diego, and San Bernardino. As the most populous county in the country,[6] Los Angeles is home to the largest number of parolees of any county in the state – nearly 31 percent of all state parolees[7] – making it first among all counties in the nation in terms of the number of people who have been released there from prison.[8]

Los Angeles County is made up of 88 separate localities that vary significantly in both their economic and racial composition. Not surprisingly, then, even within the county's roughly 4,000 square miles, parolees are highly concentrated within certain areas (Figure 7.1). The city of Los Angeles accounts for the largest share of county parolees (about 40 percent), with Long Beach, Lancaster, and Compton ranking

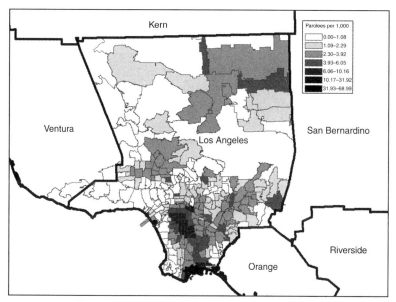

FIGURE 7.1. Concentration of parolees in Los Angeles County (per 1,000 population) by zip code.
Source: California Department of Corrections and Rehabilitation.

second, third, and fourth, respectively. And even within each municipality, individuals released from prison are further concentrated in certain neighborhoods. Just a few adjacent zip codes in the south central part of Los Angeles city host the highest concentrations of returning prisoners. In fact, more than half of those released from prison to parole in the city of Los Angeles live in zip codes that, combined, are home to just 18 percent of adult Angelinos.[9]

In order to examine community organization within Los Angeles County, I rely on data from the Social Capital Community Benchmark Survey.[10] The survey was conducted with a national sample of U.S. citizens, as well as additional samples of roughly 26,700 individuals residing in 42 communities (in 29 states) across the country.[11] Included in these community data is a random sample of 515 people in Los Angeles County. These individuals are drawn from 220 of the county's 487 residential zip codes.[12]

To begin, I merge the Los Angeles subsample from the Social Capital Survey with data on the number and rate per 100 residents of individuals released from prison by county and zip code.[13] Using this combined dataset, I can then examine the relationship between various measures of individuals' social ties and social attitudes, and the relative concentration of people released from prison to their particular geographic area. In order to control for other salient factors that vary among zip codes and also among individuals, I conduct a set of multiple regressions with robust clustered standard errors. In each model I control for the relative urbanicity and population density of the respondents' zip code, as well as respondent demographics (race, gender, education, age, citizenship status), economic well-being (whether currently employed, income below or above $30,000 per year, previous year's household income), residential mobility (length of residence in a community, whether the respondent expects to be living in the community in five years), and household indicators (whether the respondent's home is owned or rented, his or her marital status, and number of children under 18 residing in the household). (Further information on these variables is provided in Appendix I.)

Community Organization and the Concentrated Return of Prisoners
The social attributes of individuals are distinct from the social attributes of communities, and it is important to distinguish between the two levels of analysis. A given individual with extensive social networks and a high level of generalized trust may live in a community where the social landscape is otherwise sparse, and an individual may lack these social attributes despite living in an area that is marked by copious social connectedness.[14] In addition, the sample of respondents from Los Angeles County is small, and the survey asks no questions about criminal justice experience, so we cannot know whether these individuals have had a personal experience of incarceration. We also have no way of knowing whether they have a close friend or associate who has been incarcerated or who has worked inside a prison. Despite these limitations, however, the descriptive patterns evident in these models remain instructive.

I start by examining individuals' evaluations of their personal social networks. I find no relationship between zip code parole concentration and whether individuals say they have a close friend or someone in whom they can confide. Nor is parole concentration predictive of the number of close friends that individuals report or how many people in whom they say they can confide. The rate of parolees returning to one's zip code is, however, positively predictive of the frequency of informal socializing over the past 12 months (Figure 7.2). Specifically,

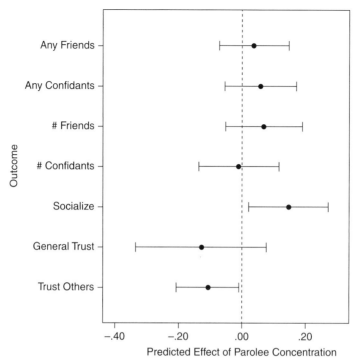

FIGURE 7.2. Parole concentration by zip code and social organization in Los Angeles County.

Note: Results are from OLS regressions and linear probability models with robust clustered standard errors. Coefficients with 95% CI. Additional controls included in all models as described in text.

Source: Los Angeles County release rates from California Department of Corrections and Rehabilitation; attitudinal data from Social Capital Benchmark Survey. N = 376 individuals in 186 zip codes.

those who live in zip codes with a higher parole concentration report that they *more often* have had friends visit them at home, have visited with relatives, have socialized with co-workers outside of work, have hung out with friends in public places, and have played cards and board games with others over the past year than those who live in zip codes with a lower parole concentration, all else equal ($p < .05$ for the scale of these five items). The magnitude of the predicted difference is sizable; holding other factors constant, an increase of 1 point in the parole rate (measured as the number of parolees per 100 adults) is associated with a 15-point increase in the informal socializing scale (ranging from 0 to 1).

Despite their more frequent informal social activities, however, individuals residing in high-parole areas are no more likely to express a sense of generalized trust. Compared with those who live in areas with fewer per capita parolees, those in high-concentration areas are no more or less likely to say that "most people can be trusted" rather than that "you can't be too careful in dealing with people." Indeed, when this question is combined in a standardized index with other questions concerning interpersonal trust – whether individuals feel they can trust their neighbors, their co-workers, their fellow religious congregants, store employees where they shop, and the local police – individuals in higher parole concentration areas actually express *less* social trust. Specifically, every 1-point increase in the zip code parolee rate predicts an 11-point decline in trust of these various groups, all else equal. Nor is this effect driven solely by distrust of the police. The relationship remains significant when trust of local police is removed from the index (p = .01).

In sum, the social patterns in Los Angeles County mirror the atomized communities that are evident in higher-security prisons, where violence is higher and resources are scarce. In zip codes that receive more returning inmates, informal social activities, such as visiting with family and hanging out with friends, is more frequent. Yet, in these same areas, feelings of generalized trust are significantly lower.

Communities and Parole Concentration across the Nation

Do the patterns evident in Los Angeles County generalize beyond this one county and state? Just as there is sizable variation across states and regions in the rate and culture of imprisonment, there is a great deal of geographic variance in the proportion of residents who were released from custody in a given year. For instance, while California released roughly 4.15 prisoners for every 1,000 residents in 2000 and Louisiana released 3.25 per 1,000, the release rate for West Virginia in that year was only 0.70 per 1,000, and the rates for Maine and Massachusetts were just 0.53 and 0.46, respectively. Within these states, parolees are likewise concentrated within particular localities. For instance, in the 10 states that experienced the most substantial prison growth during the 1980s and 1990s – Texas, Florida, California, New York, Michigan, Georgia, Illinois, Ohio, Colorado, and Missouri – 47 counties had 10 percent or more of their total population incarcerated in

2000, 13 counties had 20 percent or more incarcerated, and 2 counties had 30 percent or more residents in prison.[15]

Using population numbers from the 2000 census and zip code data on the number of prisoners released from custody across 13 states,[16] I calculate a rate of recently released prisoners for each zip code (per 100 residents). I then match individuals from the Social Capital Benchmark Survey with the rate of prisoners released to their local community. This provides a survey sample of 11,836 individuals residing in 2,083 unique zip codes.

On average, respondents to the benchmark survey live in zip codes that receive 0.35 released prisoners for every 100 community residents. However, in a given year about 2 percent of respondents receive no prisoners in their zip code, and nearly 30 percent of respondents' localities receive fewer than 0.1 returning prisoners for every 100 residents. At the opposite end of the spectrum, about 2 percent of all benchmark respondents live in zip codes that receive more than four times the sample average (more than 1.5 ex-prisoners for every 100 residents), and two percent of respondents live in zip codes that receive fully 15 for every 100 residents, or about 43 times the sample average.

In order to examine the relationship between the recent ex-prisoner release rate and individual social attitudes, controlling for other factors, I use these combined data to estimate multivariate models with the same set of both individual and zip code controls as in the Los Angeles County data. In addition, in these models I control for census region, as well as local racial composition, mean education and income, median age, average household size, and housing vacancy rate, as well as the rate of reported serious crimes using three separate variables that measure the number of reported murders, the number of aggravated assaults, and the number of all Part I crimes (murder, rape, robbery, aggravated assault, burglary, larceny, motor vehicle theft, and arson) per 1,000 county residents.[17]

The patterns that emerge in these multi-state models are similar to those evident in Los Angeles (see Figure 7.3). Individuals who reside in zip codes with higher concentrations of recent ex-prisoners are no more likely than residents of lower-concentration zip codes to say that they have close friends they "feel at ease with, can talk to about private matters, or call on for help," nor are they less likely to say that they have someone in their life "with whom [they] can share confidences or

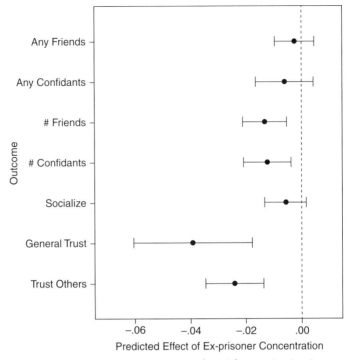

FIGURE 7.3. Ex-prisoner concentration and social organization in 13 states, by zip code.

Note: Results are from OLS regressions with robust clustered standard errors. Coefficients with 95% CI. Additional controls included in all models as described in text.

Source: Release rates from Justice Mapping and state correctional organizations; Attitudinal data from Social Capital Benchmark Survey. N = 10,151 individuals in 1,942 zip codes.

discuss a difficult decision." However, the networks of friends and confidants that individuals in higher-concentration areas report are somewhat smaller, on average, than those maintained by individuals who reside in lower-concentration areas; people who live in zip codes with high concentrations of returning prisoners report fewer close friends and confidants overall.

In addition, the rate of recently returned ex-prisoners in one's community is negatively predictive of the extent of social and generalized trust. Despite being no less likely to report frequently socializing with family and friends, individuals in high-concentration areas are less likely to agree that people can generally be trusted. Instead, they

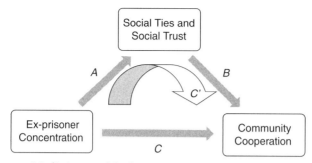

FIGURE 7.4. Mediation model of community cooperation.

are more likely to believe you should be careful in dealing with people. Specifically, a one-point increase in the rate of ex-prisoners (again measured as the number per 100 residents) predicts a 0.04 decline on this measure (scaled from 0 to 1). Likewise, on an index that combines questions about the trustworthiness of various groups, including one's neighbors, co-workers, religious congregants, store employees where they shop, and local police, higher-concentration residents are less likely to express a belief that these people can generally be trusted. On this index (again ranging from 0 to 1), a one-point increase in the ex-prisoner rate predicts about a 0.02 decline in social trust.

Social Trust and Community Cooperation

The data suggest that neighborhoods receiving a high concentration of returning prisoners have a particular set of social dynamics, which in many ways parallel the densely knit and tightly bounded organization of higher-security prisons. These patterns are intriguing, but are they also potentially important for how these communities function? Like other contextual features, such as poverty and residential instability, the concentration of ex-prisoners in a community may affect collective efficacy and community cooperation by influencing patterns of social interaction at the neighborhood level. In essence, social organization might serve as a mediator between ex-prisoner concentration and community empowerment.

I have already established that ex-prisoner concentration has a significant relationship to social ties and social trust (Path *A* in Figure 7.4). In order for mediation to be present, it must also be the case that social ties and trust have a significant relationship to cooperation (Path *B*), that

TABLE 7.1. *Mediation Models of Ex-Prisoner Concentration*

	Effect of Social Variable on Cooperation, Path B	Mediated Proportion of Release Rate on Cooperation, Path C'
General trust	0.04 (.00)	0.05
Social trust	0.25 (.02)	0.25
Number of friends	0.06 (.02)	0.04
Number of confidants	0.03 (.01)	0.01

Note: All models control for all covariates. Table entries are observed coefficients with bootstrap standard errors in parentheses.

ex-prisoner concentration has a direct effect on cooperation (Path C), and that the effect of ex-prisoner concentration on cooperation is diminished by the introduction of social ties and social trust. The indirect effect of concentration on cooperation (Path C') then tells us the portion of the context–cooperation relationship that is accounted for by social organization.

The benchmark survey asks only one question that gauges perceptions of community cooperation, and it is a somewhat imperfect measure: "If public officials asked everyone to conserve water or electricity because of some emergency, how likely is it that people in your community would cooperate?" Responses to this question are significantly predicted by the rate of released ex-prisoners in one's zip code, all else equal. Those who reside in areas with higher ex-prisoner concentrations are somewhat less likely to believe that people in their community would cooperate in the event of an emergency, if asked to do so by a public official. Specifically, an increase of one released prisoner for every 100 community members predicts a decrease in perceived community cooperation of about two percentage points ($p < .001$).

However, the relationship between the local prisoner release rate and perceptions of community cooperation, controlling for the full set of covariates, is partially mediated by social trust (Table 7.1). The data show that, in fact, levels of trust help to explain about a quarter of the relationship between ex-prisoner concentration and cooperation.[18] Evidence is weaker for the mediating role of social ties, although the number of one's close friends appears to partially mediate the effect of ex-prisoners on perceptions of community cooperation. Specifically, about 4 percent of the relationship between ex-prisoner concentration and community cooperation is explained by the extent of friendship networks $(p < .1)$.

Crime, Social Organization and Community Life

Clearly, this is only one measure of community cooperation. Moreover, this measure hinges on individual *perceptions* of cooperation on a single dimension rather than providing a more holistic or objective measure of community members' propensity or ability to engage in collective problem solving. However, these data provide preliminary evidence that social trust helps to explain the relationship between parole concentration and community cohesion.

This is particularly troubling given the many pressing needs of returning prisoners. According to recent estimates, 85 percent are chronic substance abusers and nearly 20 percent have mental health issues. For many, these issues either have never been addressed or are not actively being treated while they are on parole. In addition, about 10 percent of all returning parolees are homeless, with rates reaching 30–50 percent in cities like Los Angeles and San Francisco.[19] Many also have significant health problems, including tuberculosis and HIV. When a large number of these resource-intensive individuals return to a particular geography, it may strain local resources in ways that affect other members of the community. As Susan Mayer and Christopher Jenks note, "Disadvantaged neighbors are a disadvantage."[20]

A high concentration of returning prisoners may likewise undermine local economic stability. Estimates suggest that between 70 and 90 percent of people are unemployed when they are released from prison, and fully 50 percent are functionally illiterate.[21] This is likely to make it difficult for them to find employment. In addition, as the work of Devah Pager and others shows, job seekers are significantly disadvantaged by a criminal record, especially if they are also African American.[22] Given this reality, it is likely that high concentrations of ex-prisoners serve to depress the economic situation of particular geographies. For instance, businesses may choose not to locate in these areas, both because they prefer to be nearer to potential hiring pools and also because high-unemployment areas offer fewer potential customers with readily disposable income. The appearance of so-called food deserts – geographic areas with limited access to grocery stores and other sources of nutritious food – in low-income areas is just one example of this phenomenon.

In addition, to the extent that incarceration increases the likelihood of recidivism, receiving communities enter into an iterative feedback loop: disorder breeds crime, which leads to incarceration, which further undermines community cohesion necessary for controlling crime. There are at least three distinct ways that a high ex-prisoner concentration might increase social disorder and crime rates. First, and most obviously, individuals returning from prison bring back to their communities the particular social attitudes and behavior that they develop while incarcerated. Anti-social attitudes acquired in prison are likely to be particularly durable among those former prisoners who remain embedded in prison social networks after release, such as might occur when prison-based gangs notify street-based affiliates that a parolee is coming home.

Second, living in an area that hosts a high concentration of people returning from prison might predict individuals' social ties and orientations, even if they themselves have not been to prison; prison socialization may have a spillover or contagion effect on friends and family.[23] Because individuals develop social norms from those with whom they have "frequent or sustained contact and interaction,"[24] the geographic concentration of individuals with particular social attitudes can influence the social attitudes of those around them. This can occur through explicit teaching from one's role models and peers, as well as through the more subtle processes of behavior modeling of others in the community.

Moreover, if prisoners learn hostile or aggressive attitudes while incarcerated, they may establish those attitudes as normative within certain segments of the community to which they return. For instance, the concentration of ex-prisoners may reduce the social stigma associated with serving time in prison, which will lessen the effectiveness of incarceration as a potential deterrent to criminal behavior.[25] In Robert Putnam's work on social capital, he suggests that some communities may then become trapped in a "vicious circle, in which low levels of trust and cohesion lead to higher levels of crime, which lead to even lower levels of trust and cohesion."[26] Youth may be particularly susceptible to the influence of these subgroup community norms, as they learn what social norms and "modes of behavior"[27] are valued and embodied by those around them. In this way, social ties, particularly in disadvantaged communities, may help incubate an oppositional social culture – for instance, a "legal cynicism"[28] or the use of violence as a defensive posture.[29] Thus, social networks can actually contribute to the "contagion" of social deviance and other problem behaviors.[30] Modern studies of gangs, for instance, often focus on the role of strong social networks in the diffusion of oppositional norms.[31]

The "cultural transmission" of deviance is not a new idea.[32] Rather, scholars have long focused attention on the potential for dense social networks to promote "downward leveling norms".[33] In his studies of labor and the underclass, William Julius Wilson suggests that communities lacking organizational resources will be characterized by strong social connectedness, but that their particular social structure will facilitate rather than inhibit the emergence of social problems.[34] This idea is echoed in other work that sees neighborhood ecology as an important determinant of whether social connectedness will have prosocial or oppositional effects.[35] While in some contexts sturdy social ties can provide positive "capital," in others a "protocultural tolerance of deviant behavioral adaptation emerges, resulting in the further diffusion of violence, illicit drug use, early childrearing, and a host of other problem behaviors."[36]

Finally, the removal and return of individuals through imprisonment, what Dina Rose and Todd Clear call "coercive mobility,"[37] may also affect community social organization. Coercive mobility has a destabilizing influence on community social relations, as social networks are constantly disrupted and the roles that offenders filled prior to their removal are not taken on by others. In particular, the subtraction of a large number of individuals (primarily men) from communities weakens families, reduces the marriage prospects of women, strains parental involvement, weakens economic stability, and minimizes the ability of communities to form a stable and diverse social infrastructure.[38] Coercive mobility also decreases the supervision of young men in the area and strains the capacity of families and communities seeking to socialize and monitor youth.[39] In this way, hyper-imprisonment can actually damage the ability of communities to control crime; as Rose and Clear suggest, "Over reliance on incarceration as a formal control may hinder the ability of some communities to foster other forms of control because they weaken family and community structures.... Thus, these communities may experience more, not less, social disorganization."[40]

Certainly, the social effects of incarceration, particularly on families, are not entirely straightforward. Many incarcerated people were likely involved in activities prior to imprisonment that strained their relationships and detrimentally affected their communities. However, numerous studies have concluded that the effects of incarceration for families are a "net negative";[41] Clear argues, "When intimates are removed to prison, people often respond by isolating themselves in ways that undermine norms of cooperation and mutual support."[42] Removing residents quickly alters the density of social networks, which in turn "weakens attachment to the neighborhood and ties to neighbors."[43]

It is, of course, likewise true that former inmates can and often do have a positive impact on the communities to which they return. These individuals can provide positive examples of criminal desistance and sobriety, and many previously incarcerated people play a critical role in community-based organizations working to reduce community violence and strengthen community ties. Unfortunately, however, it is likely that most of these individuals are able to take on this social role in spite of, rather than due to, the experiences they have in prison.

Conclusion

Scholars have long been concerned with the relationship between crime and community social organization. In early "systemic" models of community social life, structural factors such as poverty, ethnic heterogeneity, and residential stability were seen as undermining neighbor networks and social bonds. This, in turn, reduced the capacity of communities to address issues of common concern.[44] More recent theories of social disorganization have also started from the idea that neighborhood well-being depends on a strong social infrastructure, which helps generate cohesion among community members.[45] For instance, the work of Robert Sampson and others suggests that "collective efficacy," defined as the willingness of community members to get involved in enforcing shared norms and monitoring behavior, leads to lower rates of crime, even in communities with high poverty rates.[46] James Coleman, one of the first to articulate the importance of shared norms of cooperation in maintaining order, wrote: "Effective norms that inhibit crime make it possible to walk freely outside at night in a city and enable old persons to leave their houses without fear for their safety."[47] When people trust one another and feel a sense of solidarity, they are more likely to watch out for each other and for their collective interests.[48]

Conversely, neighborhoods that lack social cohesion are likely to experience higher rates of crime, which may further reduce levels of trust. Putnam explores this notion in *Bowling Alone*, where he posits that a lack of social connectedness may lead individuals to develop an individualistic "kill or be killed" attitude. In response to the question "Do you agree or disagree with the following sentence: I'd do better than average in a fist fight," Putnam finds that "citizens in states characterized by low levels of social capital are readier for a fight (perhaps because they need to be), and they are predisposed to mayhem."[49] These individual social attitudes have aggregate consequences for communities, helping to explain why communities with "sparse" social networks and low rates of civic engagement have a greater risk of crime and violence.[50] In fact, Putnam concludes from a state-level regression analysis that "social capital is about as important as poverty, urbanism, and racial composition as a determinant of homicide prevalence."[51]

The primary focus of these models is whether and how the social features of a community produce or undermine social solidarity and trust, thereby contributing to or detracting from community capacity. Poverty, unemployment, and similar contextual factors are discussed as salient predictors of social organization at the community level; economic decline, population migration, and institutional ecology are all complicit. However, the emphasis in these accounts is primarily on cultural or structural rather than political forces. Even recent studies of gangs, which at one time portrayed these criminal networks as integrally linked to the local political machine,[52] have generally abandoned this idea.[53] Thus, the state as purposive actor receives little mention. Instead, informal social control is considered mostly as a precursor to and catalyst for the dissemination of particular values, rather than as a consequence of specific public policies or political institutions.[54]

In this chapter, I have focused on the explicit role of the state in shaping social community. The results I have uncovered suggest that the types of social ties that are formed and maintained in America's more violent and punitive prisons – a fragmented form of social organization marked by social groups that are both densely knit and tightly bounded – are also broadly characteristic of the communities to which ex-prisoners predominantly return.

It bears repeating that I am unable here to tell a causal story about prison effects at the community level, nor is that my purpose; my focus in this chapter has been purely descriptive. However, as Todd Clear cogently argues in a recent review of the literature:

As we travel through the host of studies bearing on the ways in which incarceration effects are felt through the range of human patterns in families, communities, and the polity, at some point the limitations of design begin to become less important than the sheer logical power of consistently problematic outcomes realized in domain after domain. What emerges is a tightly coupled system of effects, many small; but when these are aggregated, they make up an overwhelming dynamic of which incarceration is a significant part.... In another context, I referred to this system of effects as "death by a thousand cuts."[55]

Moreover, it is clear from the data that the disjointed social character of the communities to which inmates disproportionately return is likely to make it difficult for these areas to address problems of collective concern. Instead, the social effects of prison are likely to only exacerbate the existing problems of community disorganization these areas face, as large and concentrated groups of individuals exit prison.

The results I have presented suggest that prisons are not hermetically sealed storage areas that exist outside our borders. Rather, they are small enclaves of violence, disorder, and "most complete despotism"[56] that are scattered throughout our cities and towns. A growing segment of society will spend at least some length of time steeped in the increasingly harsh and often violent culture that dominates these micro-societies. For individuals leaving prison, social orientations are not likely to be confined there. Instead, individuals carry the prison experience with them when they emerge, in the form of social identities, networks, and attitudes that have the potential to further discourage generalized trust and cooperative engagement in the areas to which they return.[57]

8

The Road to Reform

> *The causal way of looking at things always answers only the question,
> "Why?" but never "To what end?" ... However, if someone asks,
> "For what purpose should we help one another, make life easier for
> each other, make beautiful music together, have inspired thoughts"
> he would have to be told, "If you don't feel the reasons, no one can
> explain them to you."*
>
> *Without this primary feeling we are nothing and had better not live
> at all.*
>
> Albert Einstein, *Collected Papers*[1]

Bedford-Stuyvesant, Brooklyn, once called the "largest ghetto in the
country,"[2] is home to more than 150,000 people. The area has undergone a great deal of development in recent years, but it still holds pockets of extreme disadvantage. It suffers high rates of crime, poverty, and
unemployment. Its residents are also disproportionately affected by
incarceration. As the Bedford-Stuyvesant Restoration Corporation, a
43-year-old community non-profit, notes: "The cycles of poverty and
low academic achievement have seemingly been intractable, channeling children into the cradle to prison pipeline. Bedford-Stuyvesant
has the highest rate of adult prison admissions in Brooklyn."[3] In
"Bed-Stuy," as in many other places around the country, prisons have
become a central institution in the lives of an extraordinary number
of people.

In light of this, it is perhaps easy to understand why some took offense at the children's play structure that the city erected behind one of the neighborhood's public housing projects. The play set was fairly typical, constructed in bright oranges and purples with a low silver slide. However, rather than depicting a castle or car or tree house, or one of a dozen other traditional children's themes, the main feature of the playground was designed to resemble a jail, complete with a large painted lock and small barred windows on a festive blue, child-sized door. In a community where a large proportion of children have at least one parent who has served time behind bars, in a neighborhood that contributes a disproportionate number of its residents to state prison populations, behind a public housing project that was notorious for gang activity, the government installed an incarceration-themed play structure for kids.

Given how many families in this community must have harbored the legitimate fear that their children would someday have to acclimate to the realities of imprisonment, the choice of playground motif was perplexing. As the parent of one six-year-old who regularly played at the playground complained, "It's a blatant message like, jail is where you'll end up at. We want to see positive images in the playgrounds."[4] To many concerned parents and community members, the message sent by the play set was that playacting the part of The Convict or The Inmate was to be expected for this particular group of youth, and even encouraged. As another local parent noted, "It was like promoting kids to go to jail."[5]

When asked about the play structure, a spokesperson for the New York City Housing Authority (NYCHA) reported that the city had received no formal complaints about it, despite at least one resident claiming that she had twice tried covering the word "JAIL" with spray paint, only to have it restored a few weeks later.[6] It was not until the national news media caught on to the story in 2010, prompting widespread public interest and outcry, that city officials ultimately painted over the large letters and replaced the theme of the structure with an outer-space motif.[7] This seemed to put an end to the sordid and slightly bizarre tale.

But what is notable about the bright orange play structure that stood for six years in this historically black, low-income neighborhood is not that public officials were so quick to get rid of it when the wider public finally took note. Rather, what is remarkable is that the city seemed to consider it so completely *unremarkable* for so long. It is difficult to imagine how the bureaucrat who ordered the playground – and there was some evidence that the jail playground had actually been special ordered for the public housing unit – failed to anticipate the potential offense that the structure might convey. However, by all reports, administrators at NYCHA thought it to be such a mundane choice that they had no immediately available record of how the equipment had been selected in the first place; a *New York Times* article noted that the housing authority "was at a loss to explain how the decision to order the play set was made."[8]

Perhaps one explanation for how the playground came to be is that, in the United States today, the so-called cradle-to-prison pipeline has taken on a distressing inevitability. In a recent report, the Bureau of Justice Statistics estimated that if recent correctional trends persisted, roughly 1 in every 9 young men born in 2001 could expect to spend at least some time in prison, but 1 in every 3 *black* males growing up in the United States today could expect to serve time at some point during his life. For a Latino boy, the lifetime risk is about 1 in 6.[9] The odds are even higher for the many minority youth being raised in America's most impoverished urban ghettos, like sections of Bed-Stuy, where they attend failing schools, live in aging public housing stock, and are exposed to disproportionate rates of crime relative to kids raised in wealthier – and whiter – suburban and rural neighborhoods.

The results presented in this study suggest that the experience of incarceration can have real consequences for the kinds of people these youth will become and the types of communities to which they will return. As Beaumont and de Tocqueville opined in 1833 after witnessing prison conditions in the American South, "In locking up the criminals nobody thinks of rendering them better, but only taming their malice; they are put in chains like ferocious beasts; and instead of being corrected, they are rendered brutal."[10] It would appear that their assessment of America's more punitive prisons holds nearly as true today.

On Punishment and Community

In this book, I have argued that the choices states make about how to respond to crime play an important role in shaping the way individuals engage with one another. Both a period of incarceration as an inmate and days spent "behind the walls" as a correctional officer result in the separation of individuals from their family networks and familiar social supports for long and intensive periods. Simultaneously, these individuals are immersed in a new institutional context that has profound implications for the character of their social networks and the types of norms these networks foster. In particular, the level of threat individuals perceive as they go about their daily lives, as well as the resources they have at their disposal, will influence the social groups they are likely to join.

As the results presented in the preceding chapters have shown, adapting to incarceration in a higher-security prison can actually increase the scope of an individual's social networks. However, these social ties may be largely criminal, as indicated by evidence that those assigned to higher-security prisons have more friends in gangs than do those assigned to less punitive prisons. Perhaps more important, these new social ties can alter social attitudes. This is most evident in norms governing interpersonal relationships. Inmates assigned to higher-custody settings are significantly more likely to report aggressive attitudes toward others and are subsequently more likely to recidivate following release.

Differences in the formal and informal culture of prison have consequences for correctional officers' adaptation processes, too. Prison work can strain officers' relationships with friends and family, and shape social interactions and work-related problem solving within the prison context. In addition, new officers assigned to higher-security prisons become less supportive of rehabilitation programs and come to perceive inmates more negatively than officers in lower-custody institutions; they are less likely to consider inmates "regular people" and more likely to perceive them as dangerous and deviant.

These findings add to a growing list of collateral consequences associated with policies of mass incarceration. First, and most basically, it has not gone without notice that imprisonment in the United States is now a substantial site of public spending (see Figure 8.1). The Vera Institute of Justice puts the annual per inmate cost to taxpayers at an average of $31,307, ranging to as high as $54,865 and $60,076 in states like New Jersey and New York, respectively.[11] In fact, much of the total growth in criminal justice costs over the recent period

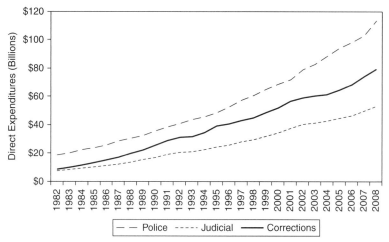

FIGURE 8.1. Direct expenditures for justice functions, 1982–2008.
Source: Justice Expenditure and Employment Abstracts, Bureau of Justice Statistics.

can be accounted for by the rapidly rising costs of corrections; compared with increases in per capita expenditures for police and judicial/legal functions, which grew by 241 and 321 percent, respectively, per capita spending on corrections increased fully 423 percent.[12] Joan Petersilia notes, however, that "these dollars have not funded more programs but rather prison staff, construction, and rising health care costs."[13] Growth in spending on state corrections has likewise outpaced increases in state expenditures for education and Medicaid. One out of every 15 general fund dollars is now spent on corrections; in some states, 1 in every 10 goes to this function.[14]

In addition to its growing fiscal burden, American prison policy levies a substantial non-monetary cost.[15] Scholars have convincingly shown that incarceration reduces job prospects,[16] harms health,[17] and decreases political trust.[18] Moreover, these individual effects have aggregate consequences. Because low-income and minority individuals are over-represented among the currently and formerly imprisoned, mass incarceration exacerbates racial and income inequality, further stratifying American society.[19] For instance, Rucker Johnson and Steve Raphael find that higher incarceration rates among black men help to account for racial disparities in HIV transmission rates among women;[20] Devah Pager finds a sizable effect of a criminal record on job prospects in the low-wage labor market, particularly for black men;[21] and Bruce Western and colleagues have shown that racial disparities in marriage rates would be halved without existing patterns of incarceration.[22]

Mass imprisonment also has explicitly political consequences. Inmates, parolees, and probationers face a "complex network of invisible punishments"[23] that include restrictions on welfare receipt, public housing eligibility, federal education grants, professional licenses, and a host of other material benefits and markers of social standing. Nearly all states also restrict voting rights to felons for some period of time. The result is that, across the country, almost 9 million U.S. citizens, or about 1 of every 40 adults, are now restricted from voting due to a felony conviction. The proportion is significantly higher among black Americans. In this group, 1 of every 13 is disenfranchised, and in three states, more than 1 in every 5 blacks is denied the right to vote.[24] Elsewhere, in work that I conducted in collaboration with Vesla Weaver, we find that the increased prevalence of incarceration has also remade the nature of Americans' subjective experience of government. When the most frequent or memorable experience citizens have with government is through its institutions of confinement, they come to see politics as something to be avoided rather than participated in.

This book adds one additional facet to this substantial list of incarceration's unintended consequences: the social effects of prison. As I have shown here, a prison is not a "deep freeze" and individuals do not enter and exit prison unchanged. Instead, time spent in prison can be deeply formative for individuals' social attitudes and beliefs.

Of equal importance, however, my intention here has been to refocus attention on what happens *inside* prison institutions. In this book, I have argued that scholars must not only attend to, and contend with, the proportion of Americans who experience prison, but also the types of prison they experience. The findings presented in this volume thus bring to light two important features of the prison experience.

First, these results make clear that prisons are *socializing* institutions. As Betty Cogwell writes, "Socialization is the process by which individuals prepare for participation *in the society in which they live*."[25] Individuals adapt to the institutional and social dynamics of their surroundings, in substantial part by transforming their own conceptions and practice of appropriate interpersonal interaction; prison culture creates "a psychological environment within the physical environment provided."²⁶ Variation in the way prison institutions are constructed has significant consequences for the way prisons are experienced by those who pass through them. Thus, the type of society we promote in prison dictates the types of citizens these institutions produce.

Second, prisons are *social* institutions. Individuals do not experience prison alone. Rather, they become part of a highly structured social context. Learning to navigate more punitive prisons entails a process of social adaptation and integration, and the particular form of social organization that develops in prison can be predicted by the context in which it is created. While the specific forms of social connectedness that are adopted and entrenched in prison may serve inmates and officers well within the culture of the prison, it does not create the types of social ties that are likely to help them reintegrate into the families and communities that will welcome them home. This explains, at least in part, the effects of higher-security prisons on the recidivism rates of inmates and on the work–family conflict experienced by officers.

In the modern era of the punitive prison, it is therefore not only the case that fewer inmates receive rehabilitation services, despite larger numbers of inmates needing such help than ever before.²⁷ Nor is it only the case that officers encounter more violence in the workplace, even as they report that they have no reliable place to turn for support when work-related issues arise. Certainly these are important consequences of the punitive turn, which each result in more people exiting prison with unmet needs. At the same time, though, America's harsher prison environments are creating *new* needs. That is, the experience of incarceration can *itself* become a factor in shaping social deficits, producing individuals who are less capable of contributing to their communities in positive ways.

Mitigating Negative Effects

The most obvious way to mitigate the negative results I have described is to reduce the number of individuals sent to prison, irrespective of the culture of the particular institution. This could be accomplished by stemming the pipeline to prison, enacting policies that address the educational deficits and acute poverty that are highly predictive of criminal offending. However, though it may be "easier to build strong children than to repair broken men,"[28] it is often difficult to convince governments to do either. Reducing the prison population can also be accomplished in the shorter term, through sentencing reforms that seek to "turn back" the criminal code and reduce the use of incarceration for non-violent and drug-related crimes.[29] Because low criminal history offenders seem particularly susceptible to the negative socializing effects of imprisonment, this would be an important first step.

In fact, California recently undertook a massive reform effort, termed "realignment," designed to lower its non-violent prison population and substantially reduce overcrowding in state prisons.[30] The reform, signed into law by Governor Jerry Brown in April 2011 under pressure from the California courts, stipulates that all newly convicted offenders as of October 1, 2011, who are "non-violent, non-serious, and non-sex offenders" will not be sent to state prison, but instead will be remanded to the custody of local jails or probation authorities. The data I have presented in this study describe the condition of the state's correctional system prior to the implementation of these new procedures. However, realignment will doubtless have important consequences for the way individuals experience the criminal justice system in California.

De-carceration is hardly a novel suggestion. However, as I have written elsewhere[31] and as others have similarly noted,[32] the danger in hailing declining incarceration rates as a singular sign of progress is that they may be accompanied by declining expenditures for in-prison services. Such is currently the case with recent prison reforms, as Robert Weisberg and Joan Petersilia report: "While prison and parole populations are decreasing across the United States, the very programs necessary for success in reentry are disappearing. We can choose our favorite metaphoric cliché: this is a perfect storm, a recipe for disaster, a crash-and-burn scenario."[33] If this is the case, then lowering the prison rate will decrease the total number of individuals who are exposed to a potentially criminogenic prison environment but will potentially increase problems for the many who will inevitably be left behind.

It is therefore critical that scholars, practitioners, and policymakers continue to take a serious look at the reigning culture and character of the modern American prison. Observers of criminal justice practice in the United States today have expressed grave concerns about the effects of "heavy-handed attempts to reduce crime."[34] As such, calls for a reduction in the imprisonment rate have long been a central feature of the reform agenda. However, in the push to decrease the use of prisons, we must not lose sight of the need to simultaneously improve them.

This study provides a critical starting point for this task, by presenting substantial evidence that the prison is not a violent place solely, or even primarily, because inmates are violent. As Donald Specter, director of the non-profit Prison Law Office, rightly noted in his 2005 testimony to the Commission on Safety and Abuse in America's Prisons, "[T]he degree of institutional violence is not dependent on the prisoners. It is a direct product of prison conditions and how the state operates its prisons.... When [violent and mentally ill] inmates are placed together in overcrowded, antiquated facilities with inadequate mental health services and nothing constructive to do, violence is inevitable."[35] Certainly, the results presented in the preceding chapters lend sizable support to this assertion. Even holding constant the prior "criminality" of inmates entering prison, America's increasingly punitive correctional institutions yield results that run counter to their crime-reduction mission.

This is not an intrinsic feature of the prison institution, though; rather, it results from a revocable choice. As Bert Useem and Anne Piehl surmise, "the causes of disorder do not lie in the inherent defects of prison, [or] unalterable 'structural' conditions...This is implied by the fact that prisons and prison systems can turn from order to disorder, or the reverse, fairly rapidly. Agency looms large: people running prisons can change the conditions that produce order. It can be created, or destroyed, by altering the *relationships* among prison management, staff, inmates, and outside authorities."[36] In order to reduce the prevalence of prison violence, and thereby change the culture that helps motivate processes of negative socialization, corrections administrators would be wise to pay attention not only to the individual offender, but to how institutional context shapes the types of relationships and communities that form within each prison.

First, a substantial reduction in overcrowding would go a long way toward alleviating the pressures of prison time. Tensions are bound to arise when people are forced to live on top of each other, triple-bunked in hallways and gymnasiums. As scholars of social connectedness have increasingly come to realize, "It turns out that what matters is not whether an environment *makes* people interact, but rather whether it gives residents the *option* to interact."[37] On this issue, David Halpern writes:

As an extensive study of neighbouring behaviour concluded: 'good fences make good neighbors.' In other words, positive social relationships rest on the ability to regulate your social interactions with others, so that you have some feeling of control over when, and how much, you interact with those concerned.[38]

Addressing other institutional factors that contribute to negative prison culture – particularly the proliferation of prison gangs – is likewise essential. This is an issue that wardens and other prison administrators are already taking seriously in most correctional systems. Increasingly, however, suppression and isolation have been the primary tactics employed to control gang behavior inside prisons.[39] For example, many systems have attempted to decrease violence by creating special housing units where members or leaders of gangs are kept separate from the rest of the facility's prisoners. Other prisons place gang-affiliated inmates or the leaders of prison gangs into isolation cells, where they are held in solitary confinement. Describing what he refers to as severe conditions inside one such segregated isolation unit, Phillip Kassel writes:

Prisoners are released from their cell merely one hour per day during four days of every five day cycle. On the fifth day they do not leave their cells at all. Out-of-cell activities – showers, personal and legal telephone calls, medical care, and two brief non-contact visitation periods per week – are invariably scheduled during prisoners' one hour release time. Library access, institutional canteen purchases, and outside property receipts are extremely restricted. Education, treatment and work opportunities are virtually non-existent.[40]

This type of "supermax" prison has proliferated in recent years as a response to prison disorder; such prisons, which were "once a novelty, have become common."[41] However, experts on the psychiatric effects of solitary confinement have found that isolating people for long periods of time can result in agitation, psychotic disorganization, and even persistent mental illness. It can likewise erode the capacity for social engagement. In one study, Stuart Grassian argues that the long-term effects of solitary confinement are "commonly manifested by a continued intolerance of social interaction, a handicap which often prevents the inmate from successfully readjusting to the broader social environment of the general population in prison and, perhaps more significantly, often severely impairs the inmate's capacity to reintegrate into the broader community upon release from imprisonment."[42] While placing people inside "prisons within a prison" might be successful at reducing short-term gang-related tensions, pursuing this goal might come at the expense of the long-term health of these individuals and their communities.

Moreover, practitioners have begun to question the efficacy of the isolation model in actually suppressing gang activity.[43] In a national survey of prison administrators, more than half expressed their belief that segregating prison gang members is ineffective in reducing prison violence.[44] (Other surveys have found somewhat higher levels of support for this and similar approaches.)[45] For wardens and correctional officers whose primary aim is securing safety and order, punitive gang suppression techniques may be seen as having the potential to backfire. In one case, separation of gang members led to "gangs seizing control of the prisons and resulted in increased levels of violence against both inmates and staff."[46] In fact, segregation of gang members may actually lead to increased gang cohesiveness, as members experience greater solidarity through heightened self-identification and proximity.[47] Similarly, relocating gang members and leaders to other prisons may help to reduce violence at the sending facility, but it can result in the spread of gangs to new facilities.[48]

In light of these concerns, some prisons have recently begun to switch gears. Rather than imposing isolation on suspected gang members, they now "actively promote integration."[49] Gang treatment programs that follow this model have been tried in a number of states, and several have been evaluated as effective.[50] For example, one program in Massachusetts provided gang members with targeted training designed to help them safely reintegrate into the general population. It reported that after two years only 17 of the 190 participants had been returned to segregation for gang activity.[51] Likewise, the administrators of a gang integration intervention at California's Pelican Bay Prison reported that just 5 percent of prisoners enrolled had failed to complete the program, only a small few had been sent back to segregation, and program participants recidivated at one-third the rate of non-participants.[52] As more of these programs emerge, developing a theory of best practices and conducting randomized controlled studies to examine their efficacy will be essential.

Many of the lessons learned from these gang interventions can also be applied to the general population. Providing all inmates with structured opportunities in which to build supportive, pro-social networks is likely to be critical in channeling individual socialization during incarceration. There are three ways this could proceed. First, contact with those in the general public might play an important role. Maintaining contact with family members outside prison might serve as one way that the pro-social norms of mainstream society can be communicated and maintained, helping inmates to (re-)engage with the norms and habits of the broader social and legal culture.[53] To facilitate this process, many correctional systems would need to alter their current practices in order to ensure that inmates, whenever possible, are imprisoned in geographic proximity to the spouses, partners, and children who might provide a positive social influence.

Second, correctional administrators might actively promote the regular (if controlled) movement of outsiders within the prison who can interact productively with groups of inmates. For instance, prison administrators might forge productive and ongoing partnerships with outside groups, making prisons systematically more accessible to non-profits, researchers, churches, and other visitors. Some prisons already do this through organizations such as Narcotics Anonymous and Alcoholics Anonymous, which form groups within prisons that are often facilitated by an outside volunteer. However, many more do not. For instance, according to data from the CCOS, fully 54 percent of California correctional officers report that community members, excluding inmates' friends and family members, either never enter the prison facility where they work or do so only rarely.

Finally, prisons might also think critically about how to safely foster positive social ties between incarcerated inmates. By allowing individuals to interact in controlled environments where cooperative behavior is encouraged, and by providing strong and clear incentives for this behavior, prison programs can encourage inmates to engage with others in shared and meaningful experiences. This, in turn, might help reduce conflict between groups.[54] Peer tutoring programs, education classes, AA meetings, group therapy, and inmate religious communities might therefore serve as important counterbalances to other types of prison associations, such as gangs, that urge the adoption of violent and aggressive attitudes. These types of programs may also help to provide "identity alternatives" to gang members and others with a criminal history,[55] giving individuals a source of self-identification that is not rooted solely in their ties to the gang or their criminal past.

Reconceptualizing prison programs in this way would require us to expand our conception of rehabilitation to incorporate the role of the inmate community. Currently, prison-based interventions and their effects are most often studied and understood as being about the individual. They are designed to "fix" people who are deemed to be broken or flawed. However, when well-conceived, these programs might do more than address the needs of individual inmates; they might also help to create and bolster new social bonds through which positive norms can develop. As Specter reasons in his testimony before Congress: "Instead of creating a culture of suppression and isolation, [programs can] provide a transition to a more normal way of life, even if it is limited to the confines of the prison. Given time and help, the prisoners adapt to this culture and recognize its value."[56] The promise of these programs is that the norms they cultivate within the group will be transferred to interpersonal interactions more broadly, influencing relationships throughout the prison and into the world beyond.

The Political Feasibility of Change

The reforms proposed in the preceding sections are ambitious; they require a fundamental reversion in our collective thinking about the purpose of imprisonment. But are they realistic? After all, countless studies have documented the "collateral consequences" of incarceration in the punitive era and there is no shortage of work citing the correlation between rehabilitation programs and reductions in recidivism. Yet it is the *politics* of crime, not crime rates alone, that have largely driven America's modern approach to crime control. As Michael Jacobson of the Vera Institute writes:

[A] powerful tautology is at work in the U.S. correctional system. New laws are constantly being passed and policies enacted that ensure more people will serve prison time each year. More people going to prison means more people coming out of prison. As greater numbers are released, almost half will wind up back in prison three years later. The result is that the politics of punishment, combined with the day-to-day workings of the correctional system, poses an apparently insurmountable obstacle to the task of reversing present trends.... This self-perpetuating system seems almost unstoppable.[57]

I (and others, including Jacobson) would argue that there is reason to be tentatively optimistic that the time for change has come[58] and that rehabilitation finally may be "back on the table."[59] A clear harbinger of this nascent change is that incarceration rates appear to have slowed over the past decade.[60] In fact, 2008 marked the first year since 1972 that the state prison population decreased. The average size of the decline was small – just less than 1 percent – but notable nonetheless in contrast to the past four decades of growth. And in 2011, 26 states had declining incarceration rates, which ranged in size from 1 to 16 percent.[61]

Several explanations have been offered for the appearance of this "window of opportunity"[62] for policy change, if indeed one has appeared. First, states faced with severe budget deficits have sensibly begun considering where to cut expenditures, and prisons are a prime target.[63] At least 15 states have already undertaken justice reinvestment strategies, which seek to identify cost-saving measures in corrections and "reinvest" some of these savings into recidivism reduction efforts. Notably, among the first to take such measures were the relatively conservative states of Texas and Kansas.[64] Scholars from the Center for Economic and Policy Research estimate that halving the incarceration rate of non-violent offenders alone would lower the cost of corrections by $16.9 billion annually. They argue that "these savings could be achieved without any appreciable deterioration in public safety."[65] Importantly, several other studies point to states that have been able to successfully reduce their correctional populations *and* increase prison-based programs in response to budget crises.[66]

A second herald of reform is a relatively recent political movement by conservatives to soften their position on crime control. As in the 1970s, when liberals and conservatives were momentarily aligned in calling for changes in the culture and practice of American corrections, the most recent period has seen bipartisan coalitions re-emerge. Indeed, a recent *Newsweek* article describes a remarkable dinner between the criminologist David Kennedy, Tea Party leader Mark Meckler (whose mother was formerly an officer with the Los Angeles Police Department and then a California correctional officer), civil rights leader Benjamin Chavis, "Texas oilman" Tim Dunn, and the MSNBC host Dylan Ratigan to discuss criminal justice reform. Kennedy described the four-hour summit as "a meeting of the minds, and of what are usually opposing cultures, that really represents the larger evolution going on right now."[67]

As *Newsweek* noted, "One rustic Italian dinner does not, of course, a revolution make." However, this "revolution" is more broadly reflected in a joint project of the conservative Texas Public Policy Foundation and the Prison Fellowship, called Right on Crime. In its public statement, the organization argues:

> Conservatives are known for being tough on crime, but we must also be tough on criminal justice spending. That means demanding more cost-effective approaches that enhance public safety. A clear example is our reliance on prisons, which serve a critical role by incapacitating dangerous offenders and career criminals but are not the solution for every type of offender. And in some instances, they have the unintended consequence of hardening nonviolent, low-risk offenders – making them a greater risk to the public than when they entered.

The organization cites an array of notable conservative voices – Rick Perry of Texas, Sam Brownback of Kansas, Tom Coburn of Oklahoma, and former president George W. Bush along with his brother, Jeb Bush, of Florida – calling for reductions in recidivism through rehabilitation programs, drug treatment, and the facilitation of post-release employment. Some of these individuals express concern about incarceration on economic grounds, but the conservative argument is often also framed as an ethical and religious one. As Chris Cannon, a former Republican member of Congress from Utah and co-founder of the Congressional Caucus to Fight and Control Methamphetamine argued, "The system has a very strong tendency to change them [offenders] for the worse. Everybody knows that, I think. Our current system is fundamentally immoral."[68]

Finally, however ironically, it may ultimately be the immense scale of the modern American prison system that will make possible its transformation. Prisons historically are relatively closed environments. Indeed, as Jonathan Simon points out, "the conditions of life in the vast expanse of male prisons in the US have become largely invisible even to the best informed Americans."[69] This has led scholars and activists to express considerable concern about the accountability of correctional systems,[70] even as they have documented a host of severe problems in American prisons, from overcrowding to abuse. These trepidations have only grown over time, as prison systems have erected "ever-higher barriers for journalists attempting to cover what happens behind prison walls."[71] By placing legal restrictions on communication between inmates, as well as between inmates and the broader public (including the media), prisons have substantially undercut the public availability of information about the daily practice of criminal justice. This disturbing trend led Justice William O. Douglas to warn:

Prisons, like all other public institutions, are ultimately the responsibility of the populace. Crime, like the economy, health, education, defense, and the like, is a matter of grave concern in our society, and people have the right and the necessity to know not only of the incidence of crime, but of the effectiveness of the system designed to control it. "On any given day, approximately 1,500,000 people are under the authority of [federal, state, and local prison] systems. The cost to taxpayers is over one billion dollars annually. Of those individuals sentenced to prison, 98% will return to society." The public's interest in being informed about prisons is thus paramount.[72]

Yet there is one way in which the prison system has actually become less obscured to Americans over time: in the modern era, the American prison system has reached such proportions that a majority of people now claim some type of personal or vicarious experience with it. In a 2006 survey by the National Center for State Courts (NCSC) of a representative sample of American adults, 54 percent of respondents said that they had either spent time in prison or jail or worked in a correctional facility, or knew someone who had. Of those who had some type of personal experience with corrections, more than half (57 percent) reported that the experience had changed their "impressions of life behind bars."[73]

It is impossible to judge the degree to which public perceptions reported in a survey reflect a true effect of personal experience on people's attitudes. However, it is clear from the NCSC data that having a personal connection to prison is significantly correlated with a variety of attitudes toward incarceration and crime control. First and foremost, those with personal or vicarious prison experience are more likely than those without such experience to believe that elected officials, law enforcement and police officers, prosecutors and district attorneys, and judges are doing a poor job of serving the public. They are also more likely to believe that prison, probation, and parole authorities are failing (chi sq. 8.21, $p < .05$).

People who have personal experience with the American prison system also think somewhat differently about criminal offenders and the best ways to address crime. Specifically, those with personal prison experience are more likely to believe that "given the right conditions, many offenders can turn their lives around and become law-abiding citizens" (chi sq. 4.65, $p < .05$).[74] In addition, when asked to choose what they believe to be the top priority in dealing with crime, those with personal prison experience are more likely than those without to specify either prevention measures (e.g., youth education) or rehabilitation programs (e.g., job training and education for offenders) and less likely to specify either punishment (e.g., longer sentences and more prisons) or enforcement (e.g., putting more police officers on the street).

These differences are equally pronounced when other characteristics of these two groups are controlled for, including race, gender, age, education, income, partisan identification, and church attendance. In a multivariate model predicting one's top criminal justice priority, having personal or vicarious prison experience predicts an increase of 10 percentage points in the likelihood of support for rehabilitation and prevention relative to support for punishment and enforcement ($p < .001$).[75] This is true even when one controls for whether the respondent or an immediate family member has been the victim of a violent crime in the past five years.[76] For a sense of the magnitude of this difference, it is worth noting that the predicted difference between Democrats and Republicans on this measure, holding other factors constant, is about 19 percentage points ($p < .001$).[77] As another point of comparison, being black relative to white predicts a decrease of about 8 percentage points ($p<.001$), all else equal.

Even more telling are data suggesting that a significant proportion of the public now doubts the ability of the criminal justice system to carry out its most fundamental responsibility: combating crime. One poll found that fully 33 percent of Americans felt that the courts and the prison system were the institutions most responsible for *increases* in crime, more so than home and schools (27 percent), pop culture and the media (14 percent), the government (12 percent), or the law enforcement system (8 percent).[78] In fact, a significant proportion of the public believes that prisons may actually exacerbate criminal tendencies in individual offenders. About a third of the public (30 percent) say that "putting offenders in prison may make them even more criminal because prisons are schools of crime."[79] The results I have presented in this study suggest that, in many cases, the public is right: prisons can perpetuate criminal offending, building criminal networks and undermining the social values that predict legal compliance. Perhaps it is this belief that will finally urge the public to begin demanding reform.

Correctional Officers and Possibilities for Change

Prisons have long been regarded as isolated and even mysterious institutions. Yet as an increasing number of Americans, along with their neighbors, brothers, uncles, fathers, and mothers, are sent to prison for some period of time or find work inside these public institutions, prisons may become less abstract and their negative effects more keenly felt. Knowing someone who has been inside a prison – or being there oneself as an inmate, correctional officer, counselor, doctor, researcher, volunteer, or visitor – may for many irrevocably alter their thinking about the role of prisons in society. As a growing number of citizens' attitudes change, the political feasibility of undertaking substantial prison reform may increase, too.

Criminal justice researchers, policymakers, and administrators interested in reconceiving corrections would also be well advised to incorporate the legitimate concerns of correctional workers into their efforts. On the front lines of the prison system, correctional officers, perhaps more than anyone else, directly affect the practice of incarceration in the way that they perform their jobs. Because of this, correctional programs and policies can have little chance of success without their buy-in.[80]

In fact, inattention to the attitudes and experiences of correctional officers can actually exacerbate existing conflicts between the prison organization and its rank-and-file staff. In one study, Nancy Jurik and Michael Musheno find that when a correctional professionalization movement fails to follow through on promises of "professional training, upward mobility and formal services for inmates … many of the officers hired in the reform era either quit their jobs or turned to union organizing to make their grievances known to the media and state's policymakers."[81] Likewise, when a prison system makes an ideological shift in prison management that is at odds with the traditional custodial role, the resulting role ambiguity can lead to significant frustration among officers; a conflicted sense of the professional role has been shown to be correlated with a variety of undesirable individual and systemic outcomes, including levels of psychological stress, job satisfaction, work–family conflict, and burnout.[82] Role conflict can also have detrimental consequences for inmates, leading officers to compensate by becoming more likely to use their discretion punitively.[83]

California provides a case study of these challenges. In May 2007 Governor Schwarzenegger and the California State Assembly passed Assembly Bill 900. According to former CDCR Secretary James E. Tilton, the legislation prompted the state to undertake "a seismic shift of focus that is geared toward … moving away from solely housing inmates in remote prisons until the date when they must be released, and toward a new model that seeks to rehabilitate offenders in custody so that [CDCR] can return them to their home communities better off than when they arrived."[84] This "philosophical shift" was marked by a revised vision statement that placed reintegration front and center, as well as the renaming of the prison system as the California Department of Corrections *and Rehabilitation* (emphasis added).

It is difficult to assess how committed California's correctional stakeholders are to the considerable work that must be undertaken in order to realize a "new day for corrections in California,"[85] and despite their stated commitment to systemic change, California's prison administrators face a herculean battle in reforming a staggering set of deeply rooted dysfunctions. As I have already described, the most recent reform effort has been through "public safety realignment."[86] The CDCR calls the reform bill "historic legislation that will enable California to close the revolving door of low-level inmates cycling in and out of state prisons."[87] Early critics of the program, however, including the American Civil Liberties Union of California, argue that too much of the associated funding is going toward the expansion of jail infrastructure rather than mental health services and drug treatment.[88]

Despite these concerns, it is surely a positive sign that CCPOA appears to be supportive of this effort, or at least has not been actively opposed to it. In part, this appears to be because the state's current governor recognizes that he cannot successfully reform the system by steamrolling the union; he must address its legitimate concerns about safety, benefits, and job security.[89] Going forward, if reforms are to succeed, CDCR must also address the long-term needs of line officers who are currently employed in the state correctional system. If the system is to downsize significantly, this will include assisting some officers with training for and securing alternative employment.

In the meantime, correctional administrators will likely go a long way toward alleviating the stress and strain caused by prison work if they focus on reducing exposure to violence; on this dimension, inmates and officers have a common interest. Working in a violent environment can take a substantial toll on officers' psychological health, and the results presented in this book add to the growing body of studies that report high levels of work-related stress and low levels of job satisfaction among correctional officers. Prison administrators have a moral responsibility to ensure that everything possible is done to keep officers protected in the workplace. This means ensuring that they have the appropriate training and the high-quality equipment they need to do their job safely and well.

Just as introducing real prison reforms will have positive consequences that go beyond the health of individual inmates to affect the larger inmate community, so, too, might transforming the experience of officers result in changes that will positively benefit the system in its entirety. California, like many states, faces persistent problems in attracting and retaining correctional staff. In fact, despite salaries that are relatively high compared with those in other state systems, there are no prisons in California that have not been faced with at least some proportion of unfilled correctional officer positions. In at least one prison, the vacancy rate was recently as high as 24 percent.[90] As a result of such elevated vacancy rates, not only are many officers working a large number of overtime hours, but a significant portion of those hours are "forced," mandated by the department in order to fill open positions during each shift. Correctional officers in California overwhelmingly perceive low levels of staffing to be a significant contributor to problems of violence in California prisons: 72 percent believe that there are not enough staff working to provide for the safety and security of inmates, and 77 percent believe that there are not enough staff working to provide for the safety and security of staff. To the extent that this exacerbates existing problems of staff retention and burnout, it will place even greater strain on the system in terms of staff retention,[91] adversely affecting the functioning of the California prison system as a whole.

Politics, Punishment, and Social Community

The importance of social communities has received a great deal of attention in recent years, yet substantial questions about it remain. For instance, the basic tenet of Robert Putnam's classic book, *Bowling Alone*, is simple: the institutions and traditions that are central to building social connectedness have declined rapidly since the 1950s and 1960s, and the country is the worse for it. As his title suggests, people are no longer bowling in bowling clubs and leagues, but are instead bowling alone. Book clubs, sewing circles, PTAs, and fraternal community groups are experiencing the same sorts of membership decay. People no longer join political organizations at the rate they once did, and associational membership has morphed from the local community meetings of yore to sporadic check writing spurred on by the direct mail campaigns of a bureaucratized non-profit industry. Informal social activity has also declined. Family dinners and dinner parties are a dying tradition, commuting time and work hours are on the rise, and neighborhood trust is a relic. For Putnam and others writing in this vein, declining social interaction means a reduction in the vital social resources it enables, including "networks, norms and social trust that facilitate coordination and cooperation for mutual benefit."[92]

In these formulations, social connectedness is a means to an end; it is a potent resource "for the public good"[93] that "makes possible the achievement of certain ends,"[94] helping communities coordinate in pursuit of common goals. Yet what is often neglected in existing debates is that social ties are neither good nor bad. Rather, like other forms of capital, social ties have contingent value;[95] the same social networks that are useful in one social context or in some ways – such as providing for individual safety in an otherwise violent and resource-poor prison (or school, or neighborhood) – may have negative utility in another regard or when transferred to a different context.[96] In addition, the formation of social networks within a society may provide benefits to some individuals or communities, while also detracting from the collective good.[97] For instance, strong social ties are commonly built within drug cartels, extremist political factions, terrorist organizations, and warring tribal societies.[98] The extent to which the social capital of these groups will be deployed for various purposes depends on the needs of the individual and the collective, needs that are determined by the context in which social ties are formed and maintained.

Put another way: relationships forged in different contexts, where different needs are felt and differing resources are available, will help to determine the various forms these relationships will take and the kind of value with which they are imbued. Making friends as a volunteer at an interfaith soup kitchen might bring about greater multi-cultural understanding, but organizations like prison and street gangs that stem from the need for safety and competition over resources surely promote less normatively desirable results. The findings presented here underscore the need to take seriously this issue of social communities' contingent value and continue to carefully map the types of processes that produce social networks of differing forms.

Equally critical is the need to continue examining the role of government in fostering social connections and in shaping citizen social organization in all of its varied forms. As Staffan Kumlin and Bo Rothstein write: "If governments want to invest in social capital, it is the quality of political institutions that must be increased, not least those that are responsible for the direct implementation of policies."[99] Previous studies have examined the unequal distributions of social capital across economic groups[100] and the critical role of the distributive side of the state – the agents and institutions tasked with the provision of benefits through social programs – in shaping individual social networks and social norms.[101] However, the social consequences of some of our most fundamental public institutions – those designed for surveillance and sanctioning – have largely escaped notice.

Prisons, like other public institutions, can produce salient social networks, consisting of meaningful social ties. However, it is difficult to argue that more punitive prisons produce the type of social capital that Putnam describes when he suggests that "a community blessed with a substantial stock of social capital ... might have powerful implications for many issues on the American national agenda – [for instance] for how we might overcome the poverty and violence of South Central Los Angeles."[102] Not only does government allow for the conditions under which oppositional subcultures arise by failing to alleviate poverty and address disorder; it actively reshapes social networks in meaningful and sometimes unintended ways.

What I have shown here is that, by cycling a large and growing group of people through an increasingly punitive criminal justice system, American prisons decrease levels of social trust, increase interpersonal hostility and aggression, amplify the scope and strength of criminal associations, and increase criminal offending. It is therefore not only the case that individuals within a society choose the type of institutions they prefer.[103] Additionally, the particular choice of public institutions will, in turn, have an active hand in shaping the scope and quality of social connections.

Enforcing legal compliance is an essential function, and a necessary part, of organized governance. However, to the extent that characteristics of modern prisons shape interpersonal ties in ways that have durable consequences for individuals and communities, it might not be only the decline of bowling leagues, political organizations, or even welfare supports that account for the changing social dynamics of the nation. Rather, America's "punitive turn," which has resulted in a growing number of citizens spending ever longer periods of time in increasingly harsh institutions, has also indelibly altered the American social landscape.

9

Epilogue (Or: How I Went to Berkeley and Wound Up in Prison)

> *'Who are YOU?' said the Caterpillar.*
> *This was not an encouraging opening for a conversation.*
> *Alice replied, rather shyly,*
> *'I – I hardly know, sir, just at present –*
> *at least I know who I WAS when I got up this morning,*
> *but I think I must have been changed several times since then.'*
> *'What do you mean by that?' said the Caterpillar sternly. 'Explain*
> *yourself!'*
> *'I can't explain MYSELF, I'm afraid, sir,' said Alice, 'because I'm not*
> *myself, you see.'*
>
> Lewis Carroll, *Alice's Adventures in Wonderland* (1865)

This was not the book I thought I would write. In fact, I had never thought much about prison before I went to graduate school. Frankly, I came to this work only accidentally, and somewhat reluctantly at first.

When I began working toward a Ph.D. at the University of California, Berkeley, I considered my research interests to be pretty mainstream social psychology and political behavior. I loved the scholarly life of graduate school and quickly adapted to the culture (and the weather) of the Bay Area. Hoping to learn the local politics and engage with my new community, I called the Oakland Public Library in the spring of my first year to ask whether they knew somewhere I could tutor for a few hours a week. The enthusiastic librarian offered to provide me the phone number of an area non-profit that worked with city schools.

However, she also knew of a college program at San Quentin State Prison that was currently recruiting volunteers.

San Quentin is California's oldest prison, built by inmates in the 1850s. Convict-laborers were housed in large wooden prison ships during construction and were then relocated to the very cells they had built. Many of the original buildings are still in use, and the structure retains the look of a great cinderblock fortress overlooking the San Francisco Bay. Situated in wealthy Marin County, San Quentin occupies what has become one of the most expensive pieces of real estate in California, and it remains one of the most notorious correctional institutions in the country. It owes this reputation in large part to the many high-profile inmates who have been housed there, from Sirhan Sirhan and Charles Manson to Eldridge Cleaver and George Jackson. It is also familiar to many Americans as the place where Johnny Cash recorded his Grammy-nominated album "At San Quentin" in 1969, which went triple platinum and helped launch his career. Designed for a capacity of about 3,000 incarcerated individuals, the facility recently reported its total population count as well over 5,000 men, more than 600 of whom have been condemned to death.[1]

Intrigued by what the librarian had told me, I scribbled down contact information for the Prison University Project (PUP), which ran the college program at San Quentin. At the time – and still, as of this writing – this was the only on-site, accredited higher-education program operating within the entire California state correctional system. Matriculation is open to any program-eligible inmate in San Quentin's general population (colloquially called genpop) who has completed high school or has a GED. PUP's student body at any given time totals more than 300 men, and every year since 2001 between 5 and 15 students have graduated from the program with an associate's degree.

I called PUP the next day and introduced myself to the program's executive director, a brilliant and seemingly indefatigable woman by the name of Jody Lewen. Like me, Jody had been a Berkeley graduate student when she started volunteering at San Quentin in the late 1990s. Just a few years after she had begun teaching at the prison, the head of the college program had unexpectedly quit. Rather than watch the organization fall apart, Jody stepped in to serve as his temporary replacement and she has been there ever since. Over the years, Jody has doggedly built the Prison University Project into a fully independent non-profit, the mission of which is to support the college program. PUP now has several full time staff members, including one former graduate of the program who has since been paroled, and it has earned a national reputation as a beacon of best practices.

On the phone that day, I told Jody a little about my interests and experience, and mentioned that I was looking for opportunities to volunteer. As it turned out, the program was looking for an instructor to teach its introductory politics course. I quickly agreed to show up the following week for training and to teach two nights a week during the coming semester. I would go on to teach there nearly every semester for the rest of my graduate career.

What I Taught (and Learned) at San Quentin

In training volunteers new to the college program, PUP staff stress that students in prison should be held to the same academic standards that define good colleges anywhere. In practice, this means that, although most inmates at San Quentin have full-time jobs doing menial work to keep the prison running – janitorial, kitchen, or maintenance – or in prison offices or on-site factories, often have no access to computers, never have access to the Internet, have no library, and cannot regularly find a quiet or private space where they can read, write, or complete homework assignments, they are still expected to show up prepared at every class and to turn in assignments on time. And somehow, incredibly, most of them generally do. (Incidentally, I find that this has drastically lowered my tolerance for excuses from students at the Ivy League university where I now teach.)

In some undeniable ways, though, PUP students are distinct from other college students. Although they are more educated than the average state prison inmate, in most other respects college students at San Quentin are fairly representative of the state prison population overall. They are disproportionately black and Latino. Most grew up in economically disadvantaged homes and have struggled with poverty and homelessness into adulthood, and many have suffered long-term addiction or mental illness. They are the proverbial underprivileged and underserved, who hail from neighborhoods where most of us don't live, won't walk at night, and wouldn't dream of sending our kids to school. As one longtime correctional administrator bitingly put it, "On a scale of zero to one, in public opinion they're zeros. Nobody cares about them; they are convicted felons."

These realities make the PUP classroom remarkable, both because it is so different from classrooms anywhere else and because it is so similar. The challenge of teaching in prison is to construct a course that does justice to the intellectual rigor of the material, while also acknowledging the unique and complicated context in which it is being taught. Navigating "Introduction to American Politics" inside prison, in particular, is a study in contradictions. How do you teach democratic theory to adult citizens of a democracy who are barred from voting? How do you describe the role of the free press as the fourth estate to a group of citizens whose media access is tightly controlled by their government? What do students make of the nation's "post-racial politics" when they look around their prison and see disproportionately black and brown faces?

Inmates are certainly no strangers to government, but their point of reference is often markedly different from that of the typical college student. Many of my students had been involved in state institutions from a very young age, first in foster care, then in group homes, juvenile detention, and then on to jail. Indeed, many had spent much of their lives under the surveillance and supervision of one or another of a host of public institutions. They had generally known a long line of professionals – foster parents, social workers, counselors, juvenile probation officers – who had, at best, come across as well-meaning but ineffective and, at worst, as uncaring, vindictive, or cruel. In our classroom discussions, students at San Quentin often referred to these experiences when they talked about "The State." They drew on their time in prison, as well as their broader experiences with police, with jails, and with criminal courts, using them as background to inform their ideas about participation and citizenship in America. Most of the students with whom I spoke saw the state as both morally bankrupt and wholly punitive rather than as an agent for the fair and reliable distribution of goods or the provision of social supports. This political learning, gleaned through citizens' direct contact with punitive political institutions, became the subject of a book that I and a colleague would eventually set out to write.[2]

At the same time, though, it became clear to me that the prison experience also encouraged a more fundamental type of socialization. Prison time had shaped my students' consciousness not just as democratic citizens, but also as moral and social beings, and as members of families, friendship networks, and communities. In conversations before and after class, students would describe how, in prison, you had to be vigilant, to "watch your back," because you never knew just by sight who was rational and who was prone to violence. They discussed the importance of keeping your wits about you and staying guarded. They repeated the famous allegory of the "new fish" coming into prison who, on his first day inside, walks right up to the biggest guy on the yard and calmly knocks him out. The idea they conveyed is that you need to establish yourself right away as the kind of person who won't be pushed around. The goal in prison is not to fit in; it is survival of the fittest.

Students also talked about how important it is to have a few guys "in your car," friends you can trust and whom you know you can count on. The bonds formed in prison are not just about companionship; they are also about safety. Among this group of men, there was a deep sense of being alone in the world, of not having any institutions or organizations to serve or protect them. Many had been repeatedly failed by social service providers, families, police, and other agents and institutions that had been ostensibly responsible for protecting them as children and then as adults. Now, in prison, they found themselves confined by their government in an environment where they were surrounded by strangers and exposed to the grinding stress of constantly lurking violence. Most felt that they were on their own to protect themselves from harm, unless they could ally themselves with peers for mutual protection. I started the project that would become this book in order to understand the effects of this kind of environment on the way people learn to relate to one another and the kinds of people they become.

Seeing Both Sides

My first serious step toward conducting this research was aimed at mapping the contours of California prison culture across individual institutions. To do this, I decided to conduct a survey of correctional officers at San Quentin and at other prisons in the state. My purpose was to examine whether officers working at different prisons, and across various security levels, had distinct attitudes and behaviors that might affect inmates' experiences of incarceration.

To get the survey off the ground, I drove to Sacramento to meet with the president and executive vice president of the California Correctional Peace Officers Association (CCPOA), to ask if they were interested in partnering with me. Mike Jimenez and Chuck Alexander greeted my proposal with a rather wry curiosity (and a fair bit of friendly sarcasm). They openly wondered why I was interested in the attitudes of law enforcement; after all, they goaded, I was studying for a "pocket protector" degree in the "People's Republic of Berkeley." After lengthy discussions, in which I assured them that I didn't have a hidden agenda that entailed criticizing officers or bashing the union, they agreed to allow me access to their members. In return, I offered to add some survey items that might be useful to them, such as questions designed to gauge officers' perceptions of their personal safety, levels of job satisfaction, and views on whether and how prison work had affected their family lives and mental health. Much to their credit, Mike and Chuck encouraged me to write honestly about whatever I found, no matter what the survey revealed.

In the cover letter that accompanied the correctional officer questionnaire, I included contact information for a dedicated cell phone line I had established. I didn't honestly expect many calls, but had set it up in case I heard from potential respondents who wanted to express reservations about the survey or needed to ask questions. My hope was that I could convince these reluctant callers to complete the survey and send it back.

To my surprise, the phone started to ring from literally the first day the survey landed in mailboxes around the state. Correctional officers often work strange hours, assigned to shifts that end late at night or in the early hours of the morning, and officers would sometimes call as they were getting into their cars, heading home. Over the ensuing weeks, that little red cell phone rang at all hours. (I began leaving it next to the bed at night, so I could grab it as soon as it rang. My long-suffering boyfriend, who is now my husband, was thrilled with this turn of events.) As I rubbed the sleep from my eyes and groped for a yellow legal pad to scribble notes, I could picture these officers driving home through California's long, low Central Valley or winding through the salt-air roads of the nearby Bay, their voices reaching out through the receding dark. The conversations that I had during those few months, as spring eased into summer, were truly fascinating. I began to think of it as my 1–800-corrections crisis line.

Like inmates, officers would talk about the constant wariness necessitated by the prison environment, as well as the detached, self-protective front that they gradually developed at work. They described this workplace persona as something like a heavy jacket that had to be donned at the start of every shift and hung up at the end of the day. Over time, though, this portative shield became a thick skin that was increasingly difficult to shed, even when officers returned to the relative haven of their private lives. One officer told me that, as a new recruit, he had once been advised to rent an apartment that was at least a half-hour's drive from the prison where he worked. This would give him enough time to "detox" on the way home, before having contact with his wife and kids. Officers sometimes also talked about the camaraderie they built with other prison staff. Like soldiers and police, they grew close to their brothers and sisters in arms, needing to trust and rely on those they would need to call should fights, riots, or other prison violence break out. Nowhere are bonds formed as tightly as in the foxhole.

Many officers also wanted to express the feeling that outsiders, myself included, had no clue what went on inside prison or how isolating prison work could be. I spoke to one man who had been working in corrections for 14 years and who described the things he had seen as "gut-wrenching" – three suicides, a stroke case, and more fights than he could count. He told me that "nobody in the public knows what goes on." Another particularly memorable phone call was from the wife of a longtime officer. Her husband was at work when she called, but still she spoke softly, as if hesitant to break a confidence. She told me how much stress her husband was under, having worked in prison for so many years, and how frustrating it was that he so rarely wanted to talk to her about it. She thought it would be good for him to fill out the survey, to take this small step toward documenting what he'd seen. She wanted to know if I could give her the words to help encourage him to participate.

Over time, completed surveys began to arrive, piling up on my desk and spilling over into wobbly stacks on the floor. In the margins of their surveys, and sometimes in multi-page letters they attached, many officers expounded on their closed-ended survey responses. They wrote, "If you feel safe in a prison, you shouldn't be there" and "There is never enough safety." Someone confessed, "I try not to let my job interfere at home, but on occasion I have been snapping in a negative way." Another officer remarked, "It's really very sad – is anywhere really safe?"

It quickly began to dawn on me that the experiences these officers were reporting quite closely paralleled the stories I had been hearing from inmates; from these two distinct groups, the same themes emerged. Among correctional officers, as among inmates, the subjective experience of prison was characterized by intense and nearly constant concerns about physical violence, a sense that the public was both unaware and indifferent to their suffering, and a feeling that there was no one advocating for or protecting them. In fact, one seeming constant among the many officers with whom I spoke was a strongly adversarial orientation toward the CDCR and a belief that officers walking the "toughest beat in the state" were essentially on their own to take care of themselves and one another. In hindsight, the similarities between officers' and inmates' experiences seem readily apparent. After all, the identities of these two seemingly opposed populations are, in a very real sense, formed and maintained by the same set of forces within the same institutional contexts.

At an early stage in this project, I was invited to attend an annual conference of the CCPOA and present some results from the correctional officer survey. During a break in the meeting, I talked to a young African-American officer who had been elected the union representative of his prison. I told him about the project, and he shared a story about something that had taken place at the prison where he works. As he described it, a relatively novice officer had been working in the cell block when he heard screaming coming from a cell down the tier. He ran over to investigate the disturbance and saw an inmate standing in front of his bunk, his face covered in blood. The prisoner, who had been clearly suffering from some form of untreated mental illness, had used his fingernails to claw at his own eyes. Both eye sockets had sustained grave damage.

The apprentice officer hesitated, not knowing how to proceed. Protocol dictated that he could not open the cell door without first asking the inmate to place his hands behind his back and put them through the bars, so he could be handcuffed. Only then could the officer go into the cell. The officer knew that, if he deviated from the rules, he could lose his job. So he called repeatedly to the inmate to comply. The inmate staggered forward, but with blood in his eyes, he couldn't find the door to his cell. In unimaginable pain, he could instead only continue to scream, as the young officer stood momentarily paralyzed on the tier.

The union representative who told me this story was trying to make me understand the kinds of impossible situations in which officers frequently find themselves. Taken out of context, it is difficult to understand how someone could be callously bound by bureaucratic rules in the face of such suffering. In the prison, though, where officers learn quickly not to trust what they see, their conditioned reaction is often to wonder if they are being tricked and whether someone is actually trying to harm them. Indeed, most officers have been *trained* to react in this way, to suspect that they are being fooled or taken advantage of. In addition, in a place where rules are strictly enforced and govern nearly every aspect of daily life, new officers do not break lightly with protocol. Many officers perceive the department as perfectly happy to throw them under the bus if they diverge from proscribed behavior when something goes wrong, even if they were trying their best to manage an unmanageable situation. Like inmates, they most often perceive the institution that is supposed to supervise and protect them as being not only inept, but also as largely indifferent to their needs.

When I hear stories like this, what inevitably comes to my mind is Alice finding herself in Wonderland. Being in prison every day must be like perpetually falling down the rabbit hole. None of the same rules apply; upside down becomes right side up; and your only choice is to figure out how to sensibly respond to a nonsense world. It becomes easier, then, to imagine how people might slowly come to find themselves making decisions that in any other context would seem peculiar, irrational, or inhumane. As I came to more fully understand the experiences of correctional officers, it became obvious to me that the effect of the prison environment on inmates was really only half of the story. If I wanted to give a full accounting of how prisons shape the social world, the officers' experience would also have to be a part of the story I was going to tell.

Reimagining Community

As I was completing this manuscript, I received a call from Jody Lewen at PUP, to tell me that a student at San Quentin had taken his own life. He was 39 years old. He was survived by his mother, siblings, and nieces and nephews on the outside, but also by a group of friends, co-workers, teachers, and classmates in prison.

Suicide is always difficult for those who are left behind. However, the suicide of an inmate is made even more traumatic for everyone by the constraints that the prison places on the ability of individuals to grieve. The policy in a California prison when an inmate unexpectedly dies dictates placing his cellmate in administrative segregation until the situation can be examined, on the assumption that the cellmate is essentially a prime murder suspect. The policy leaves little room for recognition of any real and meaningful bonds that might have existed between the two men. For inmates who have lived together, confined in a small space for years on end, losing a cellmate to suicide would most likely be devastating. Yet the cellmate, per protocol, found himself in isolation, separated from his support network at a time when what he might have needed more than ever was the emotional support of friends and peers.

The institution's suicide policy is a reflection of its governing ideology. That is to say, the policy is understandable if you take as your starting point the presumption of criminality: in prison, all harm or injury is assumed to have been deliberate, and everyone is imagined to be not just "criminal" but a potential murderer; the composite image of "The Criminal" is projected onto everyone, and every criminal therefore possesses the propensity to commit every imaginable kind of crime. Thus, when an unexplained death has occurred, everyone is a culprit until he is ruled out. The policies and practices of prison are predicated on a status quo of intense and consuming suspicion.

At the same time that I empathized with the student's cellmate, I also had great sympathy for the officer on duty, who would have been responsible for severing the rope with which this man had hung himself and for bringing his body down. That officer may also have known the inmate for years, seen him every day, and gotten to know him in at least some capacity. Indeed, despite being required by institutional policy to avoid fraternization with inmates, officers sometimes form meaningful relationships with those in their charge. When I was at San Quentin, I not infrequently saw prisoners and officers chatting amiably, as inmates came or left the education building.

I was once talking to an older officer, whom I had gotten to know fairly well over the course of a few semesters. As we were conversing, an inmate came out of a classroom and walked over to where we stood in order to pick up his identification card. The two men, both gray-haired and in their 50s, said a particularly heartfelt good-bye to one another that day. As the inmate walked away, the officer told me, somewhat nostalgically, "He's finally paroling. That guy's been here forever. Hell, he and I practically grew up together here. We were just kids when we arrived."

Inmates and correctional officers have an intensely complicated relationship. Yet, in facing the unexpected loss of an inmate, prison staff are prohibited from openly grieving, prevented by norms and codes of conduct from expressing any personal sorrow that might suggest an overly familiar relationship. This, too, strikes me as flying in the face of what we know about people's need and ability to process what must be a difficult and potentially traumatic emotional experience. Again, the rules seem to enforce a code that keeps people from recognizing and nurturing their humanity. Rules like this help me understand why people inside prisons ultimately harden themselves against caring, rather than continue to feel emotions they aren't allowed the resources or capacity to address. But if you assume that people are animals for long enough, and treat them accordingly, eventually that is how they will behave.

Moreover, the profound process of adaptation that many individuals go through in order to survive their time in prison does not wash away immediately when individuals leave. Instead, what emerges most clearly from my research and from my experiences at San Quentin is that prison culture burrows deep into the psyches of both prisoners and guards. When they pass back through the prison gate at the end of the day, or the years, or the decades spent inside, they often cannot shake the person they have become. Many still view their social world – and the choices they face within it – through the murky lens of prison life. Like all of us, they are shaped and stymied by the history of their experiences, fully internalized and deeply held. The question, then, becomes how we create institutions that encourage the kinds of thought and action we hope to achieve.

From my own experience, I offer PUP as just one small example of how prison environments, and the people they produce, can be radically transformed. Jody Lewen recently gave a lecture at the "Big Ideas Fest," a three-day conference held annually in the rugged seaside town of Half Moon Bay, California, to discuss innovation in education. She talked there about the difficulty that new students at San Quentin often face in learning to trust their teachers. In their academic lives prior to prison, PUP students have most often encountered teachers whose time and patience were limited, and who generally failed to find the energy or resources to address their pupils' often significant educational needs. School, for them, has historically been a place marked by feelings of failure and experienced as a site of profound rejection. Lewen therefore described the amazement and sometimes confusion that students express when they find out that PUP teachers work as volunteers, and when they see these teachers continue to come back to prison each week, despite regularly encountering institutional obstacles that often make the logistics of teaching in prison onerous. PUP students find it hard to believe that the program is supported by donations, that there are people on the outside who are rooting them on, people they have never met but who want them to succeed.

Even more remarkable was the way Lewen described the community ties that form between students themselves. She tells of how, early on in her time at PUP, she would occasionally stop a student on the yard to inquire after another classmate, someone who had stopped attending school. These students would often hesitate, concerned that they were being asked to "snitch" on their peers. But as the program slowly began to build a tentative trust within the community and eventually to develop a reputation among prisoners as being trustworthy, students began to grow more comfortable telling her what they knew. In fact, it didn't take long before students were taking the initiative to check up on each other, encouraging those who were having a hard time in their classes to "stick with it" and actively recruiting their cellmates and friends into the program. Lewen speaks proudly of the currently enrolled students in the college program as some of her primary recruiting tools, and how inmates now "conspire" with program staff to help motivate those who are falling behind. She paints an eloquent picture of the fierce loyalty PUP students have to the program and its staff, and the transformative relationship that prison college students can have with one another:

> The more academically advanced and psychologically self-aware students in the college program have a spectacular capacity to reach the most fearful of men. They share their own stories; they offer support and encouragement; they model healthy dependency, both on us – program staff and teachers – and on each other. They are living proof that trusting others is not only possible, but life-sustaining. All these students bear living testimony to the extraordinary resiliency of the human mind and the human heart. They form for me an endless chain of human beings who keep going back for those who have been left behind.

In the context of prison, the kind of community that the college program offers is a fragile resource, something that must be cared for and respected. In prison, the ability to trust someone can literally take on life or death meaning. Trusting a teacher or asking a peer for help means exposing the soft underbelly of one's vulnerability, which is no small thing. When students admit that there is something they do not know, or that there is something they want and are striving to earn, they put enormous faith in us not to respond with mockery or disdain. In prisons, as in classrooms more generally, I think, trust is a sacred commodity.

One story I heard in my time at San Quentin has particularly stuck with me. This was first recounted to me by a fellow volunteer and later retold to me by a student. It reportedly happened some years back to a young woman who had only recently begun volunteering with the program as the teacher of an evening class. She was in the middle of a discussion with her students when the lights briefly went out. As the story goes, the minute the lights dimmed she heard movement: chairs scraping the floor, inmates getting up and moving toward her. When the lights came back up just moments later, several of her students were standing by her desk, with their backs to her. They had come over to stand in front of her, just to make sure that no one had taken the opportunity to cause any trouble or mess with her in any way. Of course, nobody had.

I have no idea how much truth there is in this tale. I suspect that narratives like this, however apocryphal, quickly become as much shared legend and lore as they are recollection of fact. But this story, it seems to me, holds nearly as much significance if it is taken as allegory, a reflection of PUP's culture and of the shared understanding of the PUP community among its members. This is a story that both teachers and students want to retell in order to communicate to the listener the kind of environment that is created within the college program; it serves somehow to embody the feelings they have for the program and the feelings they perceive in others. Equally significant is that, having been involved with the college program for nearly 10 years, I do not find this story at all implausible. One of the first questions people often ask when I say that I taught at San Quentin is whether I was concerned about my safety. (This is generally followed by the question: "Was there a guard in the room with you?" The answer is no.) I am not naive. I recognize the histories of violence that shadow some in that room. But my usual reply is that, in fact, I did not once feel physically threatened by a student during all my time there.

For me, therefore, trying to take stock of the modern American prison means trying to unravel the story of how people make choices – the choices they make that get them to prison and the choices they make once they get there. More deeply, it has been an ongoing struggle to precisely specify what we mean by "choice." In this book, I have tried to argue that people respond to the situations in which they find themselves, given the emotional and conceptual tools that are available to them at the time; they make choices and decisions in line with the constraints, opportunities, and incentives they perceive. These perceptions, I propose, are a direct result of the institutions in which they find themselves. Understanding how and why people choose a particular path means trying to make sense of the context in which their decisions are made.

So in the end, this is also a story about the choices we make as a society – choices about how best to prosecute crime, what form our institutions of punishment will take, and how to institutionalize our basic human predispositions for both retribution and forgiveness. And the first step in making informed choices about crime control, I believe, is to honestly assess the collateral costs of what we as a nation have tried so far. I have suggested here that our national choices about incarceration over the past half-century have had very real consequences. They have had real meaning for the lives of the millions of Americans who spend time in prison, as well as for the millions more to whom those lives connect. And ultimately, the choices we make about how best to

respond to crime have consequences for us all. As one PUP student
writes, discussing the purpose of prison and the importance of the college program in shaping how he has come to see the world:

> I would like the world to know that getting tough on crime does not have to
> mean keeping those that do the crime stupid, or ignorant. Educating prisoners
> is not only good for the prisoner, it is good for society as a whole.... All you
> need to do is ask yourself, who would I rather be living in my neighborhood:
> someone who came out of prison and gained nothing from the experience
> other than being harder and more antisocial, or someone that has rehabili-
> tated and educated himself to become better thinkers, more social, and under-
> standing? Most of the prisoners will come home. Who would you rather be
> living in your neighborhood?[3]

Through my work at PUP, I began a year-long project of trying to
understand the prison environment and its effects on those who pass
through it. This book is the product of that research. For me personally, though, this project has also been about recognizing the power
and possibility of education. In the best incarnations of the classroom,
be it in prison or outside, students and teachers can immerse themselves in the world of ideas and analysis. This means that the true joy
of teaching and learning at San Quentin lies in the fact that the prison
college, itself mostly just a few simple modular buildings tucked into
a side of the rec yard and filled with scratched desks and well-worn
books, can be a place where rules apply that are different from those
that govern the prison writ large. When we are in the classroom, we all
get to exist in the "free world" for a while.

Studying incarceration in the United States has helped me to understand what prisons are. Unfortunately, the realities of prison too often
adhere to our worst imaginings. Thus, our imaginations are too often
limited to envisaging prisons as hostile and threatening environments
where allegiances to others become simultaneously crucial and cor-
rosive. But my experience has also helped me to envision what prisons
could be, and allowed me to see firsthand how caring groups of like-
minded individuals can help to change each other at the most fundamental level. How precious such a community can be, even – perhaps
especially – in the darkest corners of the world.

Appendixes

A. California Adult Prison Facilities

Facility	Date Opened	Security Level[a]	Rated Capacity	Number of Inmates	Annual Operating Budget (Millions)
California Substance Abuse Treatment Facility (SATF)	Aug. 1997	II, III, IV	3,324	7,628	230
Salinas Valley State Prison (SVSP)	May 1996	I, II, III, IV	2,224	4,555	177
High Desert State Prison (HDSP)	Aug. 1995	I, II, III, IV, RC	2,224	4,792	138
Valley State Prison for Women (VSPW)	Apr. 1995	I, II, III, IV, RC, SHU	1,980	3,810	125.2
Pleasant Valley State Prison (PVSP)	Nov. 1994	I, III, IV	2,208	5,188	195
Ironwood State Prison (ISP)	Feb. 1994	I, III	2,200	4,664	113
Centinela State Prison (CEN)	Oct. 1993	I, III	2,208	4,928	122.9
North Kern State Prison (NKSP)	Apr. 1993	I, III, RC	2,692	5,390	171
California State Prison, Los Angeles County (LAC)	Feb. 1993	I, IV, RC	2,200	4,764	100

Facility	Date Opened	Security Level[a]	Rated Capacity	Number of Inmates	Annual Operating Budget (Millions)
Calipatria State Prison (CAL)	Jan. 1992	I, IV	2,208	4,168	123
Wasco State Prison (WSP)	Feb. 1991	I, III, RC	2,984	5,935	185
Central California Women's Facility (CCWF)	Oct. 1990	I, II, III, IV, RC, Condemned	2,004	3,887	130.3
Pelican Bay State Prison (PBSP)	Dec. 1989	I, IV, SHU	2,280	3,461	180
Chuckawalla Valley State Prison (CVSP)	Dec. 1988	I, II	1,738	3,913	115
California State Prison, Corcoran (COR)	Feb. 1988	I, III, IV, SHU	3,016	4,867	115
Northern California Women's Facility (NCWF)	Inactive	–	–	–	–
R. J. Donovan Correctional Facility at Rock Mountain (RJD)	July 1987	I, III, IV, RC	2,200	4,770	144
Mule Creek State Prison (MCSP)	June 1987	I, II, III, IV	1,700	3,832	135
Avenal State Prison (ASP)	Jan. 1987	II	2,320	7,525	136
California State Prison, Sacramento (SAC)	Oct. 1986	I, II, IV	1,728	3,254	187.4
California State Prison, Solano (SOL)	Aug. 1984	II, III	2,610	6,047	158.4
Sierra Conservation Center (SCC)	1965	I, II, III, Camps	3,926	6,591	148
California Correctional Center (CCC)	1963	I, II, III, Camps	3,682	6,271	139
California Rehabilitation Center (CRC)	1962	I, II	2,314	1,626	118

Facility	Date Opened	Security Level[a]	Rated Capacity	Number of Inmates	Annual Operating Budget (Millions)
California Medical Facility (CMF)	1955	I, II, III	2,315	3,031	180
California Men's Colony (CMC)	E 1954 W 1961	I, II, III, IV	3,884	6,586	151
Deuel Vocational Institution (DVI)	1953	I, II, RC	1,787	3,748	109
California Institution for Women (CIW)	1952	I, II, III, RC, Camps	1,026	2,443	62.5
Correctional Training Facility (CTF)	1946	I, II, III	3,281	6,997	150
California Institution for Men (CIM)	1941	I, RC	3,078	6,900	232.2
California Correctional Institution (CCI)	1954 1933	I, II, IV, RC, SHU	2,781	5,907	168
Folsom State Prison (FSP)	1880	I, II, III	2,072	4,023	115
San Quentin State Prison (SQ)	1852	I, II, RC, Condemned	3,283	5,222	210
Kern Valley State Prison (KVSP)	2005	I, IV	5,120	4,791	123.3

[a] Roman numerals refer to security levels (Levels I–IV); SHU denotes security housing unit; RC, reception center.

Source: Institutional Statistics 2006/2007 fiscal year, California Department of Corrections and Rehabilitation website as of June 2007.

B. CCOS Survey Instrument and Administration Details

I conducted a field test of the survey instrument in February 2006, at a board of directors meeting of the CCPOA. Those in attendance included correctional officer representatives from every prison in the state. Each of the 90 attendees was invited to take the survey, after which a question-and-answer period was held to address any issues or concerns that participants had about the instrument. The survey was then significantly revised on the basis of these completed surveys and the comments offered by participants. The final survey instrument included 68 closed-ended questions.

In the week preceding the initial survey mailing, a full-page advertisement was placed in the *Peacekeeper*, a publication of CCPOA, informing officers about the survey, explaining its objectives, and inviting participation. A postcard and then a survey and cover letter were sent to each correctional officer at the end of March 2006, along with a stamped and self-addressed reply envelope. The cover letter explained the goals of the survey, as well as providing information about confidentiality. Two weeks after the initial mailing, a follow-up postcard was sent to every officer, as a reminder to fill out the survey. In addition, a second full-page advertisement ran in the *Peacekeeper*. At the end of June, there was a second mailing of the survey to the full sample. The second mailing included a duplicate copy of the survey, a second cover letter, and another pre-addressed business reply envelope.

As nearly as possible, surveys were sent to every correctional officer currently working in the California system. While a stratified random sample was considered, a focus group conducted with correctional officers during the field test revealed a great deal of concern that past survey efforts had "handpicked" particular people to receive surveys, in order to obtain data that would paint the prison system in an overly positive light. For this reason, it was decided that the additional time and expense of including the total population were worthwhile.

2006 CALIFORNIA CORRECTIONAL OFFICER SURVEY

This survey asks for information about you and your work with the California Department of Corrections and Rehabilitation. It also asks for your thoughts and opinions on a variety of issues concerning the prison where you are currently assigned. Please answer each question by filling in the circle next to the best choice:

Examples of <u>correct</u> ways to respond: ● Answer   OR   ⊗ Answer

When you are not sure which answer to choose, please pick whichever seems like the best option out of the choices that are given. All of your responses will be <u>strictly</u> confidential.

WORK HISTORY

1. In what year did you begin working for the California Department of Corrections?

   _____

2. At what prison do you <u>currently</u> work?

¹○ Avenal	¹⁵○ Solano
²○ CCC	¹⁶○ SATF
³○ CCI	¹⁷○ CMF
⁴○ CIM	¹⁸○ Calipatria
⁵○ CMC	¹⁹○ Centinela
⁶○ CRC	²⁰○ Chuckawalla Valley
⁷○ LA County	²¹○ CTF
⁸○ Corcoran	²²○ Deuel Vocational
⁹○ Sacramento	²³○ Folsom
¹⁰○ High Desert	²⁴○ Ironwood
¹¹○ Mule Creek	²⁵○ North Kern
¹²○ Pelican Bay	²⁶○ Pleasant Valley
¹³○ RJ Donovan	²⁷○ Salinas Valley
¹⁴○ San Quentin	²⁸○ Sierra Conservation
²⁹○ Wasco	³²○ CIW
³⁰○ NCWF	³³○ CCWF
³¹○ Valley State	³⁴○ Other _____

3. In what year did you start working at the prison where you <u>currently</u> work?

   _____

4. With which type of inmates have you worked most often <u>during the past 6 months</u>?
   ① General population (including work cadre)
   ② Medical/psychiatric
   ③ Segregation/administrative detention
   ④ Holdover/in-transit
   ⑤ Pre-trial/detention
   ⑥ Protective custody
   ⑦ Drug therapy unit
   ⑧ Reception
   ⑨ Other _____

5. With what security-level inmates have you worked most often during the past 6 months?
   ① I   ② II   ③ III   ④ IV

6. In your opinion, what percentage of the inmates at this security level do you think are:
   Very dangerous   _____ %
   Dangerous   _____ %
   Not dangerous   _____ %
   = 100 %

PERSONAL SAFETY AND SECURITY

The following questions ask you about your own safety and security while at work during the past six months.

7. I rarely feel safe when I am at work.

   ① Strongly disagree
   ② Disagree
   ③ Somewhat disagree
   ④ Undecided
   ⑤ Somewhat agree
   ⑥ Agree
   ⑦ Strongly agree

8. I have the back up support I need if things get rough.

   ① Strongly disagree
   ② Disagree
   ③ Somewhat disagree
   ④ Undecided
   ⑤ Somewhat agree
   ⑥ Agree
   ⑦ Strongly agree

9. I feel safe when working among the inmates.

   ① Strongly disagree
   ② Disagree
   ③ Somewhat disagree
   ④ Undecided
   ⑤ Somewhat agree
   ⑥ Agree
   ⑦ Strongly agree

10. A. During the past 6 months, did you occupy a position that called for the issuance of a safety vest as directed by post orders?

    ① Yes   ② No   ③ Not sure

    B. If yes, have you been issued a vest?

    ① Yes   ② No
    ③ Did not occupy a position calling for one

    C. How long ago was the vest issued to you?

    # of months ago _____

    ① Vest has not been issued
    ② Did not occupy a position calling for one

◇1◇

11. If there was a problem with the vest when it was issued, what was the problem? **(Choose all that apply)**
    ① Poor quality
    ② Ill-fitting
    ③ Not the right type of vest
    ④ Incompatible with other equipment or clothing
    ⑤ Expired
    ⑥ Other _____
    ⑦ No problem with vest
    ⑧ Vest has not been issued
    ⑨ Did not occupy a position calling for one

For the following set of questions, please indicate your evaluation <u>over the past six months</u> of the prison where you <u>currently</u> work.

12. Do you think there are enough staff working to provide for the safety and security of <u>staff</u>?
    ① Yes   ② No   ③ Not sure

13. Do you think there are enough staff working to provide for the safety and security of <u>inmates</u>?
    ① Yes   ② No   ③ Not sure

14. How likely do you think it is that a **staff member** would be assaulted in this prison?
    ① Not at all likely
    ② Somewhat likely
    ③ Likely
    ④ Very likely
    ⑤ Not sure

15. When a **staff member** has been assaulted, how often has any action been taken by the institution to discipline the inmate or inmates involved?
    ① Never
    ② Very rarely
    ③ Rarely
    ④ Now and then
    ⑤ Often
    ⑥ Very often
    ⑦ All the time

16. When action was taken in response to an instance of **inmate-on-staff** violence, how often do you feel that the action taken was adequate?
    ① Never
    ② Very rarely
    ③ Rarely
    ④ Now and then
    ⑤ Often
    ⑥ Very often
    ⑦ All the time
    ⑧ No action was taken

17. Over the past six months, how often has any type of violent incident occurred at this prison?
    ① Never
    ② Very rarely
    ③ Rarely
    ④ Now and then
    ⑤ Often
    ⑥ Very often
    ⑦ All the time

18. Over the past six months at this prison:
    A. How many times have you, personally, been the target of a direct assault against you?
       # of assaults against you _____
    B. How many times have you, personally, been <u>injured</u> in a direct assault against you?
       # of times injured _____
    C. How many times have you, personally, responded to any type of violent incident?
       # of incidents responded to _____
    D. How many times have you, personally, been <u>injured</u> while responding to any type of violent incident?
       # of times injured _____

The following questions refer to various emergency situations, including riots, food strikes, fights, fires, escapes, hostage crises, and bomb threats.

19. As far as you know, are there plans at your institution for what to do in the event of all of these types of emergencies?
    ① Yes   ② No   ③ Not sure

20. Overall, how clear are the emergency plans at this prison?
    ① Very unclear
    ② Somewhat unclear
    ③ Somewhat clear
    ④ Very clear
    ⑤ Not sure

JOB SATISFACTION

21. A. I often experience a sense that I am positively influencing other people's lives through my work.
       ① Strongly disagree
       ② Disagree
       ③ Somewhat disagree
       ④ Undecided
       ⑤ Somewhat agree
       ⑥ Agree
       ⑦ Strongly agree

    B. When I'm at work, I often feel tense or stressed.
       ① Strongly disagree
       ② Disagree
       ③ Somewhat disagree
       ④ Undecided
       ⑤ Somewhat agree
       ⑥ Agree
       ⑦ Strongly agree

◇2◇

C. I have become harsher or less trusting towards family members since I took this job.
① Strongly disagree
② Disagree
③ Somewhat disagree
④ Undecided
⑤ Somewhat agree
⑥ Agree
⑦ Strongly agree

D. I make a difference in people's lives through my work.
① Strongly disagree
② Disagree
③ Somewhat disagree
④ Undecided
⑤ Somewhat agree
⑥ Agree
⑦ Strongly agree

E. I usually feel that I am under a lot of pressure when I am at work.
① Strongly disagree
② Disagree
③ Somewhat disagree
④ Undecided
⑤ Somewhat agree
⑥ Agree
⑦ Strongly agree

F. What happens at work negatively affects my relationship with my spouse/partner or children.
① Strongly disagree
② Disagree
③ Somewhat disagree
④ Undecided
⑤ Somewhat agree
⑥ Agree
⑦ Strongly agree
⑧ Don't have spouse or children

22. How many total hours of overtime have you worked in the past six months?
_____ Hours

23. What percentage of the overtime hours worked were mandated or holdover overtime, or were worked because you anticipated being held-over?
_____ Percent

INMATE BEHAVIOR AND ACTIVITY

24. How likely do you think it is that an **inmate** would be assaulted in this prison?
① Not at all likely
② Somewhat likely
③ Likely
④ Very likely

25. Do assaults on inmates usually happen to the same inmates, or are they equally likely to happen to anybody?
① Almost always to the same inmates
② Usually to the same inmates, but sometimes to others
③ Equally likely to happen to anybody

26. What percentage of **inmate-on-inmate** violence that occurs in the prison would you say staff is aware of?
_____ Percent

27. When staff have been made aware of instances of **inmate-on-inmate** violence, how often was any action taken by the institution to discipline the inmates involved?
① Never
② Very rarely
③ Rarely
④ Now and then
⑤ Often
⑥ Very often
⑦ All the time

28. When action was taken by management in response to an instance of **inmate-on-inmate** violence, how often did you feel that the action taken was adequate?
① Never
② Very rarely
③ Rarely
④ Now and then
⑤ Often
⑥ Very often
⑦ All the time

The following questions ask you for information about gang activity at the prison where you work.

29. What percentage of inmates would you say is involved in gangs or gang activity?
_____ Percent

30. How many *different* gangs would you say operate within this prison?
# of gangs _____

31. How many of these gangs are:
White _____
Black _____
Northern Latino _____
Southern Latino _____
Other racial group _____
Mixed race or other type of gang _____

32. How often has any type of gang-related violence occurred <u>during the past six months</u>?
① Never
② A few times
③ Once a month
④ A few times a month
⑤ Once a week
⑥ A few times a week
⑦ Every working day

33. A. How often is gang-related activity motivated by problems between inmates and staff, or problems with prison conditions?
    1. Never
    2. Very rarely
    3. Rarely
    4. Now and then
    5. Often
    6. Very often
    7. All the time
    8. No such group exists

    B. Would you say that this type of gang-related activity, in response to inmate problems with staff or prison conditions, makes the prison safer, less safe, or is there no effect?
    1. Much safer
    2. Safer
    3. Somewhat safer
    4. No effect
    5. Somewhat less safe
    6. Less safe
    7. Much less safe
    8. No gangs are present at this prison

The next two questions ask you what effect you think incarceration in this prison has on most inmates.

34. Do you think that time spent as an inmate in the prison where you work makes inmates more violent, less violent, or is there no effect?
    1. Less violent
    2. Somewhat less violent
    3. No effect
    4. Somewhat more violent
    5. More violent

35. When inmates leave this prison, would you say that they are more prepared to be law abiding citizens than they were when they entered, or less prepared than when they entered?
    1. More prepared than when they entered
    2. Somewhat more prepared than when they entered
    3. No difference
    4. Somewhat less prepared than when they entered
    5. Less prepared than when they entered

WORK ENVIRONMENT

36. I receive the kind of training that I need to perform my job well.
    1. Strongly disagree
    2. Disagree
    3. Somewhat disagree
    4. Undecided
    5. Somewhat agree
    6. Agree
    7. Strongly agree

37. Management communicates clear guidelines on when the use of *non-lethal* force is appropriate.
    1. Strongly disagree
    2. Disagree
    3. Somewhat disagree
    4. Undecided
    5. Somewhat agree
    6. Agree
    7. Strongly agree

38. Management communicates clear guidelines on when the use of *lethal* force is appropriate.
    1. Strongly disagree
    2. Disagree
    3. Somewhat disagree
    4. Undecided
    5. Somewhat agree
    6. Agree
    7. Strongly agree

39. I received the kind of training I need to keep myself safe on the job.
    1. Strongly disagree
    2. Disagree
    3. Somewhat disagree
    4. Undecided
    5. Somewhat agree
    6. Agree
    7. Strongly agree

40. How would you describe your interactions with inmates at the prison where you work?
    1. Not as pleasant as most other officers
    2. About the same as most other officers
    3. More pleasant than most other officers

41. In general, how would you describe the relationship between correctional officers and inmates at your institution?
    1. Very unpleasant
    2. Unpleasant
    3. Somewhat unpleasant
    4. Undecided
    5. Somewhat pleasant
    6. Pleasant
    7. Very pleasant

FACILITIES

For the following set of questions, please indicate your evaluation <u>over the past six months</u> of the prison where you work.

42. Would you say that there have been enough visiting hours each week to accommodate visitation requests, or would you say that there have not been enough visiting hours each week?
    1. Not enough hours each week
    2. Enough hours each week
    3. Don't know

43. How <u>crowded</u> do you think it has been in the visiting areas during visiting hours?
    ① Not at all crowded
    ② Slightly crowded but not uncomfortable
    ③ Moderately crowded and becoming uncomfortable
    ④ More than moderately crowded and uncomfortable
    ⑤ Very crowded
    ⑥ Don't know

44. How <u>noisy</u> do you think it has been in the visiting areas during visiting hours?
    ① Not at all noisy
    ② Slightly noisy but not uncomfortable
    ③ Moderately noisy and becoming uncomfortable
    ④ More than moderately noisy and uncomfortable
    ⑤ Very noisy
    ⑥ Don't know

45. How often have <u>dirt or litter</u> been a major problem in the inmate dining hall or housing units?
    ① Never
    ② A few times
    ③ Once a month
    ④ A few times a month
    ⑤ Once a week
    ⑥ A few times a week
    ⑦ Every working day

46. How often have <u>rodents or insects</u> been a problem in the inmate dining hall or housing units?
    ① Never
    ② A few times
    ③ Once a month
    ④ A few times a month
    ⑤ Once a week
    ⑥ A few times a week
    ⑦ Every working day

47. In general, how would you describe the physical condition of the buildings at this prison?
    ① Poor
    ② Somewhat poor
    ③ Somewhat good
    ④ Good

The following is a list of services and programs that may be provided to inmates at your prison. Please indicate the quality of each service or program.

48. A. Educational Programs
    ① Very poor quality
    ② Poor quality
    ③ Moderate quality
    ④ Good quality
    ⑤ Very good quality
    ⑥ Don't know
    ⑦ Not offered at this institution

B. Vocational Programs
    ① Very poor quality
    ② Poor quality
    ③ Moderate quality
    ④ Good quality
    ⑤ Very good quality
    ⑥ Don't know
    ⑦ Not offered at this institution

C. Psychological Services
    ① Very poor quality
    ② Poor quality
    ③ Moderate quality
    ④ Good quality
    ⑤ Very good quality
    ⑥ Don't know
    ⑦ Not offered at this institution

D. Drug and Alcohol Treatment
    ① Very poor quality
    ② Poor quality
    ③ Moderate quality
    ④ Good quality
    ⑤ Very good quality
    ⑥ Don't know
    ⑦ Not offered at this institution

GRIEVANCE PROCEDURES

49. When I have a problem at work, there is someone I can talk to who will really help me solve it.
    ① Strongly disagree
    ② Disagree
    ③ Somewhat disagree
    ④ Undecided
    ⑤ Somewhat agree
    ⑥ Agree
    ⑦ Strongly agree

50. A. Please indicate any of the following areas in which you have had work-related problems in the last six months. **(Choose all that apply)**
    ① Harassment by a supervisor or management
    ② Job or work assignment/task
    ③ Training
    ④ Promotion/advancement
    ⑤ Performance feedback or recognition
    ⑥ Disciplinary action or misconduct allegation
    ⑦ Work schedule, attendance, leave, or pay issue
    ⑧ Issue with inmate or inmates
    ⑨ Problem with another staff member
    ⑩ Other _____

◊5◊

B. If you were to have a work-related problem in the future, would you consider contacting a supervisor to resolve it?
① Yes   ② No   ③ Not sure

C. If you would not contact a supervisor to resolve a problem at work, which of the following describes why you would not? **(Choose all that apply)**
① Do not think it will help
② Do not trust supervisor
③ Concerned about negative consequences from coworkers
④ Concerned about negative consequences from management
⑤ Think it would take too much time and effort
⑥ Other _____

D. If you were to have a work-related problem in the future, would you consider contacting CCPOA to resolve it?
① Yes   ② No   ③ Not sure

E. If you would not contact CCPOA to resolve the problem at work, which of the following describes why you would not? **(Choose all that apply)**
① Do not think it would help
② Do not trust CCPOA
③ Concerned about negative consequences from coworkers
④ Concerned about negative consequences from management
⑤ Think it would take too much time and effort
⑥ Not a member of the union
⑦ Other _____

51. When individual inmates file complaints about prison conditions, how often does this result in a formal response from staff or management?
① Never
② Very rarely
③ Rarely
④ Now and then
⑤ Often
⑥ Very often
⑦ All the time

52. When individual inmates file complaints about staff behavior, how often does this result in a formal response from staff or management?
① Never
② Very rarely
③ Rarely
④ Now and then
⑤ Often
⑥ Very often
⑦ All the time

The following questions ask you to comment on the inmate advisory council, or any other inmate self-government organization, at your institution.

53. Are you aware of the existence of an inmate advisory council (a men's or women's advisory council or other governing body) at your institution?
① Yes   ② No   ③ Not sure

54. What percentage of inmates would you say are involved with this group in any way?
_____ Percent

55. A. How often are this group's activities motivated by problems between inmates and staff, or problems with prison conditions?
① Never
② Very rarely
③ Rarely
④ Now and then
⑤ Often
⑥ Very often
⑦ All the time
⑧ Don't know/No such group exists

B. Would you say that this type of group activity, in response to inmate problems with staff or prison conditions, makes the prison safer, less safe, or is there no effect?
① Much less safe
① Less safe
② Somewhat less safe
③ No effect
④ Somewhat safer
⑤ Safer
⑥ Much safer
⑦ Don't know/No such group exists

C. When this group communicates inmate concerns to staff, how often does this result in any kind of response from staff or management?
① Never
② Very rarely
③ Rarely
④ Now and then
⑤ Often
⑥ Very often
⑦ All the time
⑧ Don't know/No such group exists

COMMUNITY LIFE

56. Are you currently enrolled in school?
① Yes   ② No

57. What would you say is the biggest obstacle to your continuing your education?
① Lack of time
② Cost
③ Lack of interest
④ Believe I don't have the academic ability
⑤ Don't have enough information

58. Do you consider yourself a
    1. Republican
    2. Independent
    3. Democrat
    4. Other party
    5. No party

59. How aware do you think people in the community surrounding the prison are of its existence?
    1. Not at all aware
    2. Slightly aware
    3. Moderately aware
    4. More than moderately aware
    5. Very aware

60. How would you describe the image of the prison in the surrounding community?
    1. Very negative
    2. Negative
    3. Somewhat negative
    4. Neutral
    5. Somewhat positive
    6. Positive
    7. Very positive

61. How often have community members, <u>excluding friends and family members of inmates</u>, entered the facility, for example as program volunteers, on tours, etc?
    1. Never
    2. A few times
    3. Once a month
    4. A few times a month
    5. Once a week
    6. A few times a week
    7. Every working day

INSTITUTIONAL GOALS

The next set of questions asks you to share <u>your own thoughts</u> about the goals of incarceration.

62. Do you feel that the purpose of a prison is rehabilitation, punishment, or both?
    1. Totally rehabilitation
    2. More rehabilitation, but still punishment
    3. Equally rehabilitation and punishment
    4. More punishment, but still rehabilitation
    5. Totally punishment

63. Do you think that most people who end up in prison are there because of personal failure, or because they did not have advantages like strong families, good education, and job opportunities?
    1. Totally personal failure
    2. Mostly personal failure, but also lack of advantages
    3. Equally lack of advantages and personal failure
    4. Mostly lack of advantages, but also personal failure
    5. Totally lack of advantages

64. A. Rehabilitation should be a central goal of incarceration.
    1. Strongly disagree
    2. Disagree
    3. Somewhat disagree
    4. Somewhat agree
    5. Agree
    6. Strongly agree

   B. The job of a prison is to keep the public safe, not to help inmates.
    1. Strongly disagree
    2. Disagree
    3. Somewhat disagree
    4. Somewhat agree
    5. Agree
    6. Strongly agree

   C. By the time most inmates enter prison, it is too late for rehabilitation programs to do them any good.
    1. Strongly disagree
    2. Disagree
    3. Somewhat disagree
    4. Somewhat agree
    5. Agree
    6. Strongly agree

   D. Inmates who want it should have access to academic training at least up to and including GED preparation.
    1. Strongly disagree
    2. Disagree
    3. Somewhat disagree
    4. Somewhat agree
    5. Agree
    6. Strongly agree

   E. Inmates who want it should have access to academic training at the college level.
    1. Strongly disagree
    2. Disagree
    3. Somewhat disagree
    4. Somewhat agree
    5. Agree
    6. Strongly agree

   F. Inmates who want it should be given access to vocational training.
    1. Strongly disagree
    2. Disagree
    3. Somewhat disagree
    4. Somewhat agree
    5. Agree
    6. Strongly agree

G. High quality rehabilitation programs would pay for themselves in the long run with decreased crime and a smaller prison population.
  ① Strongly disagree
  ② Disagree
  ③ Somewhat disagree
  ④ Somewhat agree
  ⑤ Agree
  ⑥ Strongly agree

H. Inmates who want it should have access to drug and alcohol treatment.
  ① Strongly disagree
  ② Disagree
  ③ Somewhat disagree
  ④ Somewhat agree
  ⑤ Agree
  ⑥ Strongly agree

I. Most inmates are just regular people who have made some mistakes.
  ① Strongly disagree
  ② Disagree
  ③ Somewhat disagree
  ④ Somewhat agree
  ⑤ Agree
  ⑥ Strongly agree

J. There are better ways for the state to spend money than on programs for inmates.
  ① Strongly disagree
  ② Disagree
  ③ Somewhat disagree
  ④ Somewhat agree
  ⑤ Agree
  ⑥ Strongly agree

K. Rehabilitation programs don't work because most inmates don't want to change.
  ① Strongly disagree
  ② Disagree
  ③ Somewhat disagree
  ④ Somewhat agree
  ⑤ Agree
  ⑥ Strongly agree

L. It would cost too much to provide all inmates with high quality programs.
  ① Strongly disagree
  ② Disagree
  ③ Somewhat disagree
  ④ Somewhat agree
  ⑤ Agree
  ⑥ Strongly agree

M. Inmates don't deserve to get rehabilitation programs.
  ① Strongly disagree
  ② Disagree
  ③ Somewhat disagree
  ④ Somewhat agree
  ⑤ Agree
  ⑥ Strongly agree

N. The only way to keep people from committing crimes is to get to them while they are still kids.
  ① Strongly disagree
  ② Disagree
  ③ Somewhat disagree
  ④ Somewhat agree
  ⑤ Agree
  ⑥ Strongly agree

O. If I had met a lot of the inmates I work with on the outside rather than in prison, I might be friends with them.
  ① Strongly disagree
  ② Disagree
  ③ Somewhat disagree
  ④ Somewhat agree
  ⑤ Agree
  ⑥ Strongly agree

DEMOGRAPHICS

65. What is your sex?
  ① Female   ② Male

66. In what year were you born?
  _____

67. What is the highest level of education you have attained so far?
  ① GED or High School degree
  ② Some college (no degree)
  ③ Associate's Degree
  ④ Bachelor's degree
  ⑤ Master's degree
  ⑥ Ph.D. degree
  ⑦ Advanced professional degree (medical, law)

68. Which category best describes your ethnicity? (**Choose all that apply**)
  ① American Indian or Alaska Native
  ② Asian
  ③ Black or African American
  ④ Hispanic/Latino
  ⑤ Native Hawaiian or Other Pacific Islander
  ⑥ White/Caucasian
  ⑦ Other _____

THANK YOU FOR YOUR PARTICIPATION
Many thanks for your participation in this very important survey project. Your input is extremely valuable. Please feel free to attach a separate piece of paper to write any additional comments you would like to share.
◇8◇
Case ID: _____
This ID does not allow the researchers to identify you. It is strictly for administrative use, and to prevent against duplicate surveys.

FIGURE B.1. CCOS survey instrument.

C. CCOS Response Rate by Institution

Institution	Estimated Positions Filled	Returned Surveys (No.)	Response Rate (%)
Avenal State Prison	671	161	24.0
CA Correctional Center	520	164	31.5
CA Correctional Institution	975	245	25.1
CA Institution for Men	888	236	26.6
CA Institution for Women	302	67	22.2
CA Medical Facility	526	190	36.1
CA Men's Colony	748	249	33.3
CA Rehabilitation Center	605	138	22.8
CA State Prison – Corcoran	1057	220	20.8
CA State Prison – Sacramento	747	215	28.8
CA State Prison – Solano	597	123	20.6
CA State Prison – Wasco	703	172	24.5
Calipatria State Prison	564	157	27.8
Centinela State Prison	607	139	22.9
Central CA Women's Facility	376	95	25.3
Chuckawalla Valley State Prison	331	77	23.3
Correctional Training Facility	728	182	25.0
CA State Prison – LA County	637	170	26.7
Delano II State Prison	751	136	18.1
Deuel Vocational Institution	549	157	28.6
Folsom State Prison	449	150	33.4
High Desert State Prison	671	214	31.9
Ironwood State Prison	587	150	25.6
Mule Creek State Prison	475	148	31.2
North Kern State Prison	653	137	21.0
Pelican Bay State Prison	805	271	33.7
Pleasant Valley State Prison	689	159	23.1
RJ Donovan Correctional Facility	683	184	26.9
Salinas Valley State Prison	725	181	25.0
San Quentin State Prison	805	198	24.6
Sierra Conservation Center	543	159	29.3
Substance Abuse Treatment Facility	872	203	23.3
Valley State Prison for Women	404	121	30.0

Note: Additional surveys were returned that did not specify an institution.

D. CDCR Classification Score Sheet

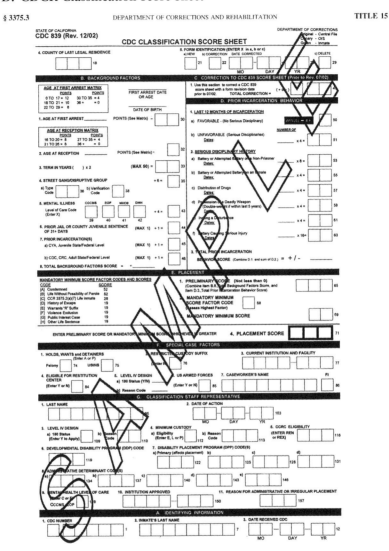

FIGURE D.1 CDCR classification score sheet.

E. Features of CDCR Security-Level Assignment

All entering or returning inmates are initially processed at a reception center (RC). During the reception period, a correctional counselor uses a Form 839 in order to classify newly received inmates according to the department's classification system.[1] The 839 is intended to be a comprehensive assessment tool: Section 61010.9 of the Director's Rules states: "The counselor shall review all relevant documents available during the RC process to complete the score sheet. Since the Placement Score usually determines the institution to which the inmate will be assigned, it is extremely important that the information considered be as complete as possible."

As described in Chapter 4, the 839 records a series of items related to both background and prior incarceration behavior. The Background Factor Score is then combined with the Prior Incarceration Behavior Score to obtain the Preliminary Score. The Preliminary Score is equal to the final Placement Score unless there is a factor in the inmate's record requiring the addition of a Mandatory Minimum. As defined in the Director's Rules, "A Mandatory Minimum Score is a numerical value identifying the least restrictive security level for an inmate who has a case factor that requires he/she be housed no lower than a specific security level."[2] If the Mandatory Minimum is applied, the final Placement Score is either the Mandatory Minimum or the Preliminary Score, whichever is greater.

In most cases, an inmate's Final Placement Score is the primary factor in determining the security-level prison to which he or she will be sent. A caseworker can, however, apply an administrative determinant to a case or otherwise suggest an irregular placement. An irregular placement is the assignment of an inmate to an institution that does not correspond to the security level of his or her Final Placement Score. A consultant's report commissioned by the state in the late 1990s concluded, "[A]dministrative determinants are 'an integral part of the score process'... [and] they serve to 'fine tune' the score system."[3] An administrative determinant can include, among other things, youthfulness or immaturity; enemies; escape potential; family ties; gang involvement; need for medical attention; need to be housed close to a court jurisdiction; mental health condition; academic program involvement; sexual orientation; or work skills.[4] System-wide,

TABLE E.1. *Factors Requiring a Mandatory Minimum*

Factor	Details	Score
Condemned	Inmate sentenced to death	52
Life without possibility of parole	Inmate sentenced to life without the possibility of parole	52
CCR 3375.2(a)(7) life inmate	Inmate excluded from placement in Level I or II facilities for • commitment offense involved multiple murders, unusual violence, or execution-type murders • history of multiple walkaways, escape from a secure perimeter or escape with force or threat of force	28
History of escape	Inmate • with any history of escape or attempted escape from a secure perimeter • who has a conviction for escape or attempted escape with force • who verbalizes an intent to escape • who has a history of walkaways without force from a non-secure perimeter facility • who has a conviction for a walkaway within the past 10 years	19
Warrants "R" suffix	Inmate with an R suffix, designating a history of specific sex offenses as provided in CCR 3377.1(b)(1)	19
Violence exclusion	Inmate with a current or prior conviction for a violent felony or sustained juvenile adjudication that does not require case-by-case consideration	19
Public interest case	Defined in CCR 3375.2(b)(20) as "high notoriety of an inmate has caused public interest in the case and requires exceptional placement"	19
Other life sentences	Inmate serving a current life sentence commitment who is excluded from minimum-custody placement until a release date is granted	19

Source: Section 61010.11.5 of the Rules and Regulations of the Director of Corrections.

about 25 percent of inmates are placed according to administrative determinants.[5] However, as administrative determinants introduce a degree of subjectivity into the placement process, all results exclude these cases.

TABLE E.2. *Percent in Dataset Placed in Each Security Level, by Classification Score*

	Percent Placed in Security Level			
	I	II	III	IV
Classification score				
0–18	70	30	0	0
19–27	25	75	0	0
28–51	4	7	90	0
52+	16	8	12	64

Note: Table excludes cases assigned a mandatory minimum, as well as those placed through administrative determinant. Rows may not add to 100% due to rounding. $N = 10,951$.

Implications of Assignment Process for Estimating Prison Effects

In the data, the majority of inmates are placed into a security level according to the range in which their score falls (see Table E.2). (When those assigned a mandatory minimum are included in the sample, a larger proportion of inmates at each security level are misplaced. This is due to the fact that most mandatory minimums either exclude inmates from a Level I facility or require inmates to be housed in a Level IV facility.) However, an individual's classification score is not a perfect predictor of placement. Not all individuals with a score above the cutoff are placed in higher-custody institutions, and not all individuals below the cutoff are placed in lower-custody settings. The most common reason for placement outside the designated security level is a "population override," used to accommodate a lack of available bed space.[6]

The "fuzzy" nature of the regression discontinuity means that estimates presented from regression equations technically show the effect of having a classification score higher than the cutoff value rather than the effect of placement into a higher-security prison. The traditional way to account for this is by estimating a two-stage least squares model.[7] In this model, a linear probability model is employed as Equation 1, in order to estimate the likelihood of placement in a higher-security prison as a function of whether the classification score falls above (coded as 1) or below the cutoff (coded as 0) and other relevant covariates. Equation 2 is then estimated similarly, but uses the coefficient for security score from Equation 1 as an instrument for assignment to a higher- or lower-security level. All results presented in Chapter 5 hold in these analyses, and the magnitudes of the effects remain relatively stable.

F. Descriptive and Predictive COMPAS Scales

	Scale	Items (#)	Description
Descriptive scale type			
Criminal and anti-social behavior	Criminal involvement	4	"Extent of involvement in the criminal justice system ... and extensiveness of the criminal history"
	History of non-compliance	4	"Focuses on the number of times the offender has failed when he or she has been placed in a community status"
	History of violence	9	"Seriousness and extent of violence in an offender's criminal history"
	Current violence	8	"Degree of violence in the present offense"
	Criminal associates	7	"Degree to which a person associates with other persons who are involved in drugs, criminal offenses, gangs"
	Early socialization failures	13	"Family problems, early school problems, and early delinquency, all of which suggest ... how the offender was socialized growing up"
	Criminal opportunity	14	"Assesses criminal opportunity ... time in high crime situation, affiliating with high risk persons ... an absence of social ties, high boredom ... and being in a high risk age group"

	Scale	Items (#)	Description
Social and personal adjustment	Substance abuse	10	"General indicator of substance abuse problems"
	Financial problems	5	"Degree to which a person experiences poverty and financial problems"
	Vocational/educational problems	11	"Degree of successes or failure in the areas of work and education"
	Family criminality	6	"The degree to which the person's family members have been involved in criminal activity, drugs, or alcohol abuse"
	Social environment	6	"Focuses on the amount of crime, disorder, and victimization potential in the neighborhood in which a person lives"
	Leisure problems/ boredom	5	"The degree to which the person experiences feelings of boredom, restlessness, feeling scattered in their leisure time, and an inability to maintain interest in a single activity for any length of time"
	Residential instability	10	"Focus on whether the offender has a stable and verifiable address, local telephone and long term local ties, as opposed to drifting and temporary living situations"
	Social adjustment problems	15	"Degree to which a person is unsuccessful and conflicted in his/her social adjustment in several of the main social institutions (school, work, family, marriage, relationships, financial)"
Social and Criminal Psychometrics	Criminal personality	13	"Main dimensions identified as components of the criminal personality"
	Criminal cognitions	10	"Brings together several cognitions that serve to justify, support, or provide rationalizations for the person's criminal behavior"
	Social isolation	8	"Degree to which the person has a supportive social network and is both accepted and well integrated into this network"

	Scale	Items (#)	Description
Predictive scale type			
Risk prediction scales	Violence	22	Risk of future violent activity
	Recidivism	17	Risk of future recidivism
	Failure to appear	14	Risk of future failure to appear
	Community non-compliance	25	Risk of future technical violation

G. Balance Statistics for Low Criminal History Subsample

As in the sample as a whole, the subsample of inmates with a low criminal history is comparable on observable covariates upon entry to prison. In terms of their level of education, type of controlling offense, number of current charges, score on a Current Violence Scale (measuring the "degree of violence in the present offense"), and term in years, the groups are on average indistinguishable. There is a slight difference in mean age between the two groups. However, as with the full sample, the difference occurs only within the two upper age cohorts: those between 31 and 40, and those older than 41 years. There is also a slight difference in the percentage of inmates incarcerated for robbery. Neither of these differences on its own is a likely explanation for the discontinuity in outcomes.

TABLE G.1 *Balance at Classification Cutoff*

	26/27	28/29	T-test p value	KS p value
Age (%)				.01
16–21	1	1		
22–30	7	2		
31–40	65	55		
41+	28	42		
Education (years)	10.6	10.8		.80
Current charge (%)				
Homicide	0	1	1	
Sex offense	1	2	.32	
Assault	22	17	.36	
Robbery	16	9	.02	
Property	30	29	.70	
Drug possession	20	15	.18	

	26/27	28/29	T-test *p* value	KS *p* value
Drug trafficking	10	15	.22	
Domestic violence	5	3	.36	
Weapons	28	33	.21	
No. of charges or offenses	1.6	1.4		.17
Violence of current charge (decile score)	5.15	4.66		.65
Term length (years)	5.2	5.2		.76

Note: Data are for low criminal history offenders with classification scores of 26 through 29.
Those placed with an administrative determinant or classified prior to 2003 are excluded.
N = 278 (134 below the cutoff and 144 above).

There is likewise no apparent difference between those just above and just below the cutoff on three scales measuring past criminality. The History of Non-Compliance Scale measures an individual's past failures at community-based corrections, such as violations of parole and failure to appear for court. The History of Violence Scale measures the number of past arrests and convictions for violent crimes, like domestic violence, assault, and homicide, as well as documented incidents of violent activity against other inmates. The Family Criminality Scale describes the criminal history of an individual's close relatives, including parents, siblings, and spouse/partner. On each of these three scales, average scores are indistinguishable between the two groups.

Items taken from the Early Socialization Failure Scale are also comparable. On average, those with classification scores just below and just above the cutoff are equally likely to have been charged with a violent felony as a juvenile and to have an equivalent number of juvenile felony charges. There is a slight difference between the two in the probability of having been incarcerated while a juvenile. However, the size of the difference is small and only marginally statistically significant. Finally, there is also little difference on measures of personal history. On measures of substance abuse, financial problems and poverty, and vocational and educational problems, the two groups are statistically equivalent.

TABLE G.2 *Balance on Criminal and Personal History*

		26/27	28/29	T-test *p* value	KS *p* value
Criminal history					
History of non-compliance	Number of times has failed when placed in a community status	3.65	3.75		.99
History of violence	Seriousness and extent of violence in criminal history	4.67	4.83		.98
Family criminality	Degree to which family members have been involved in criminal activity, drugs, or alcohol	3.71	4.23		.71
Socialization failure					
Juvenile felonies	Number of times charged with felony as juvenile	0.56	0.69		.46
Violent juvenile felonies	Ever charged with violent felony as juvenile	1.21	1.22	.85	
Juvenile incarceration	Ever incarcerated as juvenile	1.20	1.34	.04	
Personal history					
Substance abuse	Indicator of substance abuse problems	3.23	3.89		.55
Financial problems and poverty	Degree to which experiences poverty and financial problems	4.50	5.02		.79
Vocational/ educational problems	Degree of successes or failure in the areas of work and education	6.07	6.67		.15

Note: Data are for low criminal history offenders in the COMPAS database with an 839 placement score less than two points from the cutoff points for classification: 26 or 27 and 28 or 29. Those placed with an administrative determinant or classified prior to 2003 are excluded. N = 278 (134 below the cutoff and 144 above).

H. CDCR Gang Designation Form

§ 3378 DEPARTMENT OF CORRECTIONS AND REHABILITATION **TITLE 15**

STATE OF CALIFORNIA DEPARTMENT OF CORRECTIONS

NOTICE OF CRITICAL INFORMATION - PRISON GANG IDENTIFICATION

CDC 812-A (9/92)

This nonconfidential form is used to identify primary source documents in the central file which establish an inmate/parolee's current status relative to prison gang activity/association. The identification process is initiated by completing a form CDC 812 and forwarding it to the Gang Coordinator/Investigator. The Gang Coordinator/Investigator will then complete or supervise the completion of form CDC 812-A and signify to its accuracy by printing name and signing. A CDC 128-B which delineates gang activity/association shall be completed per the CDC Operations Manual.

SUPPORTING INFORMATION

Documents shall be identified by date and type such as memorandum, probation report, parole report, incident report, police report, chrono.

A. SELF ADMISSION	B. TATTOOS AND SYMBOLS
C. WRITTEN MATERIAL	D. PHOTOGRAPHS
E. STAFF INFORMATION	F. OTHER AGENCIES
G. ASSOCIATION	H. INFORMANTS (REASON FOR RELIABILITY MUST BE SPECIFIED)

I. OFFENSES (GANG RELATED)

J. LEGAL DOCUMENTS

K. VISITORS

L. COMMUNICATIONS (MAIL / NOTES)

M. DEBRIEFING REPORTS

ADDITIONAL DOCUMENTATION OR COMMENTS

GANG COORDINATOR/INVESTIGATOR

PRINT NAME OF PRISON GANG AND CURRENT STATUS: MEMBER/ ASSOCIATE/ DROPOUT/ NONE OR SAFETY CONCERNS	PRINT NAME AND SIGN	TITLE	INSTITUTION/ REGION	DATE

CDC NUMBER	INMATE/PAROLEE'S NAME	PAGE ____ OF ____

178

FIGURE H.1 CDCR gang designation form.

I. Questions from the Social Capital Benchmark Survey

Dependent Variables

Social Networks
Friends
>   FRIENDS 53. Number of close friends
>   1 No close friends
>   2 1–2 close friends
>   3 3–5 close friends
>   4 6–10 close friends
>   5 More than 10 close friends

Any Friends
>   recode of FRIENDS
>   (1 = 0) (2 through 5 = 1)

Confidants
>   CONFIDE 54. Number of people you can confide in
>   1 Nobody
>   2 One
>   3 Two
>   4 Three or more

Any Confidants
>   recode of CONFIDE
>   (1 = 0) (2 through 4 = 1)

Socialize
>   Informal social interactions (SCHMOOZ) – Q56f, 56d, 56h, 56i, and 56c (having friends visit home, visiting with relatives, socializing with co-workers outside of work, hanging out with friends in public places, playing cards and board games). At least two of these questions had to be answered for a score to be calculated. The index is calculated as the mean of the standardized responses to the five questions, based on national survey norms: IFRNDHOM, IFAMVIS, IJOBSOC, IFRNDHNG, ICARDS.
>   The following variables request frequencies "in the past twelve months":
>   CFRDVIST 56F. How often had friends over to your home
>   CFAMVISI 56D. How often visited with relatives

CJOBSOC 56H. How often socialized with co-workers outside of work

CFRDHANG 56I. How often hung out with friends in a public place

CCARDS 56C. How often played cards or board games
with others

Social Trust
General Trust
TRUST2 Can trust others vs. be careful
0 Can't be too careful
1 Depends
2 People can be trusted
Social trust (SOCTRUST) – Q6, 7a, 7b, 7c, 7d, 7f (general interpersonal trust, trust neighbors, trust co-workers, trust fellow
congregants, trust store employees where you shop, trust local
police). At least three of these answers had to be provided for
a score to be calculated. The index is calculated as the mean of
the standardized responses to the 5 questions, using national
norms to standardize: ITRUST, ITRNEI, ITRWRK, ITRREL,
ITRSHOP, ITRCOP. (Note: SOCTRUST is SOCTRST with
the polarity of the coding reversed so that higher values on
SOCTRUST indicate higher social trust.)
TRUST 6. Whether most people can be trusted or …
0 Can't be too careful
1 Depends
2 People can be trusted
TRNEI 7A. How much you can trust people in your
neighborhood
1 Trust them a lot
2 Trust them some
3 Trust them only a little
4 Trust them not at all
TRWRK 7B. How much you can trust people you work with
1 Trust them a lot
2 Trust them some
3 Trust them only a little

4 Trust them not at all

TRREL 7C. How much you can trust people at your church or place of worship

1 Trust them a lot

2 Trust them some

3 Trust them only a little

4 Trust them not at all

TRSHOP 7D. How much you can trust people who work in the stores where you shop

1 Trust them a lot

2 Trust them some

3 Trust them only a little

4 Trust them not at all

TRCOP 7F. How much you can trust the police in your local community

1 Trust them a lot

2 Trust them some

3 Trust them only a little

4 Trust them not at all

Independent Variables

Geographic Context

relative urbanicity of the respondents' zip code

    URBPCT90 Percent urban in zip code (1990)

population density of the respondents' zip code

    PO8PDNS97 Population density in zip code, 1997

racial composition of the community

    CTYWHITE Percentage white in Respondent's COMMUNITY

    CTYBLACK Percentage Black in R's COMMUNITY

    CTYHISPN Percentage Hispanic in R's COMMUNITY

    CTYASIAN Percentage Asian in R's COMMUNITY

mean education and income of the community

    CTY_EDUC Mean EDUC in R's COMMUNITY

    CTYINCOM Mean INCOME in R's COMMUNITY

and census region

    CENSREG CENSUS REGION FROM SAMPLE.

1 Northeast
2 Midwest
3 South
4 West
  recoded into dummy variables, with South excluded

Respondent Demographics

race
  HISPAN 62. Hispanic or Latino
  0 No
  1 Yes
  RACE 63. Race of Non-Hispanics
  1 White
  2 African American or Black
  3 Asian or Pacific Islander
  4 Alaskan Native/Native American
    recoded into dummy variables, with white excluded
gender
  GENDER Gender of respondent
  1 Male
  2 Female
education
  EDUC_ALL Education including GED follow-up
  1 Less than high school
  2 High school diploma/GED
  3 Some college
  4 Assoc degree (2 years) or specialized technical training
  5 Bachelor's degree
  6 Some graduate training
  7 Graduate or professional training
age
  AGE Respondent's age
    Computed from birth year provided by respondent.
citizenship
  CITIZ 64. Citizenship status
  0 No
  1 Yes

Economic Well-Being
   current employment status
      LABOR 40. Current employment status
      1 Working
      2 Temporarily laid off
      3 Unemployed
      4 Retired
      5 Permanently disabled
      6 Homemaker
      7 Student
         recoded into dummy variables, employed excluded
         employed
         laid off, unemployed
         retired, disabled, homemaker, student
   poverty
      YP_1 66A. Household income < $30K or $30K+
      1 Less than $30,000
      2 $30,000 or more
   previous year's household income
      INCOME 1999 Total household income
      0 $20,000 or less
      1 Over $20,000 but less than $30,000
      2 Less than $30,000 unspecified
      3 At least $30,00 but less than $50,000
      4 At least $50,000 but less than $75,000
      5 At least $75,000 but less than $100,00
      6 At least $100,000 or more

Residential Mobility
   length of residence in community
      LIVCOM 12. Number of years lived in your local community
      1 Less than one year
      2 One to five years
      3 Six to ten years
      4 Eleven to twenty years
      5 More than twenty years
      6 All my life
   future expected mobility

STAY 13. Expect to be living in your community in 5 years
o No
1 Yes

Household Indicators

whether home is owned or rented
OWN 15. Own or rent residence
o Rent
1 Own
marital status
MARITAL 46. Current marital status
o Never married
1 Widowed
2 Divorced
3 Separated
4 Currently married
PARTNER 46A. Living with a partner
o No
1 Yes
recoded into dummy variables, married excluded
married
partner
widowed, divorced, separated
never married
number of children under 18 residing in the household
KIDS 47. Kids 17 or younger in household

Notes

THE MODERN PRISON PARADOX

1   Craig Haney and Philip Zimbardo, "The Past and Future of U.S. Prison Policy: Twenty-Five Years after the Stanford Prison Experiment," *American Psychologist* 53, no. 7 (1998): 709–772; www.prisonexp.org/pdf/ap1998.pdf.

2   Philip G. Zimbardo, "A Situationist Perspective on the Psychology of Evil: Understanding How Good People Are Transformed into Perpetrators," in Arthur Milled (ed.), *The Social Psychology of Good and Evil: Understanding our Capacity for Kindness and Cruelty* (New York: Guilford, 2004). www.zimbardo.com/downloads/2003%20Evil%20Chapter.pdf.

3   Haney and Zimbardo, "Past and Future," 709.

4   Craig Haney, Curtis Banks, and Philip Zimbardo. "Interpersonal Dynamics in a Simulated Prison," *International Journal of Criminology and Penology* 1 (1973): 69–97; www.prisonexp.org/pdf/ijcp1973.pdf.

5   Philip Zimbardo, "Revisiting the Stanford Prison Experiment: A Lesson in the Power of Situation"; www.lucifereffect.org/about_reviews_chronicle.htm.

6   The Stanford Prison Experiment has been criticized on both ethical and methodological grounds. See, e.g., Erich Fromm, *The Anatomy of Human Destructiveness* (New York: Fawcett Books, 1973); Stephen Reicher and Alexander Haslam, "Debating the Psychology of Tyranny: Fundamental Issues of Theory, Perspective and Science," *British Journal of Social Psychology* 45 (2006); Thomas Carnahan and Sam McFarland, "Revisiting the Stanford Prison Experiment: Could Participants' Self-Selection Have Led to the Cruelty?" *Personality and Social Psychology Bulletin* 33, no. 5 (2007): 603–614.

7 Pew Center on the States, *Prison Count 2010: State Population Declines for the First Time in 38 Years* (Washington, DC: Pew Charitable Trusts, April 2010).

8 Pew Center on the States, *One in 100: Behind Bars in America.* (Washington, DC: Pew Charitable Trusts, 2008).

9 Pew Center on the States, *One in 31: The Long Reach of American Corrections* (Washington, DC: Pew Charitable Trusts, 2009).

10 International Centre for Prison Studies, *World Prison Population List*, 8th ed. (London: King's College).

11 Bruce Western and Becky Pettit, *Collateral Costs: Incarceration's Effect on Economic Mobility* (Washington, DC: Pew Charitable Trusts, 2010).

12 Becky Pettit, *Invisible Men: Mass Incarceration and the Myth of Black Progress* (New York: Russell Sage Foundation, 2012); Becky Pettit and Bruce Western, "Mass Imprisonment and the Life Course: Race and Class Inequality in U.S. Incarceration," *American Sociological Review* 69, no. 2 (2004): 151–169.

13 Pettit and Western, "Mass Imprisonment and the Life Course," 155–156.

14 Senate Joint Economic Committee Hearing, "Mass Incarceration in the United States: At What Cost?" Opening Statement of Senator Jim Webb, October 4, 2007, 110th Congress, 1st sess.

15 David Garland, *Culture of Control: Crime and Social Order in Contemporary Society* (Chicago: University of Chicago Press, 2001), 2.

16 Justice Mapping Center, "Million Dollar Blocks of Brownsville"; www.justicemapping.org/archive/26/multi-%e2%80%98million-dollar%e2%80%99-blocks-of-brownsville/.

17 Statistics on the concentration of prisoners are from various Urban Institute reports available at www.urban.org/projects/reentry-portfolio/publications.cfm.

18 Jeffrey Fagan, Valerie West, and Jan Holland, "Reciprocal Effects of Crime and Incarceration in New York City," *Fordham Urban Law Journal* 30 (2003): 1551–1602.

19 Vesla M. Weaver and Amy E. Lerman, "Political Consequences of the Carceral State," *American Political Science Review* 104, No. 4 (2010): 817–833.

20 Todd Clear, "The Effects of High Imprisonment Rates on Communities," *Crime and Justice* 37, no. 1 (2008): 97–132, at 102.

21 Bureau of Justice Statistics, "Prevalence of Imprisonment in the U.S. Population, 1974–2001" (2003); bjs.ojp.usdoj.gov/content/pub/pdf/piusp01.pdf.

22 James P. Lynch and William J. Sabol, "Prison Use and Social Control," in *Policies, Processes, and Decisions of the Criminal Justice System: Criminal Justice 2000* (Washington, DC: U.S. Department of Justice, National Institute of Justice, 2000).

23 For an overview see Patrice Villettaz, Martine Killias, and Isabel Zoder, *The Effects of Custodial vs. Non-custodial Sentences on Reoffending: A Systematic Review of the State of Knowledge* (Campbell Systematic Reviews, 2006).

24 Malcolm M. Feeley and Jonathan Simon, "The New Penology: Notes on the Emerging Strategy of Corrections and Its Implications," *Criminology* 30 (1992): 449–474.

25 James Q. Wilson, *Thinking About Crime* (New York: Basic Books, 1975).

26 Feeley and Simon, "The New Penology."

27 Amy E. Lerman and Vesla Weaver, *Policing Democracy* (Chicago: University of Chicago Press, forthcoming).

28 John Pratt, David Brown, Mark Brown, Simon Hallsworth, and Wayne Morrison (eds.), *The New Punitiveness: Trends, Theories and Perspectives*. Devon: Willin, 2005).

29 Robert Martinson, "What Works? Questions and Answers About Prison Reform," *Public Interest* (Spring 1974): 22–54.

30 Wilson, *Thinking About Crime*.

31 Garland, *Culture of Control*.

32 Edward Zamble and Frank Porporino, *Coping, Behavior, and Adaption in Prison Inmates* (New York: Springer, 1988).

33 Robert D. Putnam, *Bowling Alone: The Collapse and Revival of American Community* (New York: Simon & Schuster, 2000).

34 Includes Nevada (16.9%), Florida (16.6%), Arizona (15.5%), District of Columbia (15.5%), Delaware (15.1%), New Jersey (15.1%), New York (14.8%), Maryland (13.8%), Pennsylvania (13.7%), Louisiana (13.6%), Illinois (13.5%), Missouri (13.4%), Georgia (13.3%), California (13.2%), and Massachusetts (13.2%).

35 Bureau of Justice Statistics, "Justice Expenditure and Employment Extracts"; bjs.ojp.usdoj.gov/index.cfm?ty=dcdetail&iid=286.

36 Glen Loury, *Race, Incarceration, and American Values* (Cambridge, MA: MIT Press, 2008).

37 Ted Conover, *Newjack: Guarding Sing Sing* (New York: Vintage Books, 2001), 242–243.

38 Erving Goffman, *Asylums: Essays on the Social Situation of Mental Patients and Other Inmates* (New York: Anchor Books, 1961).

39 Joan Petersilia, *When Prisoners Come Home* (Oxford: Oxford University Press, 2003).

40 Data Analysis Unit, "Time Served on Prison Sentence: Felons First Released to Parole by Offense Calendar Year 2012" (California Department of Corrections and Rehabilitation, 2013).

41 Petersilia, *When Prisoners Come Home*.

42 Sasha Abramsky, "When They Get Out," *Atlantic Monthly* 283, no. 6 (1999): 33.

43 John Locke, *Two Treatises on Government* (1821); www.bartleby.com/169/. Thomas Hobbes, *Leviathan* (1660); oregonstate.edu/instruct/phl302/texts/hobbes/leviathan-contents.html/.

44 Locke, *Two Treatises on Government*, bk. I, ch. IX; http://www.bartleby.com/169/109.html.

45 Robert Worth, "A Model Prison" (1995), *Atlantic Monthly*; www.the-atlantic.com/past/docs/issues/95nov/prisons/prisons.htm.

46 Putnam, *Bowling Alone*.

47 Doug McAdam, *Political Process and the Development of Black Insurgency, 1930–1970* (Chicago: University of Chicago Press, 1982); Sidney Tarrow, *Power in Movement: Social Movements, Collective Action, and Politics* (New York: Cambridge University Press, 1984); David Snow and Doug McAdam, "Identity Work Processes in the Context of Social Movements: Clarifying the Identity/Movement Nexus," in Sheldon Stryker, Timothy J. Owens, and Robert W. White (eds.), *Self, Identity and Social Movements*, 41–67 (Minneapolis: University of Minnesota Press, 2000).

48 Putnam, *Bowling Alone*.

49 Amaney Jamal and Irfan Nooruddin, "The Democratic Utility of Trust: A Cross-National Analysis," *Journal of Politics* 72, no. 1 (2010): 45–59.

50 Eric Uslaner, "Producing and Consuming Trust." *Political Science Quarterly* 115 (2000–2001): 4.

51 Pierre Bourdieu and Loic J. D. Wacquant, *An Invitation to Reflexive Sociology* (Chicago: University of Chicago Press, 1992), 114.

52 For reviews and critiques, see e.g., Ted Mouw, "Estimating the Causal Effect of Social Capital," *Annual Review of Sociology* 32 (2006): 79–102; Nan Lin, "Social Networks and Status Attainment," *Annual Review of Sociology* 25 (1999): 467–487; Robert W. Jackman and Ross A. Miller, "Social Capital and Politics," *Annual Review of Political Science* 1 (1998): 47–73.

53 Ibid.

54 Putnam, *Bowling Alone*.

55 Ibid.

56 Ibid.

57 James Putzel, "Accounting for the Dark Side of Social Capital," *Journal of International Development* 9, no. 7 (1997): 939–949.

58 A. Portes and P. Landolt, "Unsolved Mysteries – The Tocqueville File II: The Downside of Social Capital," *American Prospect* 7, no. 26 (1996): 18–21.

59 Margaret Levi, "Social and Unsocial Capital: A Review Essay of Robert Putnam's Making Democracy Work," *Politics & Society* 24 (March 1996): 45–55.

60 Loic Wacquant, "Negative Social Capital: State Breakdown and Social Destitution in America's Urban Core," *Journal of Housing and the Built Environment*; Alejandro Portes, "Social Capital: Its Origins and Applications in Modern Sociology," *Annual Review of Sociology* 24 (1998): 1–24.

61 Francis Fukuyama, "Social Capital, Civil Society and Development," *Third World Quarterly* 22, no. 1 (2001): 7–20, at 8.

62 Putzel, "Accounting for the Dark Side of Social Capital."

63 See, e.g., Todd Clear, *Imprisoning Communities: How Mass Incarceration Makes Disadvantaged Neighborhoods Worse* (New York: Oxford University Press, 2007); Dina R. Rose and Todd R. Clear, "Incarceration,

Social Capital, and Crime: Implications for Social Disorganization Theory," *Criminology* 36, no. 3 (1998): 441–480.

64 Christopher Browning, Seth L. Feinberg, and Robert D. Dietz, "The Paradox of Social Organization: Networks, Collective Efficacy, and Violent Crime in Urban Neighborhoods," *Social Forces* 83, no. 2 (2004): 503–534, at 509.

65 For a brief review of the literature on crime, incarceration, and social disorganization, see Chapter 8.

66 Elliott Currie, *Crime and Punishment in America* (New York: Henry Holt, 1998), 21.

67 Senate Joint Economic Committee, "Mass Incarceration in the United States: At What Cost?"

68 John J. Donohue, "Economic Models of Crime and Punishment," *Social Research: An International Quarterly* 74, no. 2 (2007): 379–412.

69 Noval Morris, *The Future of Imprisonment* (Chicago: University of Chicago Press, 1974/1977), 2; Nils Christie, *Crime Control as Industry: Towards Gulags, Western Style?* (New York: Routledge, 1993), 23.

70 Nicola Lacey, *Criminal Justice and Democratic Systems: Inclusionary and Exclusionary Dynamics in the Institutional Structure of Late Modern Societies* (Harvard University, Minda de Gunzburg Center for European Studies, 2007), 1.

71 Nicola Lacey, *The Prisoners' Dilemma: Political Economy and Punishment in Contemporary Democracies* (New York: Cambridge University Press, 2008), 3, emphasis added.

72 International Centre for Prison Studies, *World Prison Population List.*

73 John Locke, *Second Treatise of Government* [1690] (New York: Barnes & Noble, 2004).

74 John DiIulio, *Governing Prisons* (New York: Free Press, 1987), 246.

75 Gustave Auguste De Beaumont and Alexis de Tocqueville, *On the Penitentiary System in the United States, and Its Application to France: With an Appendix on Penal Colonies* (Philadelphia: Carey, Lea & Blanchard, 1833).

76 See, e.g., T. Gorski, *Post Incarceration Syndrome and Relapse* (Homewood, IL: CENAPS Corporation, 2005); John Howard Society of Alberta, "Effects of Long Term Incarceration"; www.johnhoward.ab.ca/pub/pdf/C35.pdf.

77 See, e.g., Malcolm Braly, *On the Yard* (New York: New York Review of Books, 2002); Edward Bunker, *Little Boy Blue* (New York: St. Martin's Press, 1981); Sanyika Shakur, *Monster: The Autobiography of an LA Gang Member* (New York: Grove Press, 1993); Leon (Whitey) Thompson, *Last Train to Alcatraz* (Fiddletown, CA: Winter Book, 1988).

78 See, e.g., John Irwin, *Jail: Managing the Underclass in American Society* (Berkeley: University of California Press, 1985); Candace Kruttschnitt and Rosemary Gartner, *Marking Time in the Golden State* (New York: Cambridge University Press, 2005); Gresham Sykes, *The Society of Captives: A Study of a Maximum Security Prison* (Princeton, NJ: Princeton University Press, 1958/2007); Clemmer, *The Prison Community.*

79 Jeffrey Kluger, "Are Prisons Driving Prisoners Mad?" *Time*, January 2007.

80 Frank Porporino, "Difference in Response to Long-Term Imprisonment: Implications for the Management of Long-Term Offenders," *Prison Journal* 80 (1990): 35, 36. Cited in Craig Haney *Reforming Punishment: Psychological Limits to the Pains of Imprisonment* (Washington, DC: American Psychological Association, 2006), 163.

81 Haney, *Reforming Punishment*, 163–164.

82 Sykes, *Society of Captives*, xiii.

83 Gaes and Camp, "Unintended Consequences."

84 DiIulio, *Governing Prisons*.

85 James Austin and Patricia L. Hardyman, *Objective Prison Classification: A Guide for Correctional Agencies* (Washington, DC: National Institute of Corrections, 2004).

86 M. Lipsky, *Street-Level Bureaucracy: Dilemmas of the Individual in Public Services* (New York: Russell Sage Foundation, 1980).

87 S. Philliber, "Thy Brother's Keeper: A Review of the Literature on Correctional Officers," *Justice Quarterly* 4 (1987): 9–37.

88 J. Soss, "Lessons of Welfare: Policy Design, Political Learning and Political Action," *American Political Science Review* 93, no. 2 (1999): 363–380; Lipsky, *Street-Level Bureaucracy*.

89 Philliber, "Thy Brother's Keeper."

90 See, for instance, Paul J. Biermann "Improving Correctional Officer Safety: Reducing Inmate Weapons," (Washington, DC: U.S. Department of Justice, 2007). www.ncjrs.gov/pdffiles1/nij/grants/220485.pdf.

91 U.S. Census Bureau, *State & County Quickfacts*; retrieved January 25, 2007, from quickfacts.census.gov.

92 M. Keith Chen and Jesse M. Shapiro, "Do Harsher Prison Conditions Reduce Recidivism? A Discontinuity-Based Approach," *American Law and Economics Review* 9, no. 1 (2007): 1–29; Gerald G. Gaes and Scott D. Camp, "Unintended Consequences: Experimental Evidence for the Criminogenic Effect of Prison Security Level Placement on Post-Release Recidivism," *Journal of Experimental Criminology* 5, no. 2 (2009): 139–162.

93 Paul Gendreau and Claire Goggin, *The Effects of Prison Sentences on Recidivism* (Ottawa: Department of the Solicitor General, 1999).

94 Villettaz, Killias, and Zoder, "The Effects of Custodial vs. Non-custodial Sentences on Reoffending."

95 Lawrence L. Bench and Terry Allen, "Investigating the Stigma of Prison Classification: An Experimental Design," *Prison Journal* 83, no. 4 (2003): 367–382; Richard A. Berk and Jan de Leeuw, "An Evaluation of California's Inmate Classification System Using a Generalized Regression Discontinuity Design," *Journal of the American Statistical Association* 94, no. 448 (1999): 1045–1052; Chen and Shapiro, "Do Harsher Prison

Conditions Reduce Recidivism?"; Scott D. Camp and Gerald G. Gaes, "Criminogenic Effects of the Prison Environment on Inmate Behavior: Some Experimental Evidence," *Crime and Delinquency* 51, no. 3 (2005): 425–442; Gaes and Camp, "Unintended Consequences"; John E. Berecochea and Joel B. Gibbs, "Inmate Classification: A Correctional Program That Works?" *Evaluation Review* 15, no. 3 (1991): 333–363.

96 Craig Haney, Curtis Banks, and Philip Zimbardo, "Interpersonal Dynamics in a Simulated Prison," *International Journal of Criminology and Penology* 1 (1973): 69–97, at 90; www.prisonexp.org/pdf/ijcp1973.pdf.

97 Haney and Zimbardo, "Past and Future," 720.

98 Pierre Bourdieu, *Acts of Resistance: Against the Tyranny of the Market,* trans. Richard Nice (New York: New Press, 1999).

99 Dietlind Stolle, "The Sources of Social Capital," in M. Hooghe and D. Stolle, *Generating Social Capital: Civil Society and Institutions in Comparative Perspective* (New York: Palgrave, 2003); Marc Hooghe and Dietlind Stolle, in ibid., 35.

100 Michael Woolcock, "Social Capital and Economic Development: Toward a Theoretical Synthesis and Policy Framework," *Theory and Society* 27 (1998): 151–208, at 185.

101 Sheri Berman, "Civil Society and Political Institutionalization," *American Behavioral Scientist* 40 (1997): 562–574; M. Foley and B. Edwards, "Beyond Tocqueville: Civil Society and Social Capital in Comparative Perspective," *American Behavioral Scientist* 42, no. 1 (1998): 5–20; M. Levi, "A State of Trust," in V. Braithwaite and M. Levi (eds.), *Trust and Governance* (New York: Russell Sage Foundation, 1998); Theda Skocpol, "Unravelling from Above," *American Prospect* 25 (1996): 20–25; Sidney Tarrow, "Making Social Science Work Across Space and Time: A Critical Reflection on Robert Putnam's Making Democracy Work," *American Political Science Review* 90 (1996): 389–397.

102 A. Campbell, *How Policies Make Citizens: Senior Citizen Activism and the American Welfare State* (Princeton, NJ: Princeton University Press, 2003).

103 P. Pierson, "When Effect Becomes Cause: Policy Feedback and Political Change," *World Politics* 45 (1993): 595–628; A. L. Schneider and H. Ingram, *Policy Design for Democracy* (Lawrence: University of Kansas Press, 1997); S. Mettler, "Bringing the State Back in to Civic Engagement: Policy Feedback Effects of the G.I. Bill for World War II Veterans," *American Political Science Review* 96, no. 2 (2002); M. J. Edelman, *The Symbolic Uses of Politics* (Urbana: University of Illinois Press, 1964); Soss, "Lessons of Welfare"; Lerman and Weaver, *Policing Democracy.*

104 Bureau of Justice Statistics, *Prisoners in 2009* (Washington, DC: National Institute of Justice, 2010).

105 Devah Pager and Michelle Phelps, "Prison as a Social Context: Residential Mobility, Social Ties, and Disorder in Prison," Working paper, Princeton University.

POLITICS AND THE PUNITIVE TURN

1 Vincent Schiraldi and Jason Ziedenberg. *The Punishing Decade: Prison and Jail Estimates at the Millennium* (Washington DC: Justice Policy Institute, 2000); Bureau of Justice Statistics, *Correctional Populations in the United States, 2010*; http://bjs.gov/index.cfm?ty=pbdetail&iid=2237.

2 For a review, see Amy E. Lerman and Vesla Weaver, "Race and Crime in American Politics from Law and Order to Willie Horton and Beyond," in Michael Tonry and Sandra Bucerius (eds.), *The Oxford Handbook of Ethnicity, Crime and Immigration* (New York: Oxford University Press, forthcoming).

3 Gottschalk, *The Prison and the Gallows*; Simon, "Rise of the Carceral State"; Garland, *The Culture of Control*; Soss et al, "Governing the Poor"

4 David Jacobs and Richard Kleban, "Political Institutions, Minorities, and Punishment: A Pooled Cross-National Analysis of Imprisonment Rates," *Social Forces* 82, no. 2 (2003): 725–755.

5 Ibid., Jonathan Simon, "Rise of the Carceral State," *Social Research* 74, no. 2 (2007): 471; David Garland, *The Culture of Control* (Chicago: University of Chicago Press, 2002); Joe Soss, Richard C. Fording, and Sanford F Schram, *Disciplining the Poor: Neoliberal Paternalism and the Persistent Power of Race State* (Chicago: University of Chicago Press, 2011).

6 Kevin B. Smith, "The Politics of Punishment: Evaluating Explanations of Incarceration Rates," *Journal of Politics* 66, no. 3 (2004): 925–938, 935.

7 Amy E. Lerman and Vesla Weaver, *Policing Democracy: American Crime Control and the New Civic Underclass* (Chicago: University of Chicago Press, forthcoming), ch. 2.

8 Katherine Beckett, *Making Crime Pay: Law and Order in Contemporary American Politics* (New York: Oxford University Press, 1997); Naomi Murakawa, "Electing to Punish: Congress, Race, and the American Criminal Justice State," Ph.D. dissertation, Yale University, Department of Political Science, 2005; Murakawa, "The Origins of the Carceral Crisis: Racial Order as 'Law and Order' in Postwar American Politics," in Joseph Lowndes, Julie Novkov, and Dorian Warren (eds.), *Race and American Political Development* (New York: Routledge, 2008); Bruce Western, *Punishment and Inequality in American Democracy* (New York: Russell Sage Foundation, 2006); Michelle Alexander, *The New Jim Crow: Mass Incarceration in the Age of Colorblindness* (New York: New Press, 2010); Ian H. Lopez, "Post-Racial Racism: Racial Stratification and Mass Incarceration in the Age of Obama," *California Law Review* 98, no. 3 (2010): 1023–1073; James L. Sundquist, *Dynamics of the Party System: Alignment and Realignment of Political Parties in the United States* (Washington, DC: Brookings Institution, 1983).

9 Cited in Malcolm Feeley, *The Policy Dilemma: Federal Crime Policy and the Law Enforcement Assistance Administration, 1968–1978* (Minneapolis: University of Minnesota Press, 1981), 35.

10 Carol A. Horton, *Race and the Making of American Liberalism* (Oxford: Oxford University Press, 2005); Thomas Byrne Edsall with Mary D. Edsall, *Chain Reaction: The Impact of Race, Rights, and Taxes on American Politics* (New York: Norton, 1992).

11 Thomas E. Cronin, Tania Z. Cronin, and Michael F. Milakovich, *U.S. v. Crime in the Streets* (Bloomington: University of Indiana Press, 1981); Michael W. Flamm, *Law and Order: Street Crime, Civil Unrest, and the Crisis of Liberalism in the 1960s* (New York: Columbia University Press, 2007); Katherine Beckett, *Making Crime Pay: Law and Order in Contemporary American Politics* (New York: Oxford University Press, 1997); Bruce Western, *Punishment and Inequality in America* (New York: Russell Sage Foundation, 2006); Murakawa, "Electing to Punish"; Loic Wacquant, "The New Peculiar Institution: On the Prison as Surrogate Ghetto," *Theoretical Criminology* 4, no. 3 (2000): 377–389; Michael Tonry, *Punishing Race: A Continuing American Dilemma* (Oxford: Oxford University Press, 2011).

12 Joel B. Rosch, "Crime as an Issue in American Politics," in Erika Fairchild and Vincent J. Webb (eds.), *The Politics of Crime and Criminal Justice* (Beverly Hills, CA: Sage, 1985).

13 L. Baker, *Miranda: The Crime, the Law, the Politics* (New York: Atheneum, 1983); C. E. Smith , C. DeJong, and J. D. Burrow, *The Supreme Court, Crime, and the Ideal of Equal Justice* (New York: Peter Lang, 2003).

14 Gregory Caldeira, "Neither the Purse nor the Sword: Dynamics of Public Confidence in the Supreme Court," *American Political Science Review* 8, no. 1 (1986): 1209–1226, at 1216.

15 James B. Jacobs, "Prison Reform Amid the Ruins of Prisoners' Rights," in Michael Tonry (ed.), *The Future of Imprisonment*, 179–198 (Oxford: Oxford University Press, 2004).

16 L. M. Friedman, *Crime and Punishment in American History* (New York: Basic Books, 1993).

17 Amy Lerman and Vesla Weaver, "Race and Crime in American Politics from Law and Order to Willie Horton and Beyond," in Sandra Bucerius and Michael Tonry (eds.), *Oxford Handbook of Race, Crime and Immigration* (Oxford: Oxford University Press, forthcoming).

18 Philip A. Klinkner and Rogers M. Smith, *The Unsteady March: The Rise and Decline of Racial Equality in America* (Chicago: University of Chicago Press, 1999), 305.

19 Susan Estrich, *Getting Away with Murder: How Politics Is Destroying the Criminal Justice System* (Cambridge, MA: Harvard University Press, 1998), 67.

20 Alfred Blumstein and Allen J. Beck, "Population Growth in U.S. Prisons, 1980–1996," in M. Tonry and J. Petersilia (eds.), *Crime and Justice: A Review of the Research,* Vol. 26: *Prisons,* 17–61 (Chicago: University of Chicago Press, 1999).

21 Western, *Punishment and Inequality in America*; S. Raphael and M. Stoll, *Do Prisons Make Us Safer? The Benefits and Costs of the Prison Boom* (New York: Russell Sage Foundation, 2009); William Spelman, "Crime, Cash and Limited Options: Explaining the Prison Boom," *Criminology & Public Policy* 8, no. 1 (2009): 29–77.

22 Western, *Punishment and Inequality in America.*

23 Malcolm M. Feeley and Jonathan Simon, "The New Penology: Notes on the Emerging Strategy of Corrections and Its Implications," *Criminology* 30 (1992): 449–474; Natasha Frost, *The Punitive State: Crime, Punishment, and Imprisonment Across the United States* (New York: LFB Scholarly Publications, 2006); Garland, *Culture of Control*; John Pratt, *Punishment and Civilization: Penal Tolerance and Intolerance in Modern Society* (Thousand Oaks, CA: Sage, 2002).

24 Garland, *Culture of Control*; Loic Wacquant, "Class, Race and Hyperincarceration in Revanchist America," *Daedalus* 139, no. 3 (2010): 74–90; John Irwin, *The Warehouse Prison: Disposal of the New Dangerous Class* (Los Angeles: Roxbury, 2005).

25 Mark Mauer, *Race to Incarcerate* (New York: New Press, 1999).

26 Ibid., 42.

27 Michelle S. Phelps, "Rehabilitation in the Punitive Era: The Gap Between Rhetoric and Reality in U.S. Prison Programs," *Law and Society Review* 45, no. 1 (2011): 33–68, at 36; N. Manatu-Rupert, "Prison Reform," in D. Levinson (ed.), *Encyclopedia of Crime and Punishment,* 1226–1232 (Thousand Oaks, CA: Sage, 2002).

28 Mauer, *Race to Incarcerate,* 44.

29 Amy Lerman and Vesla Weaver, "Race and Crime in America from Law and Order to Willie Horton and Beyond," in Sandra M. Bucerius and Michael Tonry (eds.), *Oxford Handbook on Ethnicity, Crime and Immigration* (Oxford: Oxford University Press, forthcoming).

30 Beckett, *Making Crime Pay*; Michael H. Tonry, *Malign Neglect – Race, Crime, and Punishment in America* (New York: Oxford University Press, 1995); Jonathan Simon, *Governing Through Crime: How the War on Crime Transformed American Democracy and Created a Culture of Fear* (Oxford: Oxford University Press, 2007); Vesla M. Weaver, "Frontlash: Race and the Development of Punitive Crime Policy," *Studies in American Political Development* 21, no. 2 (2007): 230–265; Lerman and Weaver, "The Politics of Race and Crime in America."

31 Garland, *Culture of Control,* 9.

32 Jeremy Bentham, *Principles of Morals and Legislation* (Oxford: Clarendon Press, 1823).

33 Crime Survey, Jan, 2001. Retrieved Apr-16-2013 from the iPOLL Databank, The Roper Center for Public Opinion Research, University of Connecticut; www.ropercenter.uconn.edu/data_access/ipoll/ipoll.html.

34 Feeley and Simon, "The New Penology," 455, 452.

35 Robert Martinson, "What Works? Questions and Answers about Prison Reform," *Public Interest*, 35 (Spring 1974): 22–55, at 25.

36 Cited in Mauer, *Race to Incarcerate*, 47.

37 Beckett, *Making Crime Pay*; Franklin Zimring, "Imprisonment Rates and the New Politics of Criminal Punishment," *Punishment & Society* 3 (2001): 161–166.

38 Katherine A. Beckett and Theodore Sasson, *The Politics of Injustice: Crime and Punishment in America* (Thousand Oaks: Pine Forge Press, 2000).

39 Charles B. A. Ubah and Robert L. Robinson, Jr., "A Grounded Look at the Debate over Prison-Based Education: Optimistic Theory Versus Pessimistic Worldview," *Prison Journal* 83 (2003): 115–129.

40 Irwin, *Warehouse Prison*.

41 John DiIulio, William Bennett, and John Walters, *Body Count* (New York: Simon & Schuster, 1996).

42 Ibid.

43 John DiIulio, *Zero Prison Growth: Crime Policies for the 21st Century* (Washington, DC: Brookings Institution, 2002).

44 Elizabeth Becker, "As Ex-Theorist on Young 'Superpredators,' Bush Aide Has Regrets," *New York Times*, February 9, 2001; www.nytimes.com/2001/02/09/us/as-ex-theorist-on-young-superpredators-bush-aide-has-regrets.html?src=pm.

45 Robert Martinson, "New Findings, New View: A Note of Caution Regarding Sentencing and Reform," *Hofstra Law Review* 7 (1979): 243–258.

46 M. Welch, *Corrections: A Critical Approach* (New York: McGraw-Hall, 1996), 100.

47 Michelle S. Phelps, "Rehabilitation in the Punitive Era: The Gap Between Rhetoric and Reality in U.S. Prison Programs," *Law and Society Review* 45, no. 1 (2011): 33–68; P. Goodman, "Hero or Inmate, Camp or Prison, Rehabilitation or Labor Extraction: A Multi-Level Study of California's Prison Fire Camps," Unpublished doctoral dissertation, University of California, Irvine.

48 Goodman, "Hero or Inmate."

49 Phelps, "Rehabilitation in the Punitive Era"; Bert Useem and Anne Morrison Piehl, *Prison State: The Challenge of Mass Incarceration* (Cambridge: Cambridge University Press, 2008); Leonidas K. Cheliotis, "How Iron Is the Iron Cage of New Penology? The Role of Human Agency in the Implementation of Criminal Justice Policy," *Punishment & Society* 8 (2006): 313–340. Goodman, "Hero or Inmate"; Kelly Hannah-Moffat, "Criminogenic Needs and the Transformative Risk Subject," *Punishment & Society* 7, no, 1 (2005): 29–51; Paula Maurutto and

Kelly Hannah-Moffat, "Assembling Risk and the Restructuring of Penal Control," *British Journal of Criminology* 46, no. 3 (2006): 438–454; Gwen Robinson, "Late-Modern Rehabilitation: The Evolution of a Penal Strategy," *Punishment & Society* 10, no. 4 (2008): 429–445.

50 Fergus McNeill, Nicola Burns, Simon Halliday, Neil Hutton, and Cyrus Tata, "Risk, Responsibility and Reconfiguration: Penal Adaptation and Misadaptation," *Punishment & Society* 11, no. 4 (2009): 419–442.

51 Goodman, "Hero or Inmate": Steven Hutchinson, "Countering Catastrophic Criminology: Reform, Punishment and the Modern Liberal Compromise" *Punishment & Society* 8, no. 4 (2006): 443–467. Pat O'Malley, "Criminologies of Catastrophe? Understanding Criminal Justice on the Edge of the New Millennium," *Australian & New Zealand Journal of Criminology* 33, no. 2 (2000): 153–167; O'Malley, "Volatile and Contradictory Punishment," *Theoretical Criminology* 3, no. 2 (1999): 175–196.

52 Robert Worth, "A Model Prison," *Atlantic Monthly*, November 1995; www.theatlantic.com/past/docs/issues/95nov/prisons/prisons.htm.

53 The No Frills Prison Act, HR663, was introduced in January 1995. It called for amending the Violent Crime Control and Law Enforcement Act of 1994; see M. Curriden, "Hard Time," *ABA Journal* 81 (1995): 72–76; Nygel Lenz, "'Luxuries' in Prison: The Relationship Between Amenity Funding and Public Support," *Crime & Delinquency* 48 (2002): 499–525; P. Finn, "No-Frills Prisons and Jails: A Movement in Flux," *Federal Probation* 60 (1996): 35–45; W. Johnson, K. Bennett, and T. Flanagan, "Getting Tough on Prisoners: Results from the National Corrections Executive Survey, 1995," *Crime & Delinquency* 43 (1997): 24–48; A. Wunder, "The Extinction of Inmate Privileges: Survey Summary," *Corrections Compendium* 20 (1995): 5–24.

54 www.akrepublicans.org/pastlegs/prsb001053097.htm.

55 T. Cullen, "Assessing the Penal Harm Movement," *Journal of Research in Crime and Delinquency* 32 (1995): 338–359, at 339.

56 Mona Lynch, "Punishing Images: Jail Cam and the Changing Penal Enterprise," *Punishment & Society* 6, no. 3 (2004): 255–270, at 257.

57 David J. Rothman, "The Crime of Punishment," in T. Blomberg and S. Cohen (eds.), *Punishment and Social Control* (New York: Aldine de Gruyter, 2003).

58 Joshua Page, "Eliminating the Enemy: The Importance of Denying Prisoners Access to Higher Education in Clinton's America," *Punishment & Society* 6, no. 4 (2004): 357–378.

59 Richard Tewksbury and Jon Marc Taylor, "Eligibility for Students in Post-secondary Correctional Education Programs," *Federal Probation* 60, no. 3 (1996): 60–63; Richard Tewksbury, David J. Erickson and Jon Marc Taylor, "Opportunities Lost: The Consequences of Eliminating Pell Grant Eligibility for Correctional Education Students," *Journal of Offender Education* 31, no. 1/2 (1996): 43–56.

60 Joan Petersilia, *When Prisoners Come Home* (Oxford: Oxford University Press, 2003), 5–6.

61 Ibid., 4.

62 Bert Useem and Anne Piehl, "Prison Buildup and Disorder," *Punishment & Society* 8, no. 1 (2006): 87–115.

63 Ibid., 106.

64 Ann Chih Lin, *Reform in the Making: The Implementation of Social Policy in Prison* (Princeton, NJ: Princeton University Press, 2000), 16.

65 Katherine Beckett and Bruce Western, "Governing Social Marginality: Welfare, Incarceration, and the Transformation of State Policy," in D. Garland (ed.), *Mass Incarceration: Social Causes and Consequences* (London: Sage, 2001); N. Frost, "The Mismeasure of Punishment: Alternative Measures of Punitiveness and Their (Substantial) Consequences," *Punishment & Society* 10, no. 3 (2008): 277–300; M. Jacobson, *Downsizing Prisons: How to Reduce Crime and End Mass Incarceration* (New York: New York University Press, 2005); D. Jacobs and R. Helms, "Collective Outbursts, Politics, and Punitive Resources: Toward a Political Sociology of Spending on Social Control," *Social Forces* 77 (1999): 1497–1523; K. R. Reitz, "The New Sentencing Conundrum: Policy and Constitutional Law at Cross-Purposes," *Columbia Law Review* 105 (2005): 1082–1123.

66 Devah Pager and Michelle Phelps, "Inequality and Punishment: A Turning Point for Mass Incarceration?" Working Paper, Princeton University.

67 F. Zimring and G. Hawkins, *The Scale of Imprisonment* (Chicago: University of Chicago Press, 1991).

68 John J. DiIulio, *Governing Prisons: A Comparative Study of Correctional Management* (New York: Simon & Schuster, 1987).

69 Ibid.

70 Ibid., 118.

71 Ibid., 129.

72 Ibid., 51.

73 From C. H. Logan, "Criminal Justice Performance Measures for Prisons," in John J. DiIulio, Jr., Geoffrey P. Alpert, Mark H. Moore, George F. Cole, Joan Petersilia, Charles H. Logan, and James Q. Wilson (eds.): *Performance Measures for the Criminal Justice System* (Washington, DC: Bureau of Justice Statistics, 1993).

74 Leo Carroll, *Lawful Order: A Case Study of Correctional Crisis and Reform* (New York: Garland, 1998); Rebecca M. McLennan, *The Crisis of Imprisonment: Protest, Politics, and the Making of the American Penal State, 1776–1941* (Cambridge: Cambridge University Press, 2008); Michael C. Campbell, "Politics, Prisons, and Law Enforcement: An Examination of the Emergence of 'Law and Order' Politics in Texas," *Law & Society Review* 45, no. 3 (2011): 631–665; Campbell, "Ornery Alligators and Soap on a Rope: Texas Prosecutors and Punishment

Reform in the Lone Star State," *Theoretical Criminology* (2011); Robert Perkinson, *Texas Tough: The Rise of America's Prison Empire* (New York: Metropolitan Books, 2010); Heather Schoenfeld, "Mass Incarceration and the Paradox of Prison Conditions Litigation," *Law & Society Review* 44, nos. 3–4 (2010): 731–768.

75 Mona Lynch, *Sunbelt Justice: Arizona and the Transformation of American Punishment* (Stanford, CA: Stanford Law Books, 2010).

76 Perkinson, *Texas Tough.*

77 Lynch, *Sunbelt Justice*; McLennan, *Crisis of Imprisonment*; Campbell, "Politics, Prisons, and Law Enforcement"; Campbell, "Ornery Alligators"; Mona Lynch, "Mass Incarceration, Legal Change, and Locale," *Criminology & Public Policy* 10, no. 3 (2011): 673–698.

78 The census of facilities is sponsored by the Bureau of Justice Statistics and has been conducted by the Census Bureau via mail roughly every five years since 1974. Data from the 2000 Census include 1,668 facilities, 1,584 non-federal and 84 federal.

79 Phelps, "Rehabilitation in the Punitive Era."

80 Michelle Phelps, "The Place of Punishment: Variation in the Provision of Inmate Services Staff Across the Punitive Turn," *Journal of Criminal Justice* 40, no. 5 (2012): 348–357.

81 The first of these cases occurred in 1941 in *Ex parte Hull*, ruling that prisoners had a right to access to the federal courts. Katherine Bennett and Craig Hemmens, "Prisoner Rights," in Toni DuPont-Morales and Michael Hooper (eds.), *Handbook of Criminal Justice Administration* (New York: Marcel Dekker Publishers, 2000).

82 *Wolff v. McDonnell*, 418 U.S. 539 (1974). After *Wolff*, prisoners sought and won many cases, and the courts became the primary avenues for exposing and improving deplorable prison conditions in the United States. Half of all states were under court order within a decade, and by the 1990s, 35 states were under court order to change their prison conditions immediately.

83 James B. Jacobs, "Prison Reform Amid the Ruins of Prisoners' Rights," in Michael Tonry (ed.), *The Future of Imprisonment: Essays in Honor of Norval Morris*, 179–198 (Oxford: Oxford University Press, 2004).

84 W. C. Collins, *Jail Design and Operation and the Constitution: An Overview* (Rockville, MD: National Institute of Corrections, 1994).

85 James B. Jacobs, "The Prisoners' Rights Movement and Its Impacts, 1960–80," *Crime and Justice* 2 (1980): 429–470, at 443.

86 *Pell v. Procunier* 417 U.S. 817, 822, 823 (1974).

87 Feeley and Simon. "The New Penology"; Garland, *Culture of Control*; J. Pratt, *Penal Populism* (Abingdon: Routledge, 2007); J. Pratt, D. Brown, M. Brown, S. Hallsworth, and W. Morrison, "Introduction," in J. Pratt , D. Brown , M. Brown , S. Hallsworth, and W. Morrison (eds.), *The New Punitiveness: Trends, Theories, Perspectives* (Cullompton: Willan, 2005).

88 Feeley and Simon, "The New Penology."

89 Carl B. Clements, "Offender Classification: Two Decades of Progress," *Criminal Justice and Behavior* 23, no. 1 (1996): 121–143.

90 Ira J. Silverman and Manuel Vega, *Corrections: A Comprehensive View* (St. Paul, MN: West, 1996), 359.

91 Ibid., 135.

92 There is still a great deal of debate over how accurate these new actuarial assessments are in predicting re-offending. In particular, many argue that the indicators on which risk evaluations are based have not been sufficiently standardized. There is also some discussion over whether many actuarial instruments focus too heavily on static factors.

93 Jonathan Simon, "Reversal of Fortune: The Resurgence of Individual Risk Assessment in Criminal Justice," *Annual Review of Law and Social Science* 1 (2005): 397–421; Feeley and Simon, "The New Penology," 454.

94 Terry M. Moe, "Political Institutions: The Neglected Side of the Story," *Journal of Law, Economics and Organization* 6 (1990): 213–253.

95 Howard D. Lasswell, *Who Gets What, When and How* (Cleveland, Ohio: Meridian, 1958: first published, 1936).

96 Matthew Holden, "Exclusion, Inclusion, and Political Institutions," In R. A. W. Rhodes, Sarah A. Binder, and Bert A. Rockman (eds.), *The Oxford Handbook of Political Institutions*, (New York: Oxford University Press, June 2008): 163–190; emphasis added.

97 Émile Durkheim, *The Rules of Sociological Method* (New York: Free Press, 1938); Durkheim, *The Division of Labor in Society* [1893], trans. George Simpson (New York: Free Press, 1933).

98 John W. Kingdon, *Agendas, Alternatives and Public Policies* (Boston: Little Brown and Company, 1984).

99 Jonathan Simon, "The Society of Captives in the Era of Hyper-Incarceration," *Theoretical Criminology* 4, no. 3 (2000): 285–308, at 303.

PUBLIC POLICY AND THE CREATION OF COMMUNITY

1 Thomas Hobbes, *Leviathan* (1660); oregonstate.edu/instruct/phl302/texts/hobbes/leviathan-contents.html/.

2 Ibid., ch. 28, "Of Punishments and Rewards."

3 Ibid.

4 John Locke, *Two Treatises on Government* (1689); http://www.bartleby.com/169.

5 Locke, *Second Treatise: The Function of Civil Government*, in ibid.

6 The Fourth Amendment guarantees the right against unreasonable search and seizure, and stipulates that no warrant be issued without probable cause. The Fifth Amendment addresses capital crimes, double jeopardy, and self-incrimination, and guarantees due process of law before anyone in a criminal case may be "deprived of life, liberty, or property." The Sixth Amendment guarantees rights to a "speedy and public trial" and an impartial jury, to confront one's accusers, and to "have the Assistance of

Counsel"; the Seventh Amendment guarantees the right to trial by jury in controversies exceeding 20 dollars and that "no fact tried by a jury, shall be otherwise reexamined in any Court"; and the Eighth Amendment prohibits excessive bail, excessive fines, and cruel and unusual punishment.

7 Robert D. Putnam, *Bowling Alone: The Collapse and Revival of American Community* (New York: Simon & Schuster, 2000); H. E. Brady, S. Verba, and K. Schlozman, "Beyond SES: A Resource Model of Political Participation," *American Political Science Review* 89, no. 2 (1995): 271–294; P. Dekker, R. Koopmans, and A. van den Broek, "Voluntary Associations, Social Movements and Individual Political Behavior in Western Europe," in J. van Deth (ed.), *Private Groups and Public Life* (London: Routledge, 1997); G. Moyser and G. Parry, "Voluntary Associations and Democratic Participation in Britain," in J. van Deth (ed.), *Private Groups and Public Life* (London: Routledge, 1997); E. Clemens, "Securing Political Returns to Social Capital: Women's Associations in the United States," *Journal of Interdisciplinary History* 30, no. 4 (1999): 613–638; G. Almond and Sidney Verba, *The Civic Culture* (Princeton, NJ: Princeton University Press, 1963).

8 Putnam, *Bowling Alone.*

9 Alexis de Tocqueville, *Democracy in America* (Chicago: University of Chicago Press, 2000).

10 Samuel Huntington, "Political Development and Political Decay," *World Politics* 17, no. 3 (1965): 386–430; Samuel Huntington, *Political Order in Changing Societies* (New Haven, CT: Yale University Press, 1968).

11 James Putzel, "Accounting for the Dark Side of Social Capital," *Journal of International Development* 9, no. 7 (1997): 939–949.

12 S. Tarrow, "Making Social Science Work Across Space and Time: A Critical Reflection on Robert Putnam's Making Democracy Work," *American Political Science Review* 90 (1996): 389–397; Putzel, "Accounting for the Dark Side"; Margaret Levi, "A State of Trust," in Margaret Levi and Valerie Braithwaite (eds.), *Trust and Governance* (New York: Russell Sage Foundation, 2003); W. Maloney, G. Smith, and G. Stoker, "Social Capital and the City," in B. Edwards, M. Foley, and M. Diani (eds.), *Beyond Tocqueville: Civil Society and the Social Capital Debate in Comparative Perspective*, 1–14 (Hanover, NH: University Press of New England, 2001); Michael Woolcock, "Social Capital and Economic Development: Toward a Theoretical Synthesis and Policy Framework," *Theory and Society* 27 (1998): 151–208.

13 See, e.g., R. Hardin, "Trustworthiness," *Ethics* 107 (1996): 26–42; M. Levi, "Making Democracy Work" [book review], *Politics and Society* 24 (1996): 45–55; P. Sztompka, *Trust: A Sociological Theory* (Cambridge: Cambridge University Press, 1999).

14 Dietlind Stolle, "The Sources of Social Capital," in Marc Hooghe and Dietlind Stolle (eds.), *Generating Social Capital* (New York: Palgrave MacMillan, 2003).

15 Robert D. Putnam, *Making Democracy Work: Civic Traditions in Modern Italy* Princeton, NJ: Princeton University Press, 1993); F. Fukuyama, "Social Capital and Civil Society," *Paper presented at the IMF Conference on Second Generation Reforms*, Washington DC, George Mason University (1999) www.imf.org/external/pubs/ft/seminar/1999/reforms/fukuyama. htm; Edward Banfield, *The Moral Basis of a Backward Society* (New York: Free Press, 1958), 17–24, 83–109.

16 Almond and Verba, *Civic Culture*; Ron Inglehart, *Modernization and Postmodernization* (Princeton, NJ: Princeton University Press, 1997); Pamela Paxton, "Social Capital and Democracy: An Interdependent Relationship," *American Sociological Review* 67, no. 2 (2002); Edward N. Muller and Mitchell A. Seligson, "Civic Culture and Democracy: The Question of Causal Relationships," *American Political Science Review* 88 (1994): 635–652; Jonathan Fox, "How Does Civil Society Thicken? The Political Construction of Social Capital in Rural Mexico," *World Development* 24 (1996): 1089–1103; Margaret Levi, "Social and Unsocial Capital: A Review Essay of Robert Putnam's Making Democracy Work," *Politics and Society* 24 (1996): 45–55; Claus Offe, "How Can We Trust Our Fellow Citizens?" in M. E. Warren (ed.), *Democracy and Trust*, 42–87 (Cambridge: Cambridge University Press, 1999); Wendy M. Rahn, John Brehm, and Neil Carlson, "National Elections as Institutions for Generating Social Capital," in T. Skocpol and M. Fiorina (eds.), *Civic Engagement in American Democracy*, 111–160 (Washington, DC: Brookings Institution, 1999); Mark E. Warren, "Democratic Theory and Trust," in *Democracy and Trust*, 310–345 (Cambridge: Cambridge University Press, 1999).

17 Almond and Verba, *Civic Culture*.

18 Robert D. Putnam, *Making Democracy Work: Civic Traditions in Modern Italy* (Princeton, NJ: Princeton University Press, 1993).

19 The connection between regime type and community character has also been at the forefront of scholarship linking social capital and democratic development. For instance, the degree to which governments protect the civil and political rights of citizens may be associated with greater levels of trust and association. Conversely, the "repression level" of a government is negatively associated with these social goods (J. Booth and P. Bayer Richard, "Civil Society and Political Context in Central America," *American Behavioral Scientist* 42, no. 1 [1998]: 33–46), because such regimes foster a "culture of mistrust" (Marc Morje Howard, *The Weakness of Civil Society in Post-Communist Europe* [Cambridge: Cambridge University Press, 2003]). In repressive states, government may appear to mobilize civil society through party organizations and state-sponsored events, but these forms of participation trade the deep roots of spontaneous associational life for the flimsy facade of citizen engagement through political pomp and circumstance (Francis Fukuyama, *Trust: The Social Virtues and Creation of Prosperity* [London: Hamish Hamilton, 1995]). Similar dampening results

have been posited to occur when states take hold of privately run services (Elinor Ostrom, "Social Capital: A Fad or a Fundamental Concept?" in Partha Dasgupta and Ismail Seraeldin [eds.], *Social Capital: A Multifaceted Perspective* [Washington, DC: World Bank, 1999], 172–214; Sanford Ikea, "Urban Interventionism and Local Knowledge," *Review of Austrian Economics* 17, nos. 2/3 [2004]: 247–264). As George Will once intoned, "[S]wollen government, which displaces other institutions, saps democracy's strength. There is ... a zero-sum transaction in society: As the state waxes, other institutions wane" (quoted in Theda Skocpol, "Unravelling from Above," *American Prospect* no. 25 [March–April 1996]: 20–25).

20 Stolle, "The Sources of Social Capital," 21.

21 Loic Wacquant, "Deadly Symbiosis: When Ghetto and Prison Meet and Mesh," *Punishment & Society* 3 (2001): 95–133, at 109.

22 John J. DiIulio, *Governing Prisons: A Comparative Study of Correctional Management* (New York: Simon & Schuster, 1987).

23 Ibid., C. H. Logan, "Criminal Justice Performance Measures for Prisons," in John J. DiIulio, Jr., Geoffrey P. Alpert, Mark H. Moore, George F. Cole, Joan Petersilia, Charles H. Logan, and James Q. Wilson (eds.): *Performance Measures for the Criminal Justice System* (Washington, DC: Bureau of Justice Statistics, 1993).

24 E. Bunker, *Little Boy Blue* (New York: St. Martin's Press, 1981); L. W. Thompson, *Last Train to Alcatraz* (Fiddletown, CA: Winter Book, 1988); S. Shakur, *Monster: The Autobiography of an LA Gang Member* (New York: Grove Press, 1993); M. Braly, *On the Yard* (New York: New York Review of Books, 2002).

25 G. M. Sykes, *The Society of Captives: A Study of a Maximum Security Prison* (Princeton, NJ: Princeton University Press, 1958); J. Irwin, *Jail: Managing the Underclass in American Society* (Berkeley: University of California Press, 1985); Candace Kruttschnitt and Rosemary Gartner, *Marking Time in the Golden State* (New York: Cambridge University Press, 2005).

26 See, e.g., G. M. Sykes and S. L. Messinger, "The Inmate Social System," in G. M. Sykes, S. L. Messinger, R. A. Cloward, R. McCleery, D. R. Cressey, L. E. Ohlin, and G. H. Grosser (eds.), *Theoretical Studies in Social Organization of the Prison* (New York: Social Science Research Council, 1960); John Irwin, *Prisons in Turmoil* (Boston: Little, Brown, 1980).

27 Jonathan Simon, "The Society of Captives in the Era of Hyper-Incarceration," *Theoretical Criminology* 4, no. 3 (2000): 285–308.

28 Starting with *Simon & Schuster Inc v. New York State Crime Victims Bd* (1991), several court challenges have been successful in striking down Son of Sam laws as unconstitutional on First Amendment grounds. Many states continue to have laws on the books, however, and some states have since altered their laws in order to meet the specifications of the court that such laws be narrowly tailored.

29 Simon, "Society of Captives."
30 Joan Petersilia, *Understanding California Corrections* (Berkeley: University of California, California Policy Research Center, 2006).
31 Simon, "Society of Captives."
32 Ibid., 298.
33 Ibid., 290.
34 See, e.g., Alison Liebling and Shada Maruna (eds.), *The Effects of Imprisonment* (Cullompton: Willan, 2005); Craig Haney, "Mental Health Issues in Long-Term Solitary and 'Supermax' Confinement," *Crime & Delinquency* 49 (2003): 124–156; Kruttschnitt and Gartner, *Marking Time*; Ben Crewe, "The Prisoner Society in the Era of Hard Drugs," *Punishment and Society* 7, no. 4 (2005): 457–481.
35 Simon, "Society of Captives."
36 Crewe, "Prisoner Society."
37 Marie Gottschalk, *The Prison and the Gallows: The Politics of Mass Incarceration in America* (New York: Cambridge University Press, 2006), 166.
38 Malcolm Feeley and Edward Rubin, *Judicial Policymaking and the Modern State* (New York: Cambridge University Press, 1998).
39 Ibid., 429.
40 James B. Jacobs, "The Prisoners' Rights Movement and Its Impacts, 1960–1980," *Crime and Justice* 2 (1980): 429–470, at 431, 435.
41 Ibid., 439.
42 James B. Jacobs, "Prison Reform Amid the Ruins of Prisoners' Rights," in Michael Tonry (ed.), *Future of Imprisonment: Essays in Honor of Norval Morris* (Oxford: Oxford University Press, 2004), 183, 191.
43 Jacobs, "Prisoners' Rights Movement," 439.
44 Jacobs, "Prison Reform," 179–198.
45 Bert Useem and Peter Kimball, *States of Siege: US Prison Riots, 1971–1986* (Oxford: Oxford University Press, 1989), 10.
46 R. S. Ratner and Barry Cartwright, "Politicized Prisoners: From Class Warriors to Faded Rhetoric," *Critical Criminology* 2, no. 1 (1990): 75–92.
47 DiIulio, *Governing Prisons*.
48 Irwin, *Prisons in Turmoil*; James B. Jacobs, "Judicial Impact on Prison Reform," in T. Blomberg and S. Cohen (eds.), *Punishment and Social Control* (New York: Transaction, 2003); Loic Wacquant, *Punishing the Poor: The Neoliberal Government of Social Insecurity* (Durham, NC: Duke University Press, 2009).
49 Ibid.
50 R. S. Fong and S. Buentello, "The Detection of Prison Gang Development: An Empirical Assessment," *Federal Probation* 55 (1991): 66–69.
51 As Mark Fleisher and Scott Decker note, critics of "jacketing" – "putting an official note in an inmate's file if he is suspected of being involved in

a gang" – argue that the process is "inappropriate because it may involve suspected but unconfirmed gang activity, often reported by a snitch, which leads to incorrectly labeling an inmate as a prison gang member or associate." Mark Fleisher and Scott H. Decker, "An Overview of the Challenge of Prison Gangs," *Corrections Management Quarterly* 5, no. 10 (2001): 1–9, at 7.

52 G. M. Camp and C. G. Camp, *Prison Gangs: Their Extent, Nature, and Impact on Prisons* (Washington, DC: U.S. Government Printing Office, 1985).

53 G. W. Knox and E. D. Tromanhauser, "Gangs and Their Control in Adult Correctional Institutions," *Prison Journal* 71 (1991): 15–22.

54 R. H. Montgomery, Jr., and G. A. Crews, *A History of Correctional Violence: An Examination of Reported Causes of Riots and Disturbances* (Lanham, MD: American Correctional Association, 1998).

55 John Winterdyk and Rick Ruddell, "Managing Prison Gangs: Results from a Survey of U.S. Prison Systems," *Journal of Criminal Justice* 38, no. 4 (2010): 730–736.

56 Federal Bureau of Investigations, "National Gang Threat Assessment" (2011); www.fbi.gov/stats-services/publications/2011-national-gang-threat-assessment.

57 B. D. Baugh, *Gangs in Correctional Facilities: A National Assessment* (Laurel, MD: American Correctional Association, 1993).

58 G. W. Knox, "A National Assessment of Gangs and Security Threat Groups (STGs) in Adult Correctional Institutions: Results of the 1999 Adult Corrections Survey" (1999); retrieved March 25, 2009, from www.ngcrc.com/ngcrc/page7.htm.

59 B. L. Ingraham and C. F. Wellford, "The Totality of Conditions Test in Eighth-Amendment Litigation," in S. D. Gottfredson and S. McConville (eds.), *America's Correctional Crisis: Prison Populations and Public Policy* (New York: Greenwood Press, 1987); S. H. Decker, and B. Van Winkle, *Life in the Gang: Family, Friends, and Violence* (Cambridge: Cambridge University Press, 1996); C. R. Huff, "The Criminal Behaviour of Gang Members and Nongang At-Risk Youth," in C. R. Huff (ed.), *Gangs in America*, 2d ed., 75–102 (Thousand Oaks, CA: Sage, 1996).

60 R. G. Shelden, "A Comparison of Gang Members and Non-Gang Members in a Prison Setting," *Prison Journal* 71 (1991): 50–60. See also G. C. Gaes, S. Wallace, E. Gilman, J. Klein-Saffran, and S. Suppa, "The Influence of Prison Gang Affiliation on Violence and Other Prison Misconduct," *Prison Journal* 82, no. 3 (2002): 359–385.

61 Camp and Camp, *Prison Gangs*. See also Knox, "A National Assessment of Gangs"; H. Foss, "The Management and Intervention of Gangs," *Proceedings of the Violence and Aggression Symposium*, Saskatoon, 2000, 55–56; M. Nafekh and Y. Stys, *A Profile and Examination of Gang Affiliation Within the Federally Sentenced Offender Population* (No. R-154) (Ottawa: Research

Branch, Correctional Service of Canada, 2004); NGCRC, "A Comparison of Gang Members and Non-Gang Members from Project GANGFACT: A Special Report of the NGCRC," *Journal of Gang Research* 6, no. 2 (1999): 53–76; Shelden, "A Comparison of Gang Members."

62 David Skarbek, "Governance and Prison Gangs," *American Political Science Review* 105, no. 4 (2011): 702–716.

63 Hunt et al., "Changes in Prison Culture."

64 Irwin, *Prisons in Turmoil.*

65 Loic Wacquant, "Deadly Symbiosis: When Ghetto and Prison Meet and Merge," *Punishment & Society* 3, no. 1 (2001): 95–133, at 111.

66 David Halpern, *Social Capital* (Malden, MA: Polity Press, 2005), 260.

67 Jeremy Travis, Elizabeth Cincotta McBride, and Amy L. Solomon. "Families Left Behind: The Hidden Costs of Incarceration and Reentry," Urban Institute Justice Policy Center, 2003; www.urban.org/uploadedpdf/310882_families_left_behind.pdf.

68 Jeremy Travis, Elizabeth Cincotta McBride, and Amy L. Solomon, *Families Left Behind: The Hidden Costs of Incarceration and Re-entry* (Washington, DC: Urban Institute, 2003).

69 F. F. Furstenberg, Jr., "Fathering in the Inner-City: Paternal Participation and Public Policy," in M. S. Kimmel and M. Marsiglio (eds.), *Research on Men and Masculinities Series*, 119–147 (Thousand Oaks, CA: Sage, 1995).

70 Ibid.

71 James P. Lynch and William J Sabol, "Prison Use and Social Control," in *Policies, Processes, and Decisions of the Criminal Justice System*, Vol. 3 (Washington, DC: National Institute of Justice, 2000).

72 Ibid., 13.

73 Patrick Bayer, Randi Hjalmarsson, and David Pozen. "Building Criminal Capital Behind Bars: Peer Effects in Juvenile Corrections," *Quarterly Journal of Economics* 124, no. 1 (2009): 105–147, at 108, emphasis added.

74 For example, Kathleen Kelley Reardon, *Persuasion in Practice* (Thousand Oaks, CA: Sage, 1991).

75 J. Soss, "Lessons of Welfare: Policy Design, Political Learning and Political Action," *American Political Science Review* 93, no. 2 (1999): 363–380; S. Mettler, "Bringing the State Back In to Civic Engagement: Policy Feedback Effects of the G.I. Bill for World War II Veterans," *American Political Science Review* 96, no. 2 (2002); Mettler, *Soldiers to Citizens: The GI Bill and the Making of the Greatest Generation* (Oxford: Oxford University Press, 2005).

76 Helen M. Ingram and Anne L. Schneider, *Public Policy and the Social Construction of Deservedness* (Albany, NY: SUNY Press, 2005), 2, 5.

77 Mettler, *Soldiers to Citizens*, 13.

78 A. Schneider and H. Ingram, "Social Construction of Target Populations: Implications for Politics and Policy," *American Political Science Review* 87 (1993): 334–347; Bo Rothstein, *Just Institutions Matter: The Moral*

and Political Logic of the Universal Welfare State (Cambridge: Cambridge University Press, 1998).

79 Loic Wacquant, "Negative Social Capital: State Breakdown and Social Destitution in America's Urban Core," *Journal of Housing and the Built Environment* 13, no. 1 (1998): 25–40, at 26.

80 J. LeGrand, "Knights, Knaves and Pawns: Human Behavior and Social Policy," *Journal of Social Policy* 26 (1997): 149–169; LeGrand, *Motivation, Agency and Public Policy: Of Knights and Knaves, Pawns and Queens* (Oxford: Oxford University Press, 2003).

81 Bo Rothstein and Dietlind Stolle, "Social Capital, Impartiality and the Welfare State: An Institutional Approach," in Marc Hooghe and Dietlind Stolle (eds.), *Generating Social Capital* (New York: Palgrave Macmillan, 2003). See also Soss, "Lessons of Welfare."

82 Craig Haney and Phillip Zimbardo, "The Past and Future of U.S. Prison Policy," *American Psychologist* (July 1998): 719.

83 Roger Friedland and R. Robert Alford, "Bringing Society Back In: Symbols, Practices, and Institutional Contradictions," in Walter W. Powell and Paul J. DiMaggio (eds.), *The New Institutionalism in Organizational Analysis*, 232–263 (Chicago: University of Chicago Press, 1991), 251.

84 Jonathan Simon, *Governing Through Crime: How the War on Crime Transformed American Democracy and Created a Culture of Fear* (Oxford: Oxford University Press, 2007).

85 Alec C. Ewald, "'Civil Death': The Ideological Paradox of Criminal Disenfranchisement Law in the United States," *Wisconsin Law Review* (2002): 1045–1132.

86 *Preiser v. Rodriguez*, 441 U.S. 475, 492 (1973).

87 Catherine M. Watson, "The Presentation of Self and the New Institutional Inmate: An Analysis of Prisoners' Response to Assessment for Release," *Symbolic Interaction* 5, no. 2 (1982): 243–257.

88 Kenneth B. Clark, *Dark Ghetto: Dilemmas of Social Power* (Hanover, NH: Wesleyan University Press, 1965 /1989).

89 Melvina Sumter, "The Correctional Work Force Faces Challenges in the 21st Century," *Corrections Today* (2008); www.aca.org/research/pdf/ResearchNotes_Aug08.pdf.

90 Mark S. Fleisher and Scott H. Decker, "An Overview of the Challenge of Prison Gangs," *Corrections Management Quarterly* 5, no. 1 (2001): 1–9.

91 Ben Crouch and James W. Marquart, *An Appeal to Justice: Litigated Reform of Texas Prisons* (Austin: University of Texas Press, 1989); Irwin, *Prisons in Turmoil*; Irwin, *Jail.*

92 David Skarbek, "Governance and Prison Gangs," *American Political Science Review* 105, no. 4 (2011): 703.

93 Wacquant, "Negative Social Capital," 26.

94 Gordon Allport, *The Nature of Prejudice* (Reading, MA: Addison-Wesley, 1954), 267. See also Thomas F. Pettigrew, "Intergroup Contact Theory," *Annual Review of Psychology* 49 (1998): 65–85.

95 Allport, *The Nature of Prejudice*, 267; see also Pettigrew, "Intergroup Contact Theory."

96 Ibid., 261.

97 Stolle, "Sources of Social Capital," 34.

98 K. Newton and P. Norris, "Confidence in Public Institutions: Faith, Culture or Performance?" in S. Pharr and R. Putnam (eds.), *Disaffected Democracies*, 55–72 (Princeton, NJ: Princeton University Press, 2000).

99 Soss, "Lessons of Welfare"; Amy E. Lerman and Vesla Weaver, *Policing Democracy* (Chicago: University of Chicago Press, forthcoming).

100 Staffan Kumlin and Bo Rothstein, "Making and Breaking Social Capital: The Impact of Welfare-State Institutions," *Comparative Political Studies* 38 (2005): 339–365, 350.

101 Barbara A. Owen, *The Reproduction of Social Control* (New York: Praeger, 1988), 70–71.

102 Ibid.

103 Ibid., 53.

104 John P. May, "Introduction," in John P. May and Khalid R. Pitts, *Building Violence: How America's Rush to Incarcerate Creates More Violence* (Thousand Oaks, CA: Sage, 2000), xvii.

105 "Guards Acquitted of Staging Gladiator-Style Fights," *New York Times*, June 10, 2000; www.nytimes.com/2000/06/10/us/guards-acquitted-of-staging-gladiator-style-fights.html.

106 Bert Useem and Anne M. Piehl, "Prison Buildup and Disorder," *Punishment and Society* 8, no. 1(2006): 87–115.

107 Jody Lewen, personal communication, 2005.

108 Elaine M. Crawley, *Doing Prison Work* (Portland, OR: Willan, 2004).

109 E. D. Poole and R. M. Regoli, "Role Stress, Custody Orientation and Disciplinary Actions," *Criminology* 18, no. 2 (1980): 15–226.

110 Amy Lerman and Joshua Page, "Politicization of Punishment and Correctional Officers Attitudes toward Rehabilitation," Working paper, Princeton University, 2012.

111 Kevin L. Thomas, *Isolated Incidents: Reflections of a Correctional Officer* (Miami: 1st Books Library, 2001), 30.

112 Ioannis D. Evrigenis, *Fear of Enemies and Collective Action* (Cambridge: Cambridge University Press, 2008), 24.

113 Putnam, *Bowling Alone*.

114 Frederic Thrasher, *The Gang: A Study of 1303 Gangs in Chicago* (Chicago: University of Chicago Press, 1928).

115 Quoted in James C. Howell and Arlen Egley, Jr., "Moving Risk Factors into Developmental Theories of Gang Membership," *Youth Violence and Juvenile Justice* 3 (2005): 334.

116 Lisa Bernstein, "Opting Out of the Legal System: Extralegal Contractual Relations in the Diamond Industry," *Journal of Legal Studies* 21, no. 1 (1992): 115–157; Janet T. Landa, "A Theory of the Ethnically Homogeneous Middleman Group: An Institutional Alternative to Contract Law," *Journal of Legal Studies* 10, no. 2 (1981): 349–362; Michael Munger, "Preference Modification vs. Incentive Manipulation as Tools of Terrorist Recruitment: The Role of Culture," *Public Choice* 128 (2006): 131–146.

117 R. Waldinger, 1995. "The 'Other Side' of Embeddedness: A Case-Study of the Interplay of Economy and Ethnicity," in Martin Bulmer (ed.) *Ethnic and Racial Studies* 18 no. 3 (1995): 555–580.

118 H. Tajfel, "Experiments in Intergroup Discrimination," *Scientific American* (1970): 96–102; H. Tajfel and J. C. Turner, "The Social Identity Theory of Inter-Group Behavior," in John T. Jost and Jim Sidanius (eds.), *Political Psychology: Key Readings* (New York: Psychology Press, 1986), 276–293; M. Billig and H. Tajfel, "Social Categorisation and Similarity in Intergroup Behaviour," *European Journal of Social Psychology* 3 (1973): 27–52.

119 L. Bobo, "Group Conflict, Prejudice, and the Paradox of Contemporary Racial Attitudes," in Phyllis A. Katz and Dalmas A. Taylor (eds.), *Eliminating Racism: Profiles in Controversy* (New York: Plenum Press, 1988), 85–116; J. Sidanius and F. Pratto, *Social Dominance: An Intergroup Theory of Social Hierarchy and Oppression* (Cambridge: Cambridge University Press, 2001).

120 Evrigenis, *Fear of Enemies*, 14.

121 Pamela Paxton, "Social Capital and Democracy: An Interdependent Relationship," *American Sociological Review* 67, no. 2 (2002): 254–277.

122 Banfield, *Moral Basis of a Backward Society*.

123 Levi, "Social and Unsocial Capital."

124 Putnam, *Making Democracy Work*, 3.

125 G. Almond and S. Verba, *The Civic Culture* (Princeton, NJ: Princeton University Press, 1963); J. Brehm and W. Rahn, "Individual Level Evidence for the Causes and Consequences of Social Capital," *American Journal of Political Science* 3 (1997): 999–1023; M. Hooghe and A. Derks, "Voluntary Associations and the Creation of Social Capital: The Involvement Effect of Participation," Paper presented at the ECPR Joint Sessions, Bern, Switzerland, 1997; M. Hooghe, "Participation in Voluntary Associations and Value Indicators: The Effect of Current and Previous Participation Experiences," *Non-Profit and Voluntary Sector Quarterly* 32, no. 1 (2003): 47–69; D. Stolle and T. Rochon, "The Myth of American Exceptionalism: A Three Nation Comparison of Associational Membership and Social Capital," in J. van Deth et al. (eds.), *Social Capital and European Democracy* (London: Routledge, 1999).

126 Alejandro Portes and Julia Sensenbrenner, "Embeddedness and Immigration: Notes on the Social Determinants of Economic Action," *American Journal of Sociology* 98, no. 6 (May 1993): 1320–1350.

127 Levi, "A State of Trust"; see also Portes and Sensenbrenner, "Embeddedness and Immigration."
128 Evrigenis, *Fear of Enemies.*
129 Elijah Anderson, "The Code of the Street," *Atlantic Monthly,* May 1994.
130 Douglas S. Massey and Nancy A. Denton, *American Apartheid* (Cambridge, MA: Harvard University Press, 1993).
131 Christopher R. Browning, Seth L. Feinberg, and Robert D. Dietz, "The Paradox of Social Organization: Networks, Collective Efficacy, and Violent Crime in Urban Neighborhoods," *Social Forces* 83, no. 2 (2004): 503–534, at 508.
132 Portes, "Social Capital: Its Origins and Applications"; J. Boissevain, *Friends of Friends: Networks, Manipulators and Coalitions* (Oxford: Basil Blackwell, 1974).
133 Ruth Rosner Kornhauser, *Social Sources of Delinquency* (Chicago: University of Chicago Press, 1978).
134 Hans Toch, *Men in Crisis: Human Breakdowns in Prison* (New Brunswick, NJ: Aldine Transaction, 2008), 5.
135 e.g., Daniel Bar-Tal and Dikla Antebi, "Beliefs About Negative Intentions of the World: A Study of the Israeli Siege Mentality," *Political Psychology* 13 No. 4 (1992):633–645.
136 Ben Crouch and James W. Marquart, *An Appeal To Justice: Litigated Reform of Texas Prisons* (Austin: University of Texas Press, 1989).
137 Sensenbrenner and Sensenbrenner, "Embeddedness and Immigration."
138 Lisa Bernstein, "Opting Out of the Legal System: Extralegal Contractual Relations in the Diamond Industry," *Journal of Legal Studies* 21, no. 1 (1992): 115–157; Landa, "A Theory of the Ethnically Homogeneous Middleman Group"; Munger, "Preference Modification."

THE CULTURE AND CONSEQUENCE OF PRISON

1 Jeremy Travis, "Reentry and Reintegration: New Perspectives on the Challenges of Mass Incarceration," in M. Pattillo, D. Weiman, and B. Western (eds.), *Imprisoning America: The Social Effects of Mass Incarceration* (New York: Sage, 2004).
2 According to the demographic unit of the Department of Finance, California's population at the end of 2006 was about 37.7 million people. The U.S. census notes that about 24 percent of the state population is under 18 years of age.
3 Joshua Page, *The Toughest Beat: Politics, Punishment, and the Prison Officers Union in California* (Oxford: Oxford University Press, 2011), 3.
4 Joan Petersilia, *Understanding California Corrections* (Berkeley: University of California, California Policy Research Center, 2006).
5 Ibid.

6 Amy Lerman and Joshua Page, *Does the Front Line Reflect the Party Line? The Politicization of Punishment and Prison Officers' Perspectives toward Incarceration*, Unpublished working paper, Princeton University.

7 Lerman and Page, *Does the Front Line Reflect the Party Line?*

8 California Correctional Peace Officers Association, *Public Safety: Government's First Responsibility* (Sacramento: California Correctional Peace Officers Association, May 1995), 14.

9 Joachim Savelsberg, "Law That Does Not Fit Society: Sentencing Guidelines as a Neoclassical Reaction to the Dilemmas of Substantivized Law," *American Journal of Sociology* 97, no. 5 (1992): 1346–1381.

10 Page, *The Toughest Beat.*

11 J. Warren, "State Prison Crowding Emergency Declared," *Los Angeles Times*, October 5 2006.

12 Ibid.

13 California state budget, 2011.

14 Petersilia, *Understanding California Corrections.*

15 Federal Bureau of Investigation, "National Gang Threat Assessment"; www.fbi.gov/stats-services/publications/2011-national-gang-threat-assessment.

16 James Sterngold, "U.S. Seizes State Prison Health Care; Judge Cites Preventable Deaths of Inmates, 'Depravity' of System," *San Francisco Chronicle*, July 1, 2005.

17 California Department of Corrections (2005). The state also maintains 40 custody camps, 12 community correctional facilities, and 5 prisoner mother facilities. In addition, California has 14 federal facilities, 12 public and 2 private, and a host of county jails.

18 As of June 30, 2006, the CDCR Position Inventory by Institution reported 21,243 established positions filled, and the survey went out to a database of 21,478. Of the mailed surveys, 2,161 were returned with problematic addresses. An additional subset of 1,500 is estimated to have been sent to officers who were either retired, called to active military service, or working in fire camps. These cases were excluded from the population.

19 Section 3377 of the California Code of Regulations: Crime Prevention and Corrections.

20 Ibid.

21 Ibid.

22 Section 3377.1 of the California Code of Regulations: Crime Prevention and Corrections.

23 Paul Holland, "Statistics and Causal Inference," *Journal of the American Statistical Associations* 81, no. 396 (December 1986): 947.

24 Ibid. D. B. Rubin, "Formal Modes of Statistical Inference for Causal Effects," *Journal of Statistical Planning and Inference* 25 (1990): 279; Rubin, "Estimating Causal Effects of Treatments in Randomized and Nonrandomized Studies," *Journal of Educational Psychology* 66 (1974): 688–701.

25 Space constraints make this a necessarily cursory overview of causal inference. See Jasjeet Sekhon "The Neyman-Rubin Model of Causal Inference and Estimation" in *The Oxford Handbook of Political Methodology*, J. Box-Steffensmeier, H. Brady and D. Collier (eds) (Oxford: Oxford University Press 2007) and Sekhon "Opiates for the Matches" *Annual Review of Political Science* 12 (2009) for a more detailed discussion of the Neyman–Rubin model and the assumptions underlying causal inference in observational data. See Thad Dunning "Improving Causal Inference: Strengths and Limits of Natural Experiments" *Political Research Quarterly* 61 (2008) and Dunning "Design-Based Inference: Beyond the Pitfalls of Regression Analysis?" in *Rethinking Social Inquiry: Diverse Tools, Shared Standards*, 2nd edition, H. Brady and D. Collier (eds) (Latham, MD: Rowman and Littlefield, 2010) for more on natural experimental design and analysis.

26 Holland, "Statistics and Causal Inference"; J. Neyman, "On the Application of Probability Theory to Agricultural Experiments: Essay on Statistical Principles," Section 9, 1923; translated in *Statistical Science* 5 (1990): 465–480; Rubin, "Formal Modes of Statistical Inference"; Rubin, "Estimating Causal Effects."

27 The most common reason for placement outside the designated security level is a "population override," used to accommodate a lack of available bed space. In addition, a caseworker can suggest an irregular placement. Excluding these cases does not significantly alter the results.

28 Scholarship by Jonathan Simon and others suggests that correctional workers, as well as parole officers and police, are generally risk-averse. Thus, it seems plausible that classification officers might prefer to assign inmates to higher-custody settings where there is more oversight, in order to avoid being held responsible later should a "dangerous" person be placed in a more lenient institution where he or she ends up engaging in violence. However, this does not appear to be occurring.

29 D. Thistlethwaite and D. Campbell, "Regression-Discontinuity Analysis: An Alternative to the Ex Post Facto Experiment," *Journal of Educational Psychology* (1960): 309–317.

30 A. Ross and B. Laccy, "A Regression Discontinuity Analysis of a Remedial Education Programme," *Canadian Journal of Higher Education* 13, no. 1 (1983): 1–15; W. Van der Klaauw, "Estimating the Effect of Financial Aid Offers on College Enrollment: A Regression-Discontinuity Approach," *International Economic Review* 43, no. 4 (2002); B. Jacoband L. Lefgren, "Remedial Education and Student Achievement: A Regression-Discontinuity Analysis," *Review of Economics and Statistics* 86 (2004): 226–244.

31 R. A. Berk and D. Rauma, "Capitalizing on Nonrandom Assignment to Treatments: A Regression-Discontinuity Evaluation of a Crime Control Program," *Journal of the American Statistical Association* 78, no. 381 (1983); R. Berk and J. d. De Leeuw, "An Evaluation of California' s Inmate Classification System Using a Generalized Regression Discontinuity

Design," *Journal of the American Statistical Association* 94, no. 448 (1998): 1045–1052; M. Keith Chen and Jesse M. Shapiro, "Do Harsher Prison Conditions Reduce Recidivism? A Discontinuity-Based Approach," *American Law and Economics Review* 9, no. 1 (2007): 1–29; R. Pintoff, "The Impact of Incarceration on Juvenile Crime: A Regression Discontinuity Approach," Unpublished paper, 2004; D. Lee and J. McCrary, "Crime, Punishment, and Myopia," NBER Working Paper No. 11491 (Cambridge, MA: National Bureau of Economic Research, 2005).

32 To ensure that these differences are not responsible for the results shown in Chapter 5, all outcome analyses were conducted first for only the sub-samples of inmates who had been incarcerated as juveniles and then for those who had not. Results hold in both subgroups considered separately.

33 For a review of the literature, see Susan Philliber, "Thy Brother's Keeper: A Review of the Literature on Correctional Officers," *Justice Quarterly* 4, no. 1 (1987): 9–37.

34 J. T. Whitehead and C. A. Lindquist, "Determinants of Correctional Officers' Professional Orientation," *Justice Quarterly* 6, no. 1 (1987); K. T. Liou, "Professional Orientation and Organizational Commitment among Public Employees: An Empirical Study of Detention Workers," *Journal of Public Administration Research and Theory* 5, no. 2 (1995): 231–246; G. Bazemore and T. Dicker, "Explaining Detention Worker Orientation: Individual Characteristics, Occupational Conditions, and Organizational Environment," *Journal of Criminal Justice* 22, no. 4 (1994): 297–312; M. Kifer, C. Hemmens, and M. Stohr, "The Goals of Corrections: Perspectives from the Line," *Criminal Justice Review* 28, no. 1 (2003).

35 J. Maahs and T. Pratt, "Uncovering the Predictors of Correctional Officers' Attitudes and Behaviors: A Meta Analysis," *Corrections Management Quarterly* 5, no. 2 (2001): 13–19.

36 David Robinson, Frank J. Porporino, and Linda Simourd, "The Influence of Career Orientation on Support for Rehabilitation among Correctional Staff," *Prison Journal* 73 (1993): 162–177.

37 D. Street, "The Inmate Group in Custodial and Treatment Settings.," *American Sociological Review* 30 (1965): 40–55; L. Lombardo, *Guard Imprisoned: Correctional Officers at Work* (New York: Elsevier, 1989); Barry Brown, Robert Dupont, Nicholas Kozel, and John Spevacek, "Staff Conceptions of Inmate Characteristics," *Criminology* 9 (August–November 1971): 316–329.

38 In addition to the minimal requirements, the CDCR lists the following as "desirable qualifications" for employment as a correctional officer: a college degree, completion of criminal justice coursework, possession of Penal Code 832 (POST) Certifications, experience supervising other employees, and service in the U.S. military or as a social worker, military police officer, non-sworn correctional officer, peace officer, or fire fighter (CDCR Selection Process Brochure, 2008). Listed as "Special Personal Characteristics" for correctional work are "emotional maturity and stability; objective

understanding of persons in custody; satisfactory record as a law-abiding citizen; sobriety; demonstrated leadership ability; honesty; integrity; tact; good personal and social adjustment for correctional work; neat personal appearance; courage; alertness; willingness to work day, evening, or night shifts, weekends, and holidays, and to report for duty at any time emergencies arise. Must have integrity, dependability, good judgment, and the ability to work cooperatively with others. Must be physically and mentally able to perform the essential functions of the position" (ibid.).

39 Cadets are expected to report to their assigned institution on the Monday following graduation from the BCOA. Once they have arrived at the institution, the apprenticeship program consists of a series of intra-institutional placements that are assigned at the discretion of management. An officer is subject to reassignment about every 90 days and is not assigned a permanent post until completion of the program.

40 CDCR.ca.gov.

41 CDCR.ca.gov.

42 Personal interview with staff at the Peace Officer Selection Office.

43 Prison facilities were coded into six geographic regions: North, North Central, South Central, Los Angeles Area, South, and Far South.

44 The paucity of respondents at Levels I and II precludes analysis of other security-level effects among this subsample. However, the descriptive statistics suggest that the effects of security level on attitudes are strongest (or exclusively) for those assigned to the highest security level.

45 See, e.g., John J. DiIulio, Jr., *Governing Prisons: A Comparative Study of Correctional Management* (New York: Free Press, 1987).

46 Walter Dunbar, "Why Attica?" *Prevention of Violence in Correctional Institutions* (1973): 13; Jack E. Brent, "Tension Management and Organizational Activism: Toward a Preventive Medicine for Prison Riots," *Prevention of Violence in Correctional Institutions* (1973): 1–9.

47 Robert A. Freedberg, "County Prisons Should Promote Rehabilitation," *Morning Call*, June 19, 2006.

48 J. B. Jacobs and H. Retsky, "Prison Guard," in B. Crouch (ed.), *The Keepers: Prison Guards and Contemporary Corrections* (Springfield, IL: Thomas, 1980), 71.

49 John Dilulio, *No Escape: The Future of American Corrections* (New York: Basic Books, 1991); Charles H. Logan, "Criminal Justice Performance Measures for Prisons," in John J. DiIulio (ed.), *Study Group on Criminal Justice Performance Measures* (Bureau of Justice Statistics, Princeton Project, 1993); A. C. Lin, *Reform in the Making: The Implementation of Social Policy in Prison* (Princeton, NJ: Princeton University Press, 2000). Amy E. Lerman and Joshua Page, "The State of the Job: An Embedded Work Role Perspective on Prison Officer Attitudes," *Punishment and Society*, forthcoming.

50 Corey Weinstein, "Even Dogs Confined to Cages for Long Periods of Time Go Berserk," in John P. May and Khalid R. Pitts (eds.), *Building Violence:*

How America's Rush to Incarcerate Creates More Violence (Thousand Oaks, CA: Sage, 2000), 123.

51 DiIulio, *Governing Prisons*.

THE SOCIAL EFFECTS OF INCARCERATION

1 Edward Zamble and Frank Porporino, *Coping, Behavior, and Adaption in Prison Inmates* (New York: Springer, 1988).

2 Michael Windzio, "Is There a Deterrent Effect of Pains of Imprisonment? The Impact of 'Social Costs' of First Incarceration on the Hazard Rate of Recidivism," *Punishment and Society* 8, no. 3 (2006): 341–364.

3 D. R. Jaman, R. M. Dickover, and L. A. Bennett, "Parole Outcomes as a Function of Time Served," *British Journal of Criminology* 12 (2006): 5–34; L. H. Bukstel and P. R. Kilmann, "Psychological Effects of Imprisonment on Confined Individuals," *Psychological Bulletin* 88 (1980): 469–493; N. Walker, "The Unwanted Effects of Long-term Imprisonment," in R. Light (ed.), *Problems of Long-Term Imprisonment*, 183–199 (Aldershot: Gower).

4 L. Song and R. Lieb, *Recidivism: The Effect of Incarceration and Length of Time Served* (Olympia: Washington State Institute for Public Policy, 1993); P. Smith, C. Goggin, and P. Gendreau, *The Effects of Prison Sentences and Intermediate Sanctions on Recidivism: General Effects and Individual Differences* (Saint John, Center for Criminal Justice Studies, University of New Brunswick, 2002); P. Villettaz, M. Killias, and I. Zoder, *The Effects of Custodial vs. Non-Custodial Sentences on Reoffending: A Systematic Review of the State of Knowledge* (Lausanne: Institute of Criminology and Criminal Law, 2006).

5 See Villettaz et al., *The Effects of Custodial vs. Non-Custodial Sentences*. The authors define a custodial sanction as "any sanction where offenders are placed in a residential setting, i.e. deprived of their freedom of movement, no matter whether or not they are allowed to leave the facility during the day or at certain occasions." By contrast, a non-custodial sanction can be any non-residential or "open" sanction, such as community work, electronic monitoring, or probation.

6 Song and Lieb, *Recidivism*.

7 Jaman et al., "Parole Outcomes"; L. H. Bukstel and P. R. Kilmann, "Psychological Effects"; Walker, "Unwanted Effects."

8 Larence Bench and Terry Allen, "Investigating the Stigma of Prison Classification: An Experimental Design," *Prison Journal* 83, no. 4 (2003): 367–382; Richard A. Berk and Jan de Leeuw, "An Evaluation of California's Inmate Classification System Using a Generalized Regression Discontinuity Design," *Journal of the American Statistical Association* 94, no. 448 (2003): 1045–1052; M. Keith Chen and Jesse M. Shapiro, "Do Harsher Prison Conditions Reduce Recidivism? A Discontinuity-Based Approach," *American Law and Economics Review* 9, no. 1 (2007):

1–29; Gerald G. Gaes and Scott D. Camp, "Unintended Consequences: Experimental Evidence for the Criminogenic Effect of Prison Security Level Placement on Post-Release Recidivism," *Criminology* 5, no. 2 (2009): 139–162; John E. Berecochea and Joel B. Gibbs, "Inmate Classification: A Correctional Program That Works?" *Evaluation Review* 15, no. 3 (1991): 333–363.

9 Chen and Shapiro, "Do Harsher Prison Conditions Reduce Recidivism?"

10 R. Berk, H. Ladd, H. Graziano, and J. Back, "A Randomized Experiment Testing Inmate Classification Systems," *Criminology & Public Policy* 2, no. 2 (2003): 215–242.

11 Gaes and Camp, "Unintended Consequences."

12 Bert Useem and Anne M. Piehl, "Prison Buildup and Disorder," *Punishment and Society* 8, no. 1 (2006): 87–115.

13 Data from the Los Angeles Police Department and the LA County Sheriff's Department for January 2012–July 2012, compiled by the *Los Angeles Times*; projects.latimes.com/mapping-la/neighborhoods/violent-crime/neighborhood/list/.

14 Hans Toch, *Men in Crisis: Human Breakdowns in Prison* (New Brunswick, NJ: Aldine Transaction, 2008), 5.

15 Pat Nolan, "Testimony before the Senate Judiciary Subcommittee on Corrections and Rehabilitation on behalf of the Commission on Safety and Abuse in America's Prisons"; www.justicefellowship.org/key-issues/issues-in-criminal-justice-reform/prison-violence/861-pat-nolan-testifies-before-congress.

16 Gresham Sykes, *The Society of Captives: A Study of a Maximum Security Prison* (Princeton, NJ: Princeton University Press, 1958/2007),79–80.

17 Ibid., 77.

18 Joe Soss, "Making Clients and Citizens: Welfare Policy as a Source of Status, Belief, and Action," in Anne Larason Schneider and Helen M. Ingram (eds.), *Deserving and Entitled: Social Constructions and Public Policy* (Albany, NY: SUNY Press, 2005), 291–328.

19 Donald Braman, *Doing Time on the Outside* (Ann Arbor: University of Michigan Press, 2004).

20 Sykes, *Society of Captives*.

21 Ibid., 82.

22 Sykes, *Society of Captives*, 77.

23 Ibid., Gresham M. Sykes and Sheldon L. Messinger, "The Inmate Social System," in G. M. Sykes, S. L. Messinger, R. A. Cloward, R. McCleery, D. R. Cressey, L. E. Ohlin, and G. H. Grosser (eds.), *Theoretical Studies in Social Organization of the Prison* (New York: Social Science Research Council, 1960).

24 Clemmer, *Prison Community*.

25 The other six statements included in the lie test are the following: "I always practice what I preach"; "I have never intensely disliked anyone"; "I have played sick to get out of something"; "I always behaved myself when I

was in school"; "I feel discouraged at times"; "I have felt very angry at someone or at something."

26 Results are from principal components factor analysis with varimax rotation.

27 The interaction between classification score and classification cutoff proved insignificant and was trimmed from the final specification.

28 These estimates show clear differences in social connectedness on either side of the classification cutoff. However, they cannot be directly interpreted as the result of placement in a higher- relative to lower-security prison. This is due to the imperfect relationship between an inmate's classification score and his final security placement. Estimating a Two-Stage Least Squares (2SLS) model accounts for this "fuzziness" in the regression discontinuity design. In this model, a significant discontinuity still obtains, and the size of the effect remains relatively stable. Specifically, there is a difference of -1.5 ($p < .1$) on the Social Isolation Scale between the two groups, which again corresponds to a gap of almost a full decile (-98, $p < .05$).

29 A 2SLS regression model confirms these differences, particularly with respect to gang associations; all else equal, inmates assigned to higher- rather than lower-security prisons report significantly more friends or acquaintances who are gang members.

30 Patrick Bayer, Randi Hjalmarsson, and David Pozen, "Building Criminal Capital Behind Bars: Peer Effects in Juvenile Corrections," *Quarterly Journal of Economics* 124, no. 1 (2009): 105–147.

31 For example, Robert P. Gandossy, Jay R. Williams, Jo Cohen, and Hendrick J. Harwood, *Drugs and Crime: A Survey and Analysis of the Literature* (Washington, DC: U.S. Department of Justice, National Institute of Justice, 1980); for a more recent and nuanced analysis, see Jan M. Chaiken and Marcia R. Chaiken, "Drugs and Crime," *Crime and Justice* 13 (1990): 203–239.

32 T. Brennan, W. Dieterich, and W. Oliver, *California Department of Corrections, Parole, and Community Services Division: COMPAS Pilot Psychometric Report* (Traverse City, MI: Northpointe Institute for Public Management, 2006).

33 A fifth variable loading high on the first dimension loads weakly on the second dimension. This variable, "A hungry person has a right to steal," does not appear to fit the pattern, in that it seems substantively more similar to the second set of variables.

34 The 2SLS estimate of assignment to higher security is an increase of 1.92 on the Criminal Cognitions Scale and .67 deciles. However, in this specification the scale score remains only marginally statistically significant ($p < .1$).

35 Ronald L. Akers and Gary F. Jensen, "The Empirical Status of Social Learning Theory of Crime and Deviance: The Past, Present, and Future," in Francis T. Cullen, John P. Wright, and Kristie R. Blevins (eds.), *Taking Stock: The Status of Criminological Theory*, vol. 15 (New Brunswick, NJ:

Transaction, 2006); Travis C. Pratt, Francis T. Cullen, Christine S. Sellers, L. Thomas Winfree, Jr., Tamara D. Madensen, Leah E. Daigle, Noelle E. Fearn, and Jacinta M. Gau, "The Empirical Status of Social Learning Theory: A Meta-Analysis," *Justice Quarterly* 27 (2010): 765–802; Mark Warr, *Companions in Crime: The Social Aspects of Criminal Conduct* (Cambridge: Cambridge University Press, 2002).

36 J. M. Cohen, "Sources of Peer Group Homogeneity," *Sociology of Education* 50 (1977): 227–241.

37 Robert D. Putnam, *Bowling Alone: The Collapse and Revival of American Community* (New York: Simon & Schuster, 2000), 310–311.

38 Section 3378 of the California Code of Regulations: Crime Prevention and Corrections.

39 P. Gendreau, C. Goggin, F. Chanteloupe, and D. A. Andrews, *The Development of Clinical and Policy Guidelines for the Prediction of Criminal Behaviour in Criminal Justice Settings* (Ottawa: Ministry of the Solicitor General of Canada, 1992); P. Gendreau, T. Little, and C. Goggin, *A Meta-Analysis of the Predictors of Adult Offender Recidivism: Assessment Guidelines for Classification and Treatment* (Ottawa: Ministry of the Solicitor General of Canada, 1992); P. Gendreau, C. E. Goggin, and M. A. Law, "Predicting Prison Misconduct," *Criminal Justice and Behavior* 24, no. 4 (1992): 414–431.

40 A. P. Goldstein, *The Gang Intervention Handbook* (Champaign, IL: Research Press, 1993).

41 T. Brennan, W. Dieterich and B. Ehret, "Evaluating the Predictive Validity of the COMPAS Risk and Needs Assessment System," *Criminal Justice and Behavior* 36, no. 1 (2009): 21–40; see also T. Brennan, B. Dietrich, M. Breitenbach, and B. Mattson, *A Response to 'Assessment of Evidence on the Quality of the Correctional Offender Management Profiling for Alternative Sanctions (COMPAS)'* (Traverse City, MI: Northpointe Institute for Public Management, 2009).

42 David Farabee, Sheldon Zhang, Robert E. L. Roberts, and Joy Yang, *COMPAS Validation Study: Final Report, August 15, 2010* (UCLA, Semel Institute for Neuroscience and Human Behavior, 1993).

43 Data Analysis Unit, Offender Information Services. "California Prisoners and Parolees, 2006," California Department of Corrections and Rehabilitation (2006); www.cdcr.ca.gov/reports_research/offender_information_services_branch/Annual/CalPris/CALPRISd2006.pdf.

44 Timothy Hughes, Foris James Wilson, and Allen J. Beck, *Trends in State Parole, 1990–2000* (Washington, DC: Bureau of Justice Statistics, 2001).

45 J. Bonta and P. Gendreau, "Reexamining the Cruel and Unusual Punishment of Prison Life," *Law and Human Behavior* 14 (1990): 359.

46 "Report of the National Advisory Commission on Criminal Justice Standards, 1973," National Advisory Commission on Criminal Justice Standards and Goals.

47 G. S. Becker, "Crime and Punishment: An Economic Approach," *Journal of Political Economy* 76, no. 2 (1968): 169–217.

48 J. Q. Wilson and R. J. Herrnstein, *Crime and Human Nature* (New York: Simon & Schuster, 1985); L. F. Katz, S. D. Levitt, and E. Shustorovich, "Prison Conditions, Capital Punishment and Deterrence," *American Law and Economics Review* 5, no. 2 (2003): 318–343; D. S. Lee and J. McCrary, "Crime, Punishment, and Myopia," NBER Working Paper 11491 (Cambridge, MA: National Bureau of Economic Research, 2005).

49 H. L. Ross, *Deterring the Drinking Driver* (Lexington, MA: Lexington Books, 1981).

50 T. Tyler, *Why People Obey the Law* (Princeton, NJ: Princeton University Press, 2006), 23.

51 Ibid.

52 D. Yagil, "Beliefs, Motives and Situational Factors Related to Pedestrians' Self-Reported Behavior at Signal-Controlled Crossings," *Transportation Research Part F3* (2000): 1–13.

53 Ibid.

54 Tyler, *Why People Obey the Law*, 22.

55 For a thorough review of relevant literature, refer to the discussion in Chapter 2.

THE SOCIAL EFFECTS OF PRISON WORK

1 Gresham Sykes, *The Society of Captives: A Study of a Maximum Security Prison* (Princeton, NJ: Princeton University Press, 1958/2007), 82–83.

2 D. Glaser, *The Effectiveness of a Prison and Parole System* (Indianapolis: Bobbs-Merrill, 1964), 89.

3 Amy E. Lerman and Joshua Page, "The State of the Job: An Embedded Work Role Perspective on Prison Officer Attitudes," *Punishment and Society* 14, no. 5 (2012): 503–529.

4 Wilmar B. Schaufeli and Maria C. W. Peeters, "Job Stress and Burnout Among Correctional Officers: A Literature Review," *International Journal of Stress Management* 7, no. 1 (2000): 19–48; John R. Hepburn and Paul E. Knepper, "Correctional Officers as Human Services Workers: The Effect on Job Satisfaction," *Justice Quarterly* 10, no. 2 (1993): 315–338; Eric G. Lambert, Nancy Lynne Hogan, and Shannon M. Barton, "Satisfied Correctional Staff: A Review of the Literature on the Correlates of Correctional Staff Job Satisfaction," *Criminal Justice and Behavior* 29, no. 2 (2002): 115–143; Craig Dowden and Claude Tellier, "Predicting Work-Related Stress in Correctional Officers: A Meta-Analysis," *Journal of Criminal Justice* 32 (2004): 31–47; Michel Lariviere, "Antecedents and Outcomes of Correctional Officer Attitudes Towards Federal Inmates," Unpublished doctoral thesis, Carleton University, Ottawa, 2001.

5 CDCR.ca.gov.

6 Russ Winn, Michael Musheno, and Nancy Jurik, "The Organizational Diffusion of a Correctional Reform," *Criminal Justice Policy Review* 2 (1987): 174–190.

7 Crawley, *Prison Work*, 84.

8 Peter Moskos, *Cop in the Hood* (Princeton, NJ: Princeton University Press, 2008), 47.

9 Marvin Preston, "What Is 'Paramilitary'?" (2010), www.corrections. com/news/article/24159-what-is-paramilitary?utm_source=CCNN_ Ezine&utm_medium=email&utm_campaign=CCNN_ Ezine_2010apr21.

10 Kathleen Kelley Reardon, *Persuasion in Practice* (Thousand Oaks, CA: Sage, 1991), 139.

11 Ibid.

12 Moskos, *Cop in the Hood*, 25.

13 J. Greenhaus and N. Beutell, "Sources of Conflict between Work and Family Roles" *Academy of Management Review* 10 (1985): 76–88.

14 Ibid.

15 Elaine Crawley, *Doing Prison Work: The Public and Private Lives of Prison Officers* (Portland, OR: Willan, 2004), 238.

16 E. Lambert, N. L. Hogan, and S. M. Barton, "The Nature of Work–Family Conflict among Correctional Staff: An Exploratory Examination," *Criminal Justice Review* 29, no. 1 (2004): 145–172.

17 F. E. Cheek and M. D. Miller, "The Experience of Stress for Correction Officers: A Double-Bind Theory of Correctional Stress," *Journal of Criminal Justice* 11, no. 2 (1983): 105–112.

18 P. Finn, *Addressing Correctional Officer Stress: Programs and Strategies* (Washington, DC: National Institute of Justice, 2000).

19 Data Analysis Unit, *Employees Killed by Inmates*, (Sacramento, CA: Department of Corrections and Rehabilitation, 2005)

20 Note that numbers indicate total incidents of assault, not the number of employees assaulted.

21 N. Jurik, "Individual and Organizational Determinants of Correctional Officer Attitudes towards Inmates." *Criminology* 23 (1985): 523–539.

22 Carol Smith and John R. Hepburn, "Alienation in Prison Organizations," *Criminology* 17 (1979): 251–262.

23 F. Cullen, "The Correctional Orientation of Prison Guards: Do Officers Support Rehabilitation?" *Federal Probation* 53 (1989): 33–42.

24 While some officers work in prisons that house more than one security level, many are assigned primarily to a single population. About 88% of survey respondents indicated that they worked primarily with only one security level over the past six months. The figure excludes officers who reported having worked in more than one security level over the past six months.

25 While female inmates in California are not classified or placed according to security level, officers who work in all-female institutions were likewise

asked for their opinion as to the relative dangerousness of the inmates with whom they work. On average, officers' categorization of female inmates most closely approximates that of Level II male inmates. Slightly less than a third of women were considered to be very dangerous (31%), slightly less than a third were classified as not dangerous (30%), and the remaining group (37%) was categorized as being in the middle.

26 In addition, 21% reported a problem concerning job or work assignment/ task; 17% reported a problem with training; 11% reported a disciplinary action or misconduct allegation; and 12% reported some other type of problem not specified.

27 At the same time, however, a significant proportion of officers feel some level of job satisfaction: about 47% of officers report that they often experience the sense that they are positively influencing other people's lives, and 44% believe that they make a difference in people's lives through their work.

28 G. Bazemore and T. Dicker, "Explaining Detention Worker Orientation: Individual Characteristics, Occupational Conditions, and Organizational Environment," *Journal of Criminal Justice* 22, no. 4 (1994): 297–312.

29 F. Cullen, "The Correctional Orientation of Prison Guards: Do Officers Support Rehabilitation?" *Federal Probation* 53 (1989): 33–42; Jurik, "Individual and Organizational Determinants"; A. Paboojian and R. Teske, "Pre-Service Correctional Officers: What Do They Think About Treatment?" *Journal of Criminal Justice* 25 (1997): 425–433; P. Van Voorhis, F. T. Cullen, B. G. Link, and N. T. Wolfe, "The Impact of Race and Gender on Correctional Officers' Orientation to the Integrated Environment," *Journal of Research in Crime and Delinquency* 28 (1991): 472–500.

30 Jurik, "Individual and Organizational Determinants"; E. Poole and R. Regoli, "Role Stress, Custody Orientation and Disciplinary Actions: A Study of Prison Guards," *Criminology* 18 (1980): 215–260; F. Cullen, B. Link, N. Wolge, and J. Frank "The Social Dimensions of Correctional Officer Stress," *Justice Quarterly* 2 (1985): 505–533; Paboojian and Teske, "Pre-Service Correctional Officers."

31 F. Cullen, "The Correctional Orientation of Prison Guards: Do Officers Support Rehabilitation?" *Federal Probation* 53 (1989): 33–42; Jurik, "Individual and Organizational Determinants"; B. Crouch and G. Alpert "Sex and Occupational Socialization Among Prison Guards: A Longitudinal Study," *Criminal Justice and Behavior* 9, no. 2 (1982): 159–176; L. Zupan, "Gender-Related Differences in Correctional Officers' Perceptions and Attitudes," *Journal of Criminal Justice* 14 (1986): 349–361; Van Voorhis et al., "The Impact of Race and Gender."

32 L. Lombardo, *Guard Imprisoned: Correctional Officers at Work* (New York: Elsevier, 1989); B. Shamir and A. Drory, "Occupational Tedium Among Prison Officers," *Criminal Justice Behavior* 9 (1982): 79–99.

33 M. A. Farkas, "Correctional Officer Attitudes Toward Inmates and Working with Inmates in a 'Get Tough' Era," *Journal of Criminal Justice*

27, no. 6 (1999): 495–506; Van Voorhis et al., "The Impact of Race and Gender"; Jurik, "Individual and Organizational Determinants."

34 Farkas, "Correctional Officer Attitudes."

35 Ibid., Cullen, "Correctional Orientation of Prison Guards"; Van Voorhis et al., "The Impact of Race and Gender."

36 R. H. Teske and H. E. Williamson, "Correctional Officers' Attitudes Toward Selected Treatment Programs," *Criminal Justice and Behavior* 6, no. 1 (1979): 59–66.

37 Data are matched with GenMatch, a non-parametric matching package in R that employs a genetic algorithm to maximize the balance between treated and control group covariates. Alexis Diamond and Jasjeet S. Sekhon, "Genetic Matching for Estimating Causal Effects: A General Multivariate Matching Method for Achieving Balance in Observational Studies" (June 12, 2008); sekhon.berkeley.edu/papers/GenMatch.pdf (accessed October 12, 2010); Jasjeet S. Sekhon, "Multivariate and Propensity Score Matching Software with Automated Balance Optimization: The Matching Package for R," *Journal of Statistical Software* (forthcoming); sekhon.berkeley.edu/papers/MatchingJSS.pdf (accessed October 12, 2010). Matching is 1–1 with replacement, and ties are included as multiple weighted pairs.

38 The propensity score is estimated using logistic regression, and I match on the linear predictor rather than the predicted probabilities, as suggested in Jasjeet, "Multivariate and Propensity Score Matching Software."

39 David Duffee, "The Correction Officer Subculture and Organizational Change," *Journal of Research in Crime and Delinquency* 11 (1974): 155–172, at 169.

40 Mona Lynch, "Waste Managers? The New Penology, Crime Fighting, and Parole Agent Identity," *Law and Society Review* 32 (1998): 839–870; Laura B. Myers, "Meeting Correctional Officer Needs: An Ethical Response to Cultural Differences," *Prison Journal* 80 (2000): 184–209; William A. Reese, Russell L. Curtis, and James R. Whitworth, "Dispositional Discretion or Disparity: The Juvenile Probation Officer's Role in Delinquency Processing," *Journal of Applied Behavioral Science* 24 (1988): 81–100; Russ Winn, Michael Musheno, and Nancy Jurik, "The Organizational Diffusion of a Correctional Reform," *Criminal Justice Policy Review* 2 (1987): 174–190.

41 B. Stadnyk, *PTSD in Corrections Employees in Saskatchewan* (Saskatchewan: Registered Psychiatric Nurses Association, 2003).

42 J. B. Rogers, *FOCUS Survey and Final Report – A Summary of the Findings: Families Officers and Corrections Understanding Stress.* (2001); www.ncjrs.gov/pdffiles1/nij/grants/188094.pdf.

43 S. Stack and O. Tsoudis, "Suicide Risk among Correctional Officers: A Logistic Regression Analysis," *Archives of Suicide Research* 3, no. 3 (1997): 183–186.

44 Cheek and Miller, "The Experience of Stress."

45 Bruce Finley, "Prison Horrors Haunt Guards' Private Lives," *Denver Post*, March 24, 2007; www.denverpost.com/cI_5510659.

46 *Growth of the CCPOA* (San Francisco: Center on Juvenile and Criminal Justice, 2002); 198.170.117.218/cpp/growth_CCPOA.php.

47 Joan Petersilia, "Understanding California Corrections" (Berkeley, CA: California Policy Research Center 2006), 21.

48 Ibid., *Political Power of the CCPOA* (San Francisco: Center on Juvenile and Criminal Justice, 2002); 198.170.117.218/cpp/political_power.php.

49 *Political Power of the CCPOA*.

50 Ibid.

51 *Growth of the CCPOA*

52 Bureau of Labor Statistics, "Union Members Summary"; www.bls.gov/cps/cpslutabs.htm.

53 Ibid.

54 *Growth of the CCPOA*.

FROM INDIVIDUALS TO COMMUNITIES

1 Robert J. Sampson and Charles Loeffler, "Punishment's Place: The Local Concentration of Mass Incarceration," *Daedalus* 139, no. 3 (2010): 20–31, 23.

2 Dina R. Rose and Todd Clear, "Incarceration, Social Capital and Crime: Implications for Social Disorganization Theory," *Criminology* 36, no. 3 (2006): 441–480.

3 Todd R. Clear, "The Problem with 'Addition by Subtraction': The Prison–Crime Relationship in Low-Income Communities," in Marc Mauer (ed.), *Invisible Punishment: The Collateral Consequences of Mass Imprisonment* (New York: The New Press, 2002).

4 James Q. Wilson and George Kelling, "Broken Windows: The Police and Neighborhood Safety," *The Atlantic*, March 1, 1982; Terrence Mills and Gregory Mills, *National Evaluation of Weed and Seed Issues and Findings* (Washington, DC: National Institute of Justice, 1999); Mark H. Moore, "Problem Solving and Community Policing," in Michael Tonry and Norval Morris (eds.), *Crime and Justice: An Annual Review*, 15: 99–158 (Chicago: University of Chicago Press, 1992).

5 Steve Spiker, Andrew Marx, Rachel Diggs, and Junious Williams, *A Report on California Department of Corrections and Rehabilitation Parolees in Los Angeles County* (Oakland, CA: Urban Strategies Council, 2007).

6 LA County Population Report, portal.lacounty.gov/wps/portal/lac/about.

7 *Bureau of Justice Statistics Bulletin: Prisoners in 2004* (Washington, DC: Department of Justice, Bureau of Justice Statistics, 2005); www.ojp.usdoj.gov/bjs/pub/pdf/p04.pdf (accessed August 6, 2005).

8 Ibid.

9 *Misplaced Priorities: Los Angeles, CA*, online report of the National Association for the Advancement of Colored People; www.naacp.org/pages/los-angeles.

10 The Social Capital Community Benchmark Survey was conducted by phone in 2000 by the Saguaro Seminar at Harvard University's John F. Kennedy School of Government.

11 www.ropercenter.uconn.edu/data_access/data/datasets/social_capital_community_survey.html.

12 Twenty-eight individuals in the social capital LA county subsample have missing zip code data. Excludes Post Office box zip codes and non-residential zip codes (e.g., Walt Disney Studios, LAX Airport).

13 California Department of Corrections and Rehabilitation.

14 Dina Rose and Todd Clear, "Incarceration, Reentry and Social Capital: Social Networks in the Balance" (Washington, DC: Urban Institute, 2002), 185.

15 S. Lawrence and J. Travis, *The New Landscape of Imprisonment: Mapping America's Prison Expansion* (Washington, DC: Urban Institute, 2004).

16 Released prisoners include those who are released both with and without supervision in a given year. Data on year of release vary across states. However, there is no reason to believe that the relative proportion of individuals released to various zip codes varies substantially over time. This supposition was confirmed using over-time parole data from California.

17 All controls are from the Social Capital Benchmark Survey, with the exception of crime rates. Crime measures are from the Uniform Crime Reporting Program Data [United States], County-Level Detailed Arrest and Offense Data.

18 I test for mediation using bootstrap analyses to estimate the indirect effect of ex-prisoner concentration on cooperation through social ties and trust (Path C′). The bootstrapping method draws a large number of repeated samples with replacement from the data, computes the indirect effect for each sample, and then averages across the group of samples. All bootstrapping conducted with 5,000 samples.

19 Jeremy Travis, Amy L. Solomon and Michelle Waul, *From Prison to Home: The Dimensions and Consequences of Prisoner Reentry*, Crime Policy Report (Washington, DC: Urban Institute, 2001).

20 Susan E. Mayer and Christopher Jenks, "Growing up in Poor Neighborhoods: How Much Does It Matter?" *Science* 243, no. 4897 (1989): 1441–1445, at 1441.

21 Spiker et al., *Report on California Department of Corrections and Rehabilitation Parolees*.

22 Devah Pager, *Marked: Race, Crime and Finding Work in an Era of Mass Incarceration* (Chicago: University of Chicago Press, 2007).

23 Crane, "Epidemic Theory of Ghettos."

24 William Julius Wilson, *The Truly Disadvantaged* (Chicago: University of Chicago Press, 1987), 61. See also Ulf Hannerz, *SoulSide: Inquiries into Ghetto Culture and Community* (Chicago: University of Chicago Press, 1969/2004); Martin Sanchez Jankowski, *Islands in the Street: Gangs and American Urban Society* (Berkeley: University of California Press, 1991).

25 Rose and Clear, "Incarceration, Social Capital and Crime"; Daniel Nagin, "Criminal Deterrence Research at the Outset of the Twenty-First Century," in Michael Tonry (ed.), *Crime and Justice: A Review of Research*, Vol. 23 (Chicago: University of Chicago Press, 1998); Frank Zimring and Gordon Hawkins, *Deterrence: The Legal Threat in Crime Control* (Chicago: University of Chicago Press, 1973).

26 Robert D. Putnam, *Bowling Alone: The Collapse and Revival of American Community* (New York: Simon & Schuster, 2000), 317.

27 Ruth Rosner Kornhauser, *Social Sources of Delinquency* (Chicago: University of Chicago Press, 1978).

28 Robert Sampson and Dawn Jeglum Bartusch, "Legal Cynicism and (Subcultural?) Tolerance of Deviance: The Neighborhood Context of Racial Differences," *Law and Society Review* 32 (1998): 777–804.

29 Elijah Anderson, *Streetwise* (Chicago: University of Chicago Press, 1990); Anderson, *Code of the Street: Decency, Violence, and the Moral Life of the Inner City* (New York: W. W. Norton, 1999); Eric A. Stewart and Ronald L. Simons, "Race, Code of the Street, and Violent Delinquency: A Multilevel Investigation of Neighborhood Street Culture and Individual Norms of Violence," *Criminology* 48, no. 2 (2010): 569–605.

30 Crane, J. "The Epidemic Theory of Ghettos and Neighborhood Effects on Dropping Out and Teenage Childbearing," American Journal of Sociology 96 (1991): 1226–1259.

31 Sudhir Venkatesh, "The Social Organization of Street Gang Activity in an Urban Ghetto," *American Journal of Sociology* 103 (1997): 82–111; James Diego Vigil, *Barrio Life: Street Life and Identity in Southern California* (Austin: University of Texas Press, 1988); Joan W. Moore, *Homeboys* (Philadelphia: Temple University Press, 1978); Felix Padilla, *The Gang as an American Enterprise* (New Brunswick, NJ: Rutgers University Press, 1992); Carl Taylor, *Dangerous Society* (Ann Arbor: Michigan State University Press, 1990). Jankowski, *Islands in the Street.*

32 Richard Cloward and Lloyd E. Ohlin, *Delinquency and Opportunity: A Theory of Delinquent Gangs* (New York: Free Press, 1966); A. K. Cohen, *Delinquent Boys: The Subculture of the Gang* (New York: Free Press, 1955); Ross L. Matsueda, "The Current State of Differential Association Theory," *Crime and Delinquency* 34 (1988): 277–306, Walter B. Miller, "Lower Class Culture as a Generating Milieu of Gang Delinquency," *Journal of Social Issues* 14 (1958): 5–19.

33 Patricia Fernandez-Kelly, "Social and Cultural Capital in the Urban Ghetto: Implications for the Economic Sociology of Immigration," in

Alejandro Portes (ed.), *The Economic Sociology of Immigration: Essays on Networks, Ethnicity and Entrepreneurship.* (New York: Russell Sage Foundation, 1995), 213–247.

34 Wilson, *The Truly Disadvantaged*; Wilson, *When Work Disappears* (New York: Knopf, 1996).

35 Crane, "Epidemic Theory of Ghettos."

36 Christopher Browning, Seth L. Feinberg, and Robert D. Dietz, "The Paradox of Social Organization: Networks, Collective Efficacy, and Violent Crime in Urban Neighborhoods," *Social Forces* 83, no 2 (2004): 503–534, at 508.

37 Rose and Clear, "Incarceration, Social Capital and Crime."

38 Todd R. Clear, "Communities with High Incarceration Rates," in Michael Tonry (ed.), *Crime and Justice: A Review of Research*, Vol. 37 (Chicago: Chicago University Press, 2009); Bruce Western, *Punishment and Inequality in America* (New York: Russell Sage Foundation, 2006); Donald Braman, *Doing Time on the Outside: Incarceration and Family Life in America* (Ann Arbor: University of Michigan Press, 2004); Adrian Nicole LeBlanc, *Random Family: Love, Drugs, Trouble and Coming of Age in the Bronx* (New York: Scribner, 2004).

39 James Lynch and William Sabol, "*Did Getting Tough on Crime Pay?*" Crime Policy Report (Washington, DC: Urban Institute, 1997); Rose and Clear, "Incarceration, Social Capital and Crime"; Robert J. Sampson, "Urban Black Violence: The Effects of Male Joblessness and Family Disruption," *American Journal of Sociology* 93, no. 2 (1987): 348–382.

40 Rose and Clear, "Incarceration, Social Capital and Crime."

41 Clear, "Effects of High Imprisonment Rates," 105.

42 Ibid., 107.

43 Ibid., 117.

44 Clifford R. Shaw and Henry McKay, *Juvenile Delinquency and Urban Areas* (Chicago: University of Chicago Press, 1969); John Kasarda and Morris Janowitz, "Community Attachment in Mass Society," *American Sociological Review* 39 (1974): 328–339.

45 James Coleman, "Social Capital in the Creation of Human Capital," *American Journal of Sociology* 94 (1988): S95 S120; Robert Sampson, Stephen Radenbush, and Felton Earls, "Neighborhoods and Violent Crime: A Multilevel Study of Collective Efficacy," *Science* 277 (August 15, 1997): 918–924; Richard Rosenfeld, Steven Messner, and Eric P. Baumer, "Social Capital and Homicide," *Social Forces* 80, no. 1 (2001): 283–310.

46 Sampson et al., "Neighborhoods and Violent Crime"; Rose and Clear, "Incarceration, Social Capital and Crime."

47 Coleman, "Social Capital in the Creation of Human Capital," 94.

48 Fred DuBow and D. Emmons, "The Community Hypothesis," in D. A. Lewis (ed.), *Reactions to Crime* (Beverly Hills, CA: Sage, 1981).

49 Putnam, *Bowling Alone*, 310.

50 See, e.g., Rosenfeld et al., "Social Capital and Homicide"; Bruce P. Kennedy, Ichiro Kawachi, Deborah Prothow-Stith, Kimberly Lochner, and Vanita Gupta, "Social Capital, Income Inequality, and Firearm Violent Crime," *Social Science and Medicine* 47, no. 1 (1998): 7–17; Matthew R. Lee and Shaun A. Thomas, "Civic Community, Population Change, and Violent Crime in Rural Communities," *Journal of Research in Crime and Delinquency* 47, no. 1 (2010): 118–147.

51 Putnam, *Bowling Alone*, 308–309.

52 Frederic Thrasher, *The Gang: A Study of 1303 Gangs in Chicago* (Chicago: University of Chicago Press, 1928).

53 There are, of course, notable exceptions, including Jankowski's 1991 *Islands in the Street*, which devotes a chapter to the issue of gangs and government. Curiously, however, criminal justice activities are excluded from this discussion and are discussed only in a separate chapter.

54 Wilson, *When Work Disappears*.

55 Clear, "Effects of High Imprisonment Rates," 109.

56 Gustave de Beaumont and Alexis de Tocqueville, *On the Penitentiary System in the United States and Its Application in France*, trans. Francis Lieber (Carbondale: Southern Illinois University Press, 1964), 79.

57 Joan Petersilia, *When Prisoners Come Home* (Oxford: Oxford University Press, 2003), 52.

THE ROAD TO REFORM

1 Alice Calaprice (ed.), *The Ultimate Quotable Einstein* (Princeton NJ: Princeton University Press, 2011), 418.

2 Barry Stein, *Rebuilding Bedford-Stuyvesant, Community Economic Development in the Ghetto* (Cambridge, MA: Center for Community Development, 1975).

3 Bedford-Stuyvesant Restoration Corporation; data.ed.gov/node/17315.

4 Ida Siegal, "Playground Jail Removed after Bed-Stuy Parents Fume" (March 26, 2010); www.nbcnewyork.com/news/local/Play-Jail-in-Bed-Stuy-Housing-Development-has-parents-fuming-89079147.html.

5 Cara Buckley and Mick Meenan, "Playground 'Jail' Drawing Outrage, Gets a Face-Lift" (March 25, 2010); www.nytimes.com/2010/03/25/nyregion/25jail.html?_r=1&ref=publichousing.

6 Jake Pearson, Elizabeth Hays, and Helen Kennedy, "Brooklyn Residents' Complaints about Playground Designed as Prison Are Finally Heard" *New York Daily News* (March 24, 2010); www.nydailynews.com/ny_local/brooklyn/2010/03/24/2010-03-24_brooklyn_housing_proj-ect_residents_say_city_tot_lot_with_play_jail_treats_kid_li.html?r=ny_local&utm_source=feedburner&utm_medium=feed&utm_campaign=Feed%3A+nydnrss%2Fny_local+%28NY+Local%29.

7 Black and Brown News staff, "'Jail Playground' Found at BK Public Housing Property; Design Changed" (March 21, 2010); blackandbrown-news.com/bbn-exclusive-jail-playground-found-at-bk-public-housing-property-design-changed/.

8 Elissa Gootman and Cara Buckley, "Playground's Jail Theme Is Gone, but Perplexity Lingers," *New York Times* (March 25, 2010); www.nytimes.com/2010/03/26/nyregion/26jail.html.

9 Thomas P. Bonczar, "Prevalence of Imprisonment in the U.S. Population, 1974–2001," Bureau of Justice Statistics, 2003; bjs.ojp.usdoj.gov/content/pub/pdf/piuspo1.pdf.

10 G. Beaumont and A. Tocqueville, *On the Penitentiary System in the United States and Its Application in France* [1833] (Chicago: Vail-Ballou Press, 1964).

11 Christian Henrichson and Ruth Delaney, "The Price of Prisons: What Incarceration Costs Taxpayers," Vera Institute of Justice, January 2012; www.vera.org/download?file=3495/the-price-of-prisons-updated.pdf.

12 Kristen A. Hughes, *Justice Expenditures and Employment in the United States* (Washington, DC: Bureau of Justice Statistics, 2003).

13 Joan Petersilia, *When Prisoners Come Home* (Oxford: Oxford University Press, 2003), 5.

14 Pew Center on the States, *One in 100: Behind Bars in America* (Washington, DC: Pew Charitable Trusts, 2008).

15 Rucker Johnson and Steve Raphael, "The Effects of Male Incarceration Dynamics on AIDS Infection Rates among African-American Women and Men," *Journal of Law & Economics* 52, no. 2 (May 2009): 251–293.

16 Devah Pager, *Marked: Race, Crime and Finding Work in an Era of Mass Incarceration* (Chicago: University of Chicago Press, 2007).

17 Kason Schnittker and Andrea John, "Enduring Stigma: The Long-Term Effects of Incarceration on Health," *Journal of Health and Social Behavior* 48, no. 2 (2007): 115–130. Michael Massoglia, "Incarceration, Health, and Racial Disparities in Health," *Law and Society Review* 42, no. 2 (2008): 275–306.

18 Amy Lerman and Vesla Weaver, *Policing Democracy* (Chicago: University of Chicago Press, forthcoming).

19 Bruce Western, *Punishment and Inequality in America* (New York: Russell Sage Foundation, 2006); Bruce Western and Becky Pettit, *Collateral Costs: Incarceration's Effect on Economic Mobility* (Washington, DC: Pew Charitable Trusts, 2010).

20 Johnson and Raphael, "The Effects of Male Incarceration."

21 Pager, *Marked*.

22 Bruce Western, Leonard M. Lopoo, and Sara McLanahan, "Incarceration and the Bonds Among Parents in Fragile Families," in Mary Patillo, David Weiman, and Bruce Western (eds.), *Imprisoning America: The Social Effects of Mass Incarceration* (New York: Russell Sage Foundation, 2004).

23 Marc Mauer, *Invisible Punishment: The Collateral Consequences of Mass Imprisonment* (New York: New Press, 2002), 12.

24 Christopher Uggen and Sarah Shannon, *State Level Estimates of Felon Disenfranchisement in the United States, 2010* (Washington, DC: Sentencing Project, 2012).

25 Betty E. Cogwell "Some Structural Properties Influencing Socialization," *Administrative Science Quarterly* 13, no. 3 (1968): 417–440, at 418; emphasis added.

26 *Stanford Prison Experiment: A Simulation Study of the Psychology of Imprisonment Conducted at Stanford University*; www.prisonexp.org/.

27 Joan Petersilia, "Prisoner Reentry: Public Safety and Reintegration Challenges," *Prison Journal* 81, no. 3 (2001): 360–375.

28 Frederick Douglas, quoted in Nicholas D. Kristof, "A Poverty Solution That Starts with a Hug," *New York Times*, January 7, 2012.

29 Marc Mauer, "Sentencing Reform: Amid Mass Incarceration – Guarded Optimism," *Criminal Justice* 26, no. 1 (2011): 27–36.

30 Assembly Bill (AB) 109 and AB 117.

31 Lerman and Weaver, *Policing Democracy*.

32 Robert Weisberg and Joan Petersilia, "The Dangers of Pyrrhic Victories Against Mass Incarceration," *Daedalus* 139, no. 3 (2010): 124–133.

33 Ibid., 130.

34 Robert J. Sampson, "Crime and Public Safety: Insights from Community-Level Perspectives on Social Capital," in Susan Saegert, J. Phillip Thompson, and Mark R. Warren (eds.), *Social Capital and Poor Communities* (New York: Russell Sage Foundation, 2001), 89–114, 101.

35 Donald Specter, "Making Prisons Safe: Strategies for Reducing Violence," Testimony to the Commission on Safety and Abuse in America's Prisons; law.wustl.edu/Journal/22/p125Specter.pdf.

36 Bert Useem and Anne Piehl, "Prison Buildup and Disorder," *Punishment and Society* 8, no. 1 (2006): 87–115, at 94; emphasis added.

37 David Halpern, *Social Capital* (Malden, MA: Polity Press, 2005), 265.

38 Halpern, *Social Capital*; internal citations omitted.

39 G. M. Camp and C. G. Camp, *Prison Gangs: Their Extent, Nature, and Impact on Prisons* (Washington, DC: U.S. Government Printing Office, 1985); G. W. Knox, "A National Assessment of Gangs and Security Threat Groups (STGs) in Adult Correctional Institutions: Results of the 1999 Adult Corrections Survey," *Journal of Gang Research* 7, no. 3 (2000): 1–45; John Winterdyk and Rick Ruddell, "Managing Prison Gangs: Results from a Survey of U.S. Prison Systems," *Journal of Criminal Justice* 38, no 4 (2010): 730–736.

40 Philip Kassel, "The Gang Crackdown in Massachusetts' Prisons: Arbitrary and Harsh Treatment Can Only Make Matters Worse" [electronic version], *New England Journal on Criminal and Civil Confinement* 24 (1998): 37–64, at 42.

41 Useem and Piehl, "Prison Buildup and Disorder."

42 Stewart Grassian, "Psychiatric Effects of Solitary Confinement," *Journal of Law and Policy* 22 (2006): 325–383.

43 Mark S. Fleisher and Scott H. Decker, "An Overview of the Challenge of Prison Gangs," *Corrections Management Quarterly* 5, no. 10 (2001): 1–9.

44 G. W. Knox, "A National Assessment of Gangs and Security Threat Groups (STGs) in Adult Correctional Institutions: Results of the 1999 Adult Corrections Survey," *Journal of Gang Research* 7 (2000): 1–45.

45 John Winterdyk and Rick Ruddell, "Managing Prison Gangs: Results from a Survey of U.S. Prison Systems," *Journal of Criminal Justice* 38, no. 4 (2010): 730–736.

46 B. Parry, "Prison Gang Management: California's Approach," *The State of Corrections* (1999): 39–44, cited in Chantal De Placido, Terri L. Simon, Treena D. Witte, Deqiang Gu, and Stephen C. P Wong, "Treatment of Gang Members Can Reduce Recidivism and Institutional Misconduct," *Law and Human Behavior* 30, no. 1 (2006): 93–114.

47 Kassel, "The Gang Crackdown."

48 J. Warick, "Gangs Feed on Anger, Thrive on Brutality," Part 1 of *Street Gangs*, *StarPhoenix*, January 2004; cited in De Placido et al., "Treatment of Gang Members."

49 While approaches vary widely in size and form, they have several common features, as Donald Specter describes: First, they create housing units that are relatively small, consisting of between 15 and 20 prisoners. Second, the adult programs allow the prisoner to choose to participate, although one program conditions that choice on the decision to inform against his former gang. Third, they create a set of expectations that include mandatory integration with prisoners of other races and gangs and a very low tolerance of misbehavior. Fourth, prisoners are given extensive orientation about these expectations. Fifth, prisoners are provided with counseling services to help them control anger and violence and foster healthy relationships. These services come in the form of formal group sessions, but also informally through guidance provided by specially selected staff in the units. Finally, prisoners are provided with real and substantial incentives to complete the program. This may include contact visits with their family, jobs, and a safe environment when they return to the general population. Specter, "Making Prisons Safe."

50 De Placido et al., "Treatment of Gang Members"; W. Toller and B. Tsagaris, "A Practical Approach Combining Security and Human Services," *Corrections Today* 58, no. 6 (1996): 110–112; H. Foss, "The Management and Intervention of Gangs," *Proceedings of the Violence and Aggression Symposium*, Saskatoon, 55–56; M. Gaseau, "States That Take a Case by Case Approach to Gang Management."

51 Toller and Tsagaris, "A Practical Approach."

52 Specter, "Making Prisons Safe."

53 C. W. Thomas, "Prisonization or Resocialization? A Study of External Factors Associated with the Impact of Imprisonment," *Journal of Research in Crime and Delinquency* 10 (1973): 13–21.

54 Gordon Allport, *The Nature of Prejudice* (Reading, MA: Addison-Wesley, 1954), 267. See also Thomas F. Pettigrew, "Intergroup Contact Theory," *Annual Review of Psychology* 49 (1998): 65–85.

55 Kassel, "The Gang Crackdown."

56 Donald Specter, "Making Prisons Safe: Strategies for Reducing Violence," *Journal of Law & Policy* 22 (2006): 125–134.

57 Michael Jacobson, *Downsizing Prisons* (New York: New York University Press, 2005), 29.

58 Francis T. Cullen, "The Twelve People Who Saved Rehabilitation: How the Science of Criminology Made a Difference," *Criminology* 43 (2005): 1–42; Mona Lynch, "The Contemporary Penal Subject(s)," in M. Frampton et al. (eds.), *After the War on Crime: Race, Democracy, and a New Reconstruction* (New York: New York University Press, 2008).

59 Jonathan Simon, "Introduction," in M. Frampton et al. (eds.), *After the War*, p. 10.

60 Devah Pager and Michelle Phelps, "Inequality and Punishment: A Turning Point for Mass Incarceration?" Working paper, Princeton University.

61 Devah Pager and Michelle Phelps, "The End of Mass Incarceration? The Social, Political, and Economic Correlates of States' Declining Incarceration Rates." Working paper, Princeton University.

62 John Kingdon, *Agendas, Alternatives and Public Policies* (Reading, MA: Addison-Wesley, 1995).

63 Vera Institute of Justice, *The Continuing Fiscal Crisis in Corrections: Setting a New Course* (New York: Vera Institute of Justice, 2010); J. Wool and D. Stemen, *Changing Fortunes or Changing Attitudes?* (New York: Vera Institute of Justice, 2004).

64 Ibid.

65 John Schmitt, Kris Warner, and Sarika Gupta, *The High Budgetary Cost of Incarceration* (Washington, DC: Center for Economic and Policy Research, June 2010).

66 Jacobson, *Downsizing Prisons*; Sara Steen and Rachel Bandy, "When the Policy Becomes the Problem: Criminal Justice in the New Millennium," *Punishment & Society* 9 (2007): 5–26.

67 Andrew Romano, "Liberal Academic, Tea Party Leader Rethinking Crime Policy," *Newsweek*, April 16, 2012.

68 Marc Levin, "Effective Justice: What Conservatives Are Saying about Criminal Justice Reform" (January 14, 2010); www.texaspolicy.com/pdf/2010-01-PP02-conservativesaresaying-ml.pdf.

69 Jonathan Simon, "The Society of Captives in the Era of Hyper-Incarceration," *Theoretical Criminology* 4, no. 3 (2000): 285–308.

70 Lerman and Weaver, *Policing Democracy;* see also Richard Harding, *Private Prisons and Public Accountability* (New Brunswick, NJ: Transaction, 1997); Nicole B. Casarez, "Furthering the Accountability Principle in Privatized Federal Corrections: The Need for Access to Private Prison Records," *University of Michigan Journal of Law Reform* (1994–1995): 249.

71 Marie Gottschalk, "Money and Mass Incarceration: The Bad, The Mad, and Penal Reform," *Criminology and Public Policy* 8, no. 1 (2009): 97–109.

72 Pell v. Procunier, 417 U.S. 817 (1974).

73 NCSC Sentencing Attitudes Survey, March 2006. Retrieved September 12, 2012, from the iPOLL Databank, The Roper Center for Public Opinion Research, University of Connecticut; www.ropercenter.uconn.edu/data_access/ipoll/ipoll.html.

74 Ibid.

75 Question wording: "Please tell me which of the following four options you think should be the top priority for dealing with crime. Would you say prevention, such as youth education programs (or) rehabilitation, such as job training and education for offenders (or) punishment, such as longer sentences and more prisons (or) enforcement, such as putting more police officers on the street." Coded 0 if punishment or enforcement and 1 if prevention or rehabilitation.

76 In this survey, 9% of respondents reported that they had been the victim of this type of crime in the past five years.

77 Having personal experience with prison also significantly predicts a more negative evaluation of correctional authorities by about four percentage points on a scale ranging from "excellent" to "poor" (coded 0 and 1, respectively) ($p < .05$). Question wording: "I'd like your opinion of the job some different groups in the criminal justice system are doing serving the public. What about prison, probation and parole authorities. Are they doing an excellent job, a good job, only a fair job, or a poor job (serving the public)?" Coded 0–1. Question wording for personal experience: "Have you or anyone you know spent time in prison or jail, or worked in a correctional facility?" Coded 0 if no and 1 if yes.

78 Wirthlin Quorum Survey, September 1994. Retrieved August 31, 2012, from the iPOLL Databank, The Roper Center for Public Opinion Research, University of Connecticut; www.ropercenter.uconn.edu/data_access/ipoll/ipoll.html.

79 Crime in America Survey, May 1996. Retrieved August 31, 2012, from the iPOLL Databank, The Roper Center for Public Opinion Research, University of Connecticut; www.ropercenter.uconn.edu/data_access/ipoll/ipoll.html.

80 David Duffee, "The Correction Officer Subculture and Organizational Change," *Journal of Research in Crime and Delinquency* 11 (1974): 155–172, at 160.

81 Nancy C. Jurik and Michael C. Musheno, "The Internal Crisis of Corrections: Professionalization and the Work Environment," *Justice Quarterly* 3, no. 4 (1986): 457–480, at 475.

82 Wilmar B. Schaufeli and Maria C. W. Peeters, "Job Stress and Burnout Among Correctional Officers: A Literature Review," *International Journal of Stress Management* 7, no. 1 (2000): 19–48; John R. Hepburn and Paul E. Knepper, "Correctional Officers as Human Services Workers: The Effect on Job Satisfaction," *Justice Quarterly* 10, no. 2 (1993): 315–338; Eric G. Lambert, Nancy Lynne Hogan, and Shannon M. Barton, "Satisfied Correctional Staff: A Review of the Literature on the Correlates of Correctional Staff Job Satisfaction," *Criminal Justice and Behavior* 29, no. 2 (2002): 115–143; Craig Dowden and Claude Tellier, "Predicting Work-Related Stress in Correctional Officers: A Meta-Analysis," *Journal of Criminal Justice* 32 (2004): 31–47; Michel Lariviere, "Antecedents and Outcomes of Correctional Officer Attitudes Towards Federal Inmates," Unpublished doctoral thesis, Carleton University, Ottawa, 2001.

83 Eric D. Poole and Robert M. Regoli, "Role Stress, Custody Orientation, and Disciplinary Actions: A Study of Prison Guards," *Criminology* 18, no. 2 (1980): 215–226.

84 James E. Tilton, *Prison Reforms: Achieving Results* (Sacramento: California Department of Corrections and Rehabilitation, 2008).

85 Governor Arnold Schwarzenegger, quoted by Don Thompson, "Youth Prisons Get New Chief," Associated Press, July 2, 2005.

86 Public Safety Realignment, California Department of Corrections and Rehabilitation (July 15, 2011); www.cdcr.ca.gov/About_CDCR/docs/Realignment-Fact-Sheet.pdf.

87 Public Safety Realignment, California Department of Corrections and Rehabilitation; www.cdcr.ca.gov/realignment/.

88 Allen Hopper, Margaret Dooley-Sammuli, and Kelli Evans. "Public Safety Realignment: California at a Crossroads," American Civil Liberties Union (March 2012); www.aclu.org/criminal-law-reform/aclu-california-releases-statewide-anaylsis-realignment.

89 Joshua Page, "Cutting Corrections and Helping Officers," California Progress Report (May 5, 2011); www.californiaprogressreport.com/site/cutting-corrections-and-helping-officers.

90 Author's calculations from data obtained from the Department of Corrections and Rehabilitation Office of Personnel Services, October 2006.

91 Thomas Wright, "Correctional Employee Turnover: A Longitudinal Study," *Journal of Criminal Justice* 21 (1993): 131–142.

92 Robert D. Putnam, *Bowling Alone: The Collapse and Revival of American Community* (New York: Simon & Schuster, 2000).

93 James Putzel, "Accounting for the Dark Side of Social Capital," *Journal of International Development* 9, no. 7 (1997): 939–949.

94 James S. Coleman, "Social Capital in the Creation of Human Capital," *American Journal of Sociology* 94 (1988): S95–S120.

95 Loïc Wacquant, "Negative Social Capital: State Breakdown and Social Destitution in America's Urban Core," *Journal of Housing and the Built Environment* 13, no. 1 (1998): 25–40.

96 Amaney Jamal, "When Is Social Trust a Desirable Outcome? Examining Levels of Trust in the Arab World," *Comparative Political Studies* 40, no. 11 (2007): 1328–1349, at 1329.

97 Alejandro Portes, "Social Capital: Its Origins and Applications in Modern Sociology," *Annual Review of Sociology* 24 (1998): 1–24.

98 William F. Whyte, *Street Corner Society* (Chicago: University of Chicago Press, 1937); Diego Gambetta, *The Sicilian Mafia: The Business of Private Protection* (Cambridge, MA: Harvard University Press, 1996), 8; Eli Berman and David Laitin, "Religion, Terrorism, and Public Goods: Testing the Club Model," *Journal of Public Economics* 92 (2008): 1942–1967.

99 Staffan Kumlin and Bo Rothstein, "Making and Breaking Social Capital: The Impact of Welfare-State Institutions," *Comparative Political Studies* 38, no. 4 (2005): 339–365, at 362.

100 P. Bourdieu, "The Forms of Capital," in J. Richardson (ed.), *Handbook of Theory and Research for the Sociology of Education*, 241–258 (Westport, CT: Greenwood Press, 1986); N. Lin, "Inequality in Social Capital," *Contemporary Sociology* 29, no. 6 (2000): 785–795.

101 For instance, Bo Rothstein, *Just Institutions Matter: The Moral and Political Logic of the Universal Welfare State* (Cambridge: Cambridge University Press, 1998); Bo Rothstein and Dietlind Stolle, "Social Capital, Impartiality and the Welfare State: An Institutional Approach," in Marc Hooghe and Dietlind Stolle (eds.), *Generating Social Capital* (New York: Palgrave Macmillan, 2003).

102 Robert D. Putnam, *Making Democracy Work: Civic Traditions in Modern Italy* Princeton, NJ: Princeton University Press, 1993), 35–36.

103 Eric M. Uslaner, "Trust, Democracy and Governance: Can Government Policies Influence Generalized Trust?" in Marc Hooghe and Dietlind Stolle (eds.), *Generating Social Capital* (New York: Palgrave Macmillan, 2003).

EPILOGUE

1 Data Analysis Unit, *California Prisoners and Parolees 2010* (Sacramento, CA: Department of Corrections and Rehabilitation, 2011).

2 Amy Lerman and Vesla Weaver, *Policing Democracy* (Chicago: University of Chicago Press, forthcoming).

3 Hector Oropeza, "A Letter from Hector," *Newsletter* (San Quentin, CA: Prison University Project, 2005); prisonuniversityproject.org/sites/default/files/newsletters/PUP_Newsletter_Nov2005.pdf.

FEATURES OF CDCR SECURITY-LEVEL ASSIGNMENT

1 Form 840 serves this purpose for each regularly scheduled reclassification of an inmate, and 841 for an inmate returning for a parole violation.

2 Section 61010.11.5 of the California Code of Regulations: Crime Prevention and Corrections.

3 SB 491 Senate Bill – Bill Analysis (1997). Sacramento, California State Senate Assembly Committee on Public Safety.

4 Section 61010.11.6 of the Director's Rules advises caseworkers: "An administrative determinant identifies both temporary and permanent case factors and alerts staff to safety and security considerations which may limit the inmate's eligibility for placement. If there are not enough boxes to identify all applicable administrative determinants, give priority to those most related to security and safety."

5 SB 491 Senate Bill – Bill Analysis (1997); R. Berk, "Conducting a Randomized Field Experiment for the California Department of Corrections: The Experience of the Inmate Classification Experiment," National Institute of Justice, NRC Panel on Evaluation Research for Criminal Justice Programs, 2004.

6 J. Petersilia, *Understanding California Corrections* (University of California at Irvine, Center for Evidence Based Corrections, 2006).

7 M. Keith Chen and Jesse M. Shapiro, "Do Harsher Prison Conditions Reduce Recidivism? A Discontinuity-Based Approach," *American Law and Economics Review* 9, no. 1 (2007): 1–29.

Index

Note: Material in figures or tables is indicated by italic page numbers.

social institutions, prisons as, 173
social isolation, feelings of.
    See also social effects of
    incarceration
    correctional officers, 58, 61–62
    punitive prisons, 8
    social isolation,
        measurement, 101–103
    Social Isolation Scale,
        criminal history and,
        103–104, 224–225
    Social Isolation Scale,
        items in, 102
    Social Isolation Scale, robustness
        tests, 105–106
    Social Isolation Scale, sense of
        belonging and, 104–105
    Social Isolation Scale, social
        networks and, 104–105
social networks.
    See also prison gangs
    collective efficacy and, 159
    community disorganization theory
        and, 163–165
    community organization and
        return of prisoners, 154–156,
        157–158, 159–161, 163–164
    correctional officers, social effects
        of environment, 55–56
    criminogenic attitude adoption
        and, 8, 99, 112–113
    effect on Social Isolation Scale
        (COMPAS), 104–105
    effects of prisoner
        classification, 107–108
    family ties, difficulty maintaining
        in prison, 106–107, 164, 170
    government role in fostering social
        connections, 188
    loneliness and, 8
    measurement with COMPAS
        survey, 100
    nonviolent first-time prisoners,
        community ties, 54–55
    parolees' social ties in
        communities, 162

prison peer groups, effect on
    recidivism, 55
social capital and, 13, 187–188
state influence on composition of
    networks, 54–56
state influence on context of social
    interaction, 56
social trust, effect of ex-prisoners
    in communities, 11,
    156, 159–161
socializing institutions, prisons as,
    48, 170–173, 193–194
spending for criminal justice.
    See cost of criminal
    justice
Stanford Prison Experiment,
    1–3, 8, 20
state influence
    composition of social
        networks, 54–56
    context of social interaction, 56
    role in fostering social
        connections, 188
    social attitudes, 14, 54–56
Supreme Court and criminal justice,
    26, 40
symbolic politics of crime control,
    overview, 26–32

Take Back Our Streets Act, 33
Texas
    control model of prisons,
        36–37
    incarceration rates, 36
    incarceration rates and geographic
        location, 5
    justice reinvestment
        strategy, 180
    tradition of being "Texas
        Tough," 38–39
"three strikes" policies, 27
trust, generalized
    effect of ex-prisoners in
        communities, 11, 151,
        156, 158–159
    effect of harsher prisons, 7, 150